Justification as the Speech of the Spirit

Justification as the Speech of the Spirit

A Pneumatological and Trinitarian Approach to Forensic Justification

JEFFREY K. ANDERSON

Foreword by Peter Gräbe

WIPF & STOCK · Eugene, Oregon

JUSTIFICATION AS THE SPEECH OF THE SPIRIT
A Pneumatological and Trinitarian Approach to Forensic Justification

Copyright © 2021 Jeffrey K. Anderson. All rights reserved. Except for brief quotations in critical publications or reviews, no part of this book may be reproduced in any manner without prior written permission from the publisher. Write: Permissions, Wipf and Stock Publishers, 199 W. 8th Ave., Suite 3, Eugene, OR 97401.

Wipf & Stock
An Imprint of Wipf and Stock Publishers
199 W. 8th Ave., Suite 3
Eugene, OR 97401

www.wipfandstock.com

All Scripture quotations, unless otherwise indicated, are taken from the Holy Bible, New International Version®, NIV®. Copyright ©1973, 1978, 1984, 2011 by Biblica, Inc.™ Used by permission of Zondervan. All rights reserved worldwide. www.zondervan.com The "NIV" and "New International Version" are trademarks registered in the United States Patent and Trademark Office by Biblica, Inc.™

PAPERBACK ISBN: 978-1-7252-9402-8
HARDCOVER ISBN: 978-1-7252-9401-1
EBOOK ISBN: 978-1-7252-9403-5

08/04/21

This book is dedicated to my wife, Trisha Marie Anderson. It was Trisha who first suggested I combine the Hebrew concept of *YHWH dābār* ("the word of the Lord"), the classic Protestant teaching on forensic justification, and speech-act theory. Without her help this volume would never have been completed. Trisha, "the boundary lines" have indeed "fallen in pleasant places for me" (Ps 16:6). You are the "goodness" God had stored up for me, and which he bestowed "in the sight of all" (Ps 31:19). You truly do "surpass them all" (Prov 31:28). I am more grateful with every year that passes.

With *all* my heart,
Jeffrey

Contents

Foreword by Peter Gräbe — ix
Preface — xxi
Acknowledgments — xxiii

1.0	Abstract	1
2.0	Introduction: The Problem to Be Addressed	3
3.0	Methodology	7
4.0	A History of God's Righteousness	13
5.0	God's Declaration in Justification and the Role of the Holy Spirit	103
6.0	Speech-Act Theory: God's Words of Power	127
7.0	Conclusion	168

Bibliography — 177

Foreword

Although I am familiar with Dr. Anderson's work, I was again deeply impressed as I reviewed the scope and depth of his research in this publication. He is indeed a scholar in the fullest sense of the word. In his preface, Dr. Anderson notes that a major stimulus for the writing of this book was his persuasion that the traditional Protestant doctrine of justification by faith is still valid today and does not need to be redefined from a pneumatological perspective as attempted by Dr. Frank Macchia. In this foreword, I want to point to the trinitarian scope of Paul's message of justification by faith. In Paul's letter to the Romans, the gospel, the power of God, and the concept of justification by faith are all intertwined and closely connected to the Holy Spirit. Luther discovered in Rom 1:16–17 the doctrine of justification by faith and recognized that it is the heart of the gospel message. This insight gave rise to the Protestant Reformation, one of the largest renewal movements in the history of the church!

THE GOSPEL IS THE POWER OF GOD

In Rom 1:16–17, Paul formulates the theme of his letter. After a personal confession, "I am not ashamed of the gospel," he shares with us what the gospel is all about.[1] Like a master artist, a few strokes of the pen say everything. He is not ashamed of the gospel (οὐ γὰρ ἐπαισχύνομαι τὸ εὐαγγέλιον) "for it is the power of God for salvation to everyone who believes, to the Jew first and also to the Greek" (δύναμις γὰρ θεοῦ ἐστιν εἰς σωτηρίαν παντὶ τῷ πιστεύοντι, Ἰουδαίῳ τε πρῶτον καὶ Ἕλληνι).

---

1. For a discussion of Paul's gospel, see Stanton, "Paul's Gospel."

The Old Testament from Genesis to Jeremiah portrays the creative and effective power of God's Word.[2] Let's review a few passages:

Genesis 1:3	And God said, "Let there be light," and there was light.
Psalm 147:15	He sends his command to the earth; his word runs swiftly.
Isaiah 40:8	The grass withers and the flowers fall, but the word of our God stands forever.
Isaiah 55:10–11	As the rain and the snow come down from heaven, and do not return to it without watering the earth and making it bud and flourish, so that it yields seed for the sower and bread for the eater, so is my word that goes out from my mouth: It will not return to me empty, but will accomplish what I desire and achieve the purpose for which I sent it.
Jeremiah 23:29	"Is not my word like fire," declares the LORD, "and like a hammer that breaks a rock in pieces?"

The gospel is *God's* power. In Romans 1:1 Paul writes about the gospel of God (εὐαγγέλιον θεοῦ). Power belongs to the essence of God ("Wesen Gottes").[3] Mark 14:62 describes God's name as ἡ δύναμις ("the Mighty One"). In the Old Testament, the power of Yahweh is often revealed as he acted in history to achieve salvation for his people. In early Christian thought, God's saving power referred in the first place to the resurrection of Jesus: "By his power God raised the Lord from the dead, and he will raise us also" (1 Cor 6:14; see also 2 Cor 13:4[4] and Phil 3:10[5]). The creative power of God, who gives life to the dead and calls things that are not as though they were (Rom 4:17), was active in Paul's preaching. Paul, therefore, did not rely on his own rhetorical skills to persuade his hearers, but on the power of the Spirit:

> My message and my preaching were not with wise and persuasive words,
> but with a demonstration of the *Spirit's power*,
> so that your faith might not rest on men's wisdom, but on *God's power*. (1 Cor 2:4–5)

Δύναμις (power) is a concept that refers to the Spirit—just look at the way in which the Spirit's power (ἐν ἀποδείξει πνεύματος καὶ δυνάμεως) and God's

---

2. Cranfield, *Commentary*, 87–88.
3. Wilckens, *Brief*, 82–83.
4. For to be sure, he was crucified in weakness, yet he lives by God's power.
5. I want to know Christ and the power of his resurrection . . .

power (ἀλλ' ἐν δυνάμει θεοῦ) are used synonymously in the passage quoted above. Paul also refers to the power of the Spirit in the following passages:

> I will not venture to speak of anything except what Christ has accomplished through me in leading the Gentiles to obey God by what I have said and done—by the *power of signs and miracles*, through the *power of the Spirit*. So from Jerusalem all the way around to Illyricum, I have fully proclaimed the gospel of Christ. (Rom 15:18–19)

> Does God *give you his Spirit* and *work miracles among you* because you observe the law, or because you believe what you heard? (Gal 3:5)

IN THE GOSPEL GOD'S RIGHTEOUSNESS IS REVEALED

The flow of the argument in Romans 1: 15–17 can be summarized as follows:

> Paul is eager to preach the gospel to those in Rome.
> Why?
> Because he is not embarrassed by the gospel.
> Why?
> Because the gospel is God's own power resulting in salvation for all.
> Why?
> Because in the gospel God's righteousness is revealed.[6]

In the gospel God's righteousness is revealed (δικαιοσύνη γὰρ θεοῦ ἐν αὐτῷ ἀποκαλύπτεται). This statement is contrasted in verse 18 with God's wrath which is revealed (ἀποκαλύπτεται γὰρ ὀργὴ θεοῦ) from heaven against all the godlessness and wickedness of human beings. In his contribution on the forensic metaphors in Romans, Andrie B. du Toit emphasizes the forensic dimension of δικαιοσύνη γὰρ θεοῦ and points to its association with a court trial.[7] The phrase δικαιοσύνη θεοῦ can be rendered on a deep semantic level by the phrase "God's justification/acquittal (of sinners)." Contrary to the trials in Romans 1:18–32 and 2:1–16, a positive verdict is expected. No human being can earn a "not guilty" verdict; we can only appropriate it in faith.

A feature of modern languages is that they use prepositions where ancient languages used cases. In the original Greek, there is no preposition:

---

6. Matera, *Romans*, 34.
7. Du Toit, "Forensic Metaphors," 232.

justification (δικαιοσύνη) is simply followed by the genitive form of the word for God (θεοῦ). The genitive indicates a close relationship; the kind of relationship must be determined from the context.

The "righteousness of Yahweh" (צדקת יהוה) in the Old Testament refers to his relationship with his people within the context of the covenant.[8] Kertelge emphasizes the importance of the covenant context also for the New Testament. Believers who have been justified by God have entered a new reality; they experience a new relationship with God, a relationship in which believers obey Jesus Christ as their Lord.[9] Justified-by-God human beings have not only been acquitted, they have also experienced the reality of the new creation.[10] Udo Schnelle formulates this idea beautifully: "Through faith in Jesus Christ, God grants participation in the new being. Human beings thus stand before God as undeserving recipients of a gift, as persons who are no longer compelled to find their own way in this world .... Rather, as those justified by faith and having their origin in God, they can do God's will in the world."[11] In his commentary on Romans (2010) Frank Matera, a prominent Catholic New Testament scholar, interprets δικαιοσύνη θεοῦ as a subjective genitive ("God's own righteousness") and not as a genitive of origin ("the righteousness that comes from God"). He points out, however, that this righteousness should not be understood as God's retributive justice, but as God's saving justice and covenant loyalty. In the Psalms and in the book of Isaiah, God's righteousness (δικαιοσύνη, LXX) is sometimes equated with his salvation (σωτηρία, LXX):

> My *righteousness* draws near swiftly,
> my *salvation* will go out, ...
> But my *righteousness* will be forever,
> and my *salvation* for generations of generations. (Isa 51:5, 8)

Righteousness is here not a static quality of a God who judges people, but the dynamic quality of a God granting salvation. Frank Matera summarizes his interpretation as follows:

> This interpretation of the righteousness of God puts the emphasis where it ought to be (on God's saving justice) without neglecting the righteousness that God grants as a free gift. For when the righteousness of God is revealed, those who respond

---

8. Kertelge, "δικαιοσύνη," 790.

9. Kertelge, *Rechtfertigung*, 127.

10. Kertelge formulates: "Die Gerechtsprechung des Sünders hat nicht nur forensische, sondern als forensische auch 'effektive' Bedeutung" (*Rechtfertigung*, 123).

11. Schnelle, *Paul*, 471.

in faith receive the gift of God's righteousness. . . . Everything begins and ends with faith. Thus Paul writes that God's righteousness is revealed 'from faith to faith.'[12]

I now want to turn to the most consequential interpretation of God's righteousness in the history of the Church. In the preface to the complete edition of Martin Luther's Latin writings of 1545, Luther mentions an event that changed his whole life. While he was meditating on Romans 1:16–17, it dawned on him that God's righteousness (*iustitia dei*) does not refer to a justice that condemns but to the salvation that God freely grants to those who believe.[13] Luther writes:

> At last, by the mercy of God, meditating day and night, I gave heed to the context of the words, namely, "In the righteousness of God is revealed, as it is written, 'He who through faith is righteous shall live.'" There I began to understand that the righteousness of God is that by which the righteous lives by a gift of God, namely by faith. And this is the meaning: the righteousness of God is revealed by the gospel, namely, the passive righteousness with which merciful God justifies us by faith, as it is written, "He who through faith is righteous shall live." Here I felt that I was altogether born again and had entered paradise itself through open gates. There a totally other face of the entire Scripture showed itself to me. Thereupon I ran through the Scriptures from memory. I also found in other terms an analogy, as, the word of God, that is, what God does in us, the power of God, with which he makes us strong, the wisdom of God, with which he makes us wise, the strength of God, the salvation of God, the glory of God. And I extolled my sweetest word with a love as great as the hatred with which I had before hated the word "righteousness of God." Thus that place in Paul was for me truly the gate to paradise.[14]

This insight into Scripture gave rise to the greatest renewal movement in church history, the Protestant Reformation. Luther was convinced that Paul's message about the justification of the sinner by faith alone is the center of everything the Bible says about salvation.

Although these words were written in 1545, they are still as fresh and beautiful as the morning dew. They are still so inspiring because Luther formulated the gospel message in both its simplicity and its power. Believers

---

12. Matera, *Romans*, 36.
13. Stuhlmacher, *Revisiting Paul's Doctrine*, 34.
14. Luther, *Luther's Works*, 34:337.

can just stand in awe before a righteous and loving God. Luther's words are truly trinitarian: everything flows from God the Father; simultaneously everything circles around the gospel message of the crucified and risen Christ. Concepts associated with the Spirit permeate Luther's words: "faith," "to be born again," "power," and "love."

THE SIGNIFICANCE OF ROMANS 5–8

Romans 5–8 is very important for our discussion. Andrie B. du Toit captured the significance of this passage with the heading: "As people who have been declared not guilty we have been made completely new."[15] Frank Matera gives Romans 5:1—8:39 the title, "The experience of salvation in the light of God's righteousness."

In his commentary on Romans, C. E. B. Cranfield emphasizes the close relationship between Romans 1:16b-17 and the ensuing chapters. The theme of Romans is stated in Romans 1:16b-17. The revelation of the righteousness which is from God by faith alone—"He who is righteous by faith" is then expounded in 1:18—4:25 and the life promised for those who are righteous by faith (the phrase "shall live" in 1:17) is expounded in 5:1—8:39.[16]

Romans 8 is one of the finest passages in Paul's letters. In this chapter, Paul alludes to and develops key themes discussed in the previous three chapters (5–7). Douglas Moo points to a ring composition in which Romans 8:18-39 alludes to the themes of 5:1-11, and 8:1-17 recalls 5:12-21.[17]

In Romans 6:1, Paul refers to an objection raised against his law-free gospel: "What shall we say, then? Shall we go on sinning so that grace may increase?" Paul answers this objection by pointing out that believers have died to sin "by their baptismal participation in Christ's death"[18] and "just as Christ was raised from the dead through the glory of the Father, we too may live a new life" (Rom 6:3). The new life is the life of the Spirit of God who dwells in believers and enables them to live a life pleasing to God.

> The theological themes of Romans 5–8 have the following structure:
>
> Eschatological hope grounded in justification and reconciliation (Rom 5)
> The ethical life of the justified (Rom 6)
> The plight of the unredeemed (Rom 7)

---

15. In the original Afrikaans: "As vrygespreektes is ons splinternuwe mense."
16. Cranfield, *Commentary*, 748.
17. For a detailed discussion, see Moo, *Letter to the Romans*, 316–528.
18. Matera, *Romans*, 186.

Eschatological hope grounded in the Spirit (Rom 8)[19]

Is Paul's message of justification by faith apart from doing the works of the law an invitation to an immoral life? Romans 8 presents a clear answer: those who have been justified by faith experience the power of the Spirit, who enables them to live holy lives. Righteousness by faith has its counterpart in the life of faith enabled by the Spirit. Paul experienced the power of the Spirit both in his own life as well as in the communities who accepted his message of justification by faith alone. The written code of the law cannot enable people to obey its instructions. The Spirit, however, is a life-giving force—the presence of the living God in believers' lives. Let us listen to Romans 8:1–4:

> Therefore, there is now no condemnation for those who are in Christ Jesus, because through Christ Jesus the law of the Spirit of life set me free from the law of sin and death. For what the law was powerless to do in that it was weakened by the sinful nature, God did by sending his own Son in the likeness of sinful man to be a sin offering. And so he condemned sin in sinful man, in order that the righteous requirements of the law might be fully met in us, who do not live according to the sinful nature but according to the Spirit.

Romans 8 is permeated by references to the Spirit and plays a pivotal role in Paul's argument. Prior to chapter 8, Paul refers only four times to the Spirit in 1:9, 2:29, 5:5, and 7:6. In chapter 8 there are nineteen references to the Spirit. The Spirit not only empowers those who have been justified by faith to live holy lives, but also assures believers of the final glory they will experience at the resurrection of the dead. Paul assures us in Romans 8:11: "And if the Spirit of him who raised Jesus from the dead is living in you, he who raised Christ from the dead will also give life to your mortal bodies through his Spirit, who lives in you." In describing the role of the Spirit, Paul uses an agricultural term, ἀπαρχή, the first of the harvest that was dedicated to God ensuring that the whole harvest will follow (8:23: "we ourselves, who have the firstfruits of the Spirit"). "For Paul, the Spirit is the 'firstfruits' of a harvest that believers will reap when their bodies are redeemed from death at the general resurrection of the dead (8:23)."[20]

Romans 8:18 formulates the theme of the last section of Romans 8: "I consider that our present sufferings are not worth comparing with the glory that will be revealed in us." Paul returns to the key theme of hope for

---

19. Matera, *Romans*, 188.
20. Matera, *Romans*, 210.

eschatological glory, a theme he introduced in 5:1–11 and took up again in 5:21: "so that, just as sin reigned in death, so also grace might reign through righteousness to bring eternal life through Jesus Christ our Lord." In Romans 5, Paul finds the reason for the hope for future glory in the believers' present experience of justification and reconciliation. In chapter 8, however, Paul writes about believers' final hope in the context of the experience of the Spirit, the firstftruits of salvation. Paul's theology reaches a climax in Romans 8 as he underscores the cosmic scope of salvation embracing not only the justified, but the whole of creation. In this way, Paul enhances and develops the message of hope introduced in chapter 5.[21]

SAVED BY THE TRIUNE GOD: A FEW EXAMPLES OUTSIDE ROMANS

In the preceding analysis of the passages from Romans, we have seen the trinitarian scope of Paul's message of justification. In the remaining corpus Paulinum, the experience of salvation is also ascribed to the work of the Father, the Son, and the Spirit. Look at the detailed description of salvation in Titus 3:4–7:

> But when the kindness and love of *God our Savior* appeared,
>   he saved us, not because of righteous things we had done,
> but because of *his mercy*. He saved us through the washing of
> rebirth and renewal by the *Holy Spirit*,
>   whom he poured out on us generously through *Jesus Christ our Savior*,
>   so that, *having been justified* by his grace, we might become
> heirs having the hope of eternal life.

This passage is part of a broader context in which Paul urges Titus to remind the believers to do what is good. He reminds his readers that they were also foolish and disobedient before "the kindness and love of God our Savior appeared." Salvation is founded on God and his mercy and not on any righteous deeds. Salvation is only possible because of the death and resurrection of Jesus Christ "our Savior." In this passage, Paul focuses, however, on the activity of the *Holy Spirit*. God "saved us through the washing of rebirth and renewal by the Holy Spirit, whom he poured out on us generously." When Paul talks about the Holy Spirit, he creates an image of abundance. Believers have been made completely new, they have been put in right relation with God and now have the hope of eternal life. Just note all

---

21. Matera, *Romans*, 186.

the positive concepts in this passage: kindness, love, mercy, renewal, generosity, hope, eternal life. The gospel is indeed wonderful news.

Images from two Old Testament passages can be discerned in this passage. The image of "pouring out the Spirit" stems from Joel 2:28: "I will pour out my Spirit on all people. Your sons and daughters will prophesy, your old men will dream dreams, your young men will see visions."

The other Old Testament passage that lies behind the language of this text is Ezekiel 36:25–28, where the Lord promises to wash his people with clean water and cleanse them from all impurities and from all their idols. This image of cleansing is then followed by the promise of sending the Spirit:

> I will give you a new heart and put a new spirit in you; I will remove from you your heart of stone and give you a heart of flesh. And I will put my Spirit in you and move you to follow my decrees and be careful to keep my laws ... you will be my people, and I will be your God. (Ezek 36:26–28)

This is new covenant language. God expected his people to follow the decrees of the covenant given on Mount Sinai. History proved, however, that Israel was unable to obey the Lord's commands. Despite Israel's disobedience, the holy God decided not to abandon his covenant people but promised a new covenant (Jer 31:31–34). The Lord announced through his prophet Ezekiel that he would give his people a new heart and would put his Spirit in them, enabling them to keep his laws.[22]

I conclude with one more example of Paul's trinitarian view of salvation:

> But you were washed, you were sanctified, you were justified in the name of the Lord Jesus Christ and by the Spirit of our God. (1 Cor 6:11)

These words conclude the passage starting in 1 Corinthians 6:1. It came to Paul's attention that members of the congregation pursued lawsuits against fellow believers. Paul reminded his readers that "the wicked will not inherit the kingdom of God." He named some of those wicked people—the sexually immoral, idolaters, drunkards, slanderers, swindlers—and pointed out that some members of the congregation belonged to the sinners he had just mentioned. Then follows the passage we are considering: "But you were washed, you were sanctified, you were justified . . . ." The passive form of the verbs is called the "divine passive." Out of respect for the divine, God is not named but implied: "God has effected the salvation expressed by these rich metaphors 'in the name of the Lord Jesus Christ and by his Spirit.'"[23] The

---

22. Gräbe, *Power of God*, 56–57.
23. Fee, *God's Empowering Presence*, 129.

salvation of sinners is brought about by the triune God: "God the Father saves, through the work of Christ, effected experientially by the Spirit."[24]

The believers were no longer thieves or drunkards or slanderers because they were washed. They were sanctified and justified by *God*. This was made possible by the death and resurrection of *Jesus Christ*. It is, however, the *Spirit* who made sanctification and justification *a reality in their lives*. Gordon Fee describes the work of the Spirit in Paul's soteriology so well:

> The Spirit appropriates God's salvation in the life of the believer in such a way that new life and behavior are the expected result; and without the latter, the effective work of the Spirit in the believer's life, there has been no true salvation—in any meaningful sense for Paul.[25]

CONCLUSION: THE TRINITARIAN SCOPE OF PAUL'S MESSAGE OF JUSTIFICATION BY FAITH

The "Joint Declaration on the Doctrine of Justification" by the Lutheran World Federation and the Roman Catholic Church states:

> In faith we together hold the conviction that justification is the work of the triune God. The Father sent his Son into the world to save sinners. The foundation and presupposition of justification is the incarnation, death, and resurrection of Christ. *Justification thus means that Christ himself is our righteousness, in which we share through the Holy Spirit in accord with the will of the Father.* Together we confess: By grace alone, in faith in Christ's saving work and not because of any merit on our part, we are accepted by God and receive the Holy Spirit, who renews our hearts while equipping and calling us to good works.[26]

The gospel message of justification by faith is profoundly *theocentric*. It is rooted in the Old Testament covenant and the belief in the just and faithful and caring God. The familiar words of John 3:16 say it so well: "For God so loved the world . . ."

This well-known statement does not end here. "For God so loved the world *that he gave his only Son*." The message of justification by faith is the message of the crucified and risen Christ. Because of the sacrifice of

---

24. Fee, *God's Empowering Presence*, 128.
25. Fee, *God's Empowering Presence*, 132.
26. LWF and RCC, *Joint Declaration*, §15; italics in the original.

Jesus every person who puts his/her trust in him can hear the verdict: "Not guilty!" Or better still, "righteous."

In Romans 1:16–17, the wonder of the gospel is portrayed with just a few words. We read about the righteousness of God freely given to those who believe, and Paul quotes Habakkuk 2:4, "He who through faith is righteous shall live." In a deeply personal way Paul shares with his readers that he is not ashamed of the gospel, because it is the *power of God*. The gospel message is not a mere theoretical statement. When the gospel message is preached, the power of the Holy Spirit is at work.[27]

As Luther comprehended the gospel, he felt that he "was altogether born again and had entered paradise itself through open gates." John Wesley encountered the power of the gospel in a similar way. He wrote in his journal:

> In the evening I went very unwillingly to a society in Aldersgate Street, where one was reading Luther's preface to the Epistle to the Romans. About a quarter before nine, while he was describing the change which God works in the heart through faith in Christ, I felt my heart strangely warmed. I felt I did trust in Christ, Christ alone, for salvation; and an assurance was given me that He had taken away my sins, even mine, and saved me from the law of sin and death.[28]

The Spirit is God's gift to those who have been justified ("God has poured out his love into our hearts by the Holy Spirit, whom he has given us" Rom 5:5).[29] In a masterful way, Paul unfolds his statement in Romans 1:16–17 in the ensuing chapters, reaching a climax in Romans 8, the chapter of the Spirit. The Spirit makes justification a present reality in the lives of believers and enables them to live holy lives. Justification and sanctification find a unity *in the activity of the Spirit*.[30] Sanctification shows that justification is a reality in the life of a believer.

The work of the Spirit reaches beyond this life. Paul assures us that because we have the "firstfruits of the Spirit," we can eagerly await sharing in the glory of God when our bodies are raised from the dead (Rom 8:23). The

---

27. For more information on the connection between the concept of power (δύναμις) and the Holy Spirit see Gräbe, *Power of God*, 245–55.

28. Wesley, "I Felt My Heart."

29. See also Gal 3:2, "Did you receive the Spirit by observing the law, or by believing what you heard?" and Gal 5:5, "But by faith we eagerly await through the Spirit the righteousness for which we hope."

30. Kertelge, *Rechtfertigung*, 278.

Spirit is a present reality in believers' lives as he enables them to address God in the intimate way that Jesus did: "Abba, Father" (Rom 8:15).

Let us continue to teach and preach the gospel message of justification by faith with a new sense of urgency. Let us not be ashamed of the gospel, because it is *the power of God*. Viewed from the perspective of the triune God, this is still the message that brings about the experience of the new birth and allows believers (in the words of Martin Luther) to enter paradise itself through open gates.

Preface

Over the last couple decades, an increasing number of voices have noted the absence of an overt pneumatology in the Protestant doctrine of justification by faith. I first became aware of this theological void in the summer of 2005 while taking a PhD course on contemporary theologies from Frank Macchia. Among the required readings was an essay Frank wrote for *Theology Today*, in which he laid out his attempt to fill the gap and redefine justification, giving it a robust pneumatological basis. It was a common practice to have students write a short response to the various readings—usually something around five hundred words long. I submitted a nine thousand-word rebuttal. Frank, in turn, responded graciously (but firmly) to my comments that though he welcomed disagreements, he was concerned that I had not actually engaged his argument, I had talked past him. He was right. All I had done was dismiss his proposal out-of-hand and restate the classic forensic view of justification.

Looking back, I still think I was right, and that Frank's conclusions were in error, but I have come to genuinely appreciate the concerns he raised. The following work is a significantly condensed version of my attempt to respond to those concerns and the questions raised by Frank and others. However, as will become clear, I still affirm the traditional Protestant view of the Father's legal declaration about the believer, based on the work of the Son. While it is true the Protestant Reformers did not offer a fully trinitarian statement on justification, we should recall that a pneumatology of justification was *not* the among the central issues of dispute. The Reformers were embattled on multiple fronts, so their efforts were devoted to addressing the issues that were pressed upon them. Thus, they did not attempt to articulate a view of justification that specifically highlighted the role of the Holy Spirit. Yet, silence on a topic does not imply a position on that topic.

The original version of this project was nearly eight hundred pages long, far too unwieldy to be much practical help. However, one of the driving goals of that work was to provide a clear exegetical basis for the theological claims. Roughly three hundred pages were specifically devoted to the exegesis of four biblical texts, making the result an exercise in systematic theology and Pauline theology. I have dropped the exegetical sections from this edition, but the desire to have the theology rooted in the Bible has not wavered.

Jonathan Edwards wrote that God's great redemptive work of "saving and renewing poor and perishing souls" is a thing "most beautiful . . . a most glorious work."[1] The Bible's teaching of justification is indeed "most beautiful." It is one of things Christian leaders are called upon to "watch closely" (1 Tim 4:16). It is meant to be a source of genuine encouragement to believers, and it is intended to refute those who teach false doctrine (Titus 1:9). Thus, justification is both intensely practical and esthetically beautiful. It displays the beauty of God's holiness, "which is infinitely excellent; yea it is infinite beauty, brightness, and glory itself."[2] It is my hope that you will see some of that "infinite beauty" as you read about God's glorious work of justification.

Psalm 115:1

Jeffrey Anderson
September 23, 2020

---

1. Edwards, *Religious Affections*, loc. 408.
2. Edwards, *Religious Affections*, loc. 408.

Acknowledgments

It is customary to say thank you to friends and colleagues at the beginning of a book like this. In the past, I have often found such acknowledgements to be a bit repetitious. But after working through the process of researching, writing, and publishing a dissertation, and then distilling that down to about of third of its original size, I have a much greater appreciation for why authors so frequently thank their husbands, wives, children, friends, etc. It takes a toll on them. You miss events you would otherwise attend, and when you do make it to family occasions sometimes, your mind is preoccupied. Not always, mind you, but often enough that it affects others, so a publication like this really doesn't come about without the aid of many others.

I want to thank Peter Gräbe, my former advisor and now friend. He demonstrated unearthly patience and graciousness toward me as a student, and now unfailing warmth and interest as a friend and colleague. A special thank you to Corné Bekker and James Flynn, the dean and associate dean at Regent University's School of Divinity. They are a genuine pleasure to work with and for. It is very hard to overstate the value of sheer competence. Both men exude competence in their respective roles, as they provide leadership and direction for the school.

To Daniel Gilbert and Alex Mekonnen: the three of us all started full time on the same day. According to Plato, genuine friendship must be based upon mutual affection, respect, love, and far more. You two, along with Mary Beth and Roman, were one of the nicest surprises when we came to Virginia. Trish and I deeply value your friendship and warmth. And, Daniel, I appreciate your willingness to put up with my humor.

To Ryan, Brandon, and Kady, my sons and daughter-in-law. Psalm 127:3 tells us, "Sons are a heritage from the Lord, children a reward from him." *You* are my heritage, the greatest reward I could hope for. I am proud of you all, more than I can say. It was a pleasure to have everyone living with us during the summer months of 2020. I eagerly look forward to what God has in store for all of you in the next chapter of your lives.

And finally, to Dale and Baby-Jimmy: you fill me (Opa) and Grandma with joy and delight! You are a "crown" for us (Prov 17:6). I love watching *Transformers: Prime* with you and chasing you around the back yard. You have been my best helper with the bird feeders and the sprinklers. Opa loves you so very much!

1.0

Abstract

In recent decades, the Protestant doctrine of justification has undergone unprecedented levels of criticism, originating from many different sectors. Although the concerns expressed are many and varied, one recurring theme is the absence of any overt pneumatology within the doctrine. Since the early centuries, the church has believed *opera trinitatis ad extra sunt indivisa* (i.e., that "the external works of the Trinity are undivided"). However, during the Reformation, when justification began to take such a central role, it was understood as a legal declaration by the Father based on the redemptive work of the Son. Given the earlier dictum, such a formulation raises the question: Where is the Holy Spirit in such a formulation? If every act God performs is necessarily a trinitarian act, then where is the Holy Spirit in this construction? It would appear, *prima facie*, that Luther developed and passed on a "pneumatologically barren" notion of justification. Consequently, the past three decades have seen numerous attempts to redefine the meaning of the word *justification*, usually along pneumatological lines. Further, a significant number of these reformulations attempt to recast justification as a broad umbrella-term that covers nearly all of soteriology, rather than as a specific forensic term within the *ordo salutis*. My contention is that the conclusions drawn from the above (valid) question are, at best, premature and, at worst, misguided. The heart of this project is to show that justification, as it came from the Protestant Reformers, is already a pneumatologically rich concept. The major obstacle is in the traditional framing, or wording, of the doctrine, so that it *appears* to be lacking pneumatology. However, through the use of speech-act theory and some observations from biblical theology, it can be demonstrated that the Protestant doctrine of forensic justification is genuinely *spirit*ual—truly trinitarian.

2.0

Introduction

The Problem to Be Addressed

The history of justification is long and involved, characterized by almost unremitting controversy. Yet it is the very complexity of the subject that demands it be handled with care. In the first few centuries of the church, justification did not play the kind of pivotal role it would during the Reformation era. Instead, topics such as the Holy Trinity or the dual natures of Christ took center stage during those formative years.[1] As an article of faith, during the first three and a half centuries of the Christian era, justification was more often assumed than argued. It would have to wait until the early part of the fifth century, when Augustine took up the topic, before it took on any real prominence; and it would wait still another millennium before it became *the* central doctrine for Protestantism—"the article upon which the Church stands or falls."[2] Additionally, during the Reformation

---

1. Tavard, *Justification*, 116ff.

2. Although popularly attributed to Luther, the earliest we find this statement is 1618 by Johann Alsted where he writes, "The article of justification is said to be the article by which the church stands or falls" (Alsted, *Theologia scholastica didacta*, 711; as cited in McGrath, *Iustitia Dei*, Kindle loc. 34). However, according to Randall Pederson, *articulus iustificationis dicitur articulus stantis et cadentis ecclesiae* was a common proverb among early Lutheran and Reformed authors and, according to Balthasar Meisner, it was, in fact, attributed to Luther. See Pederson, *Unity in Diversity*, 146n233; Secker, ed., *Lutheran Confessions*, 260. According to Alister McGrath, the closest *written* statement from Luther is, "Because if this article [of justification] stands, the church

era, justification was disputed like no other doctrine.[3] The slow development of the doctrine notwithstanding, today justification continues to be among the most contested topics within the theological world. R. C. Sproul has aptly noted that the controversies surrounding justification have not reached such a fevered pitch since the days of the Protestant Reformation.[4] When one considers the disputes over justification within the so-called "New Perspective(s) on Paul" (NPP), or those surrounding the "Joint Declaration on the Doctrine of Justification" between Roman Catholics and the Lutheran World Federation in 1999, as well as recent conflicts within the evangelical church between authors like John Piper[5] and Robert Gundry,[6] not to mention the innovative contributions from Pentecostal/Charismatic authors like Frank Macchia, Amos Yong, and L. Lyle Dabney, or the highly visible conflict over the justification between N.T. Wright[7] and John Piper,[8] or even the dispute among conservative Presbyterians over the "Federal Vision" or "Auburn Avenue Theology" with its implications for the doctrine of justification—Sproul's claim does not appear to be overstated.

It is obvious that no single work could appropriately survey all the above movements and ideas. Therefore, the goals of this project are far more modest. First and foremost, the aim will be to show that the traditional Protestant idea of forensic justification is an accurate representation of the biblical message. Second, and contrary to the claims of many recent contemporary theologians, I will seek to demonstrate that the Protestant understanding is actually pneumatologically informed—a view wherein the Holy Spirit is not merely present in some "static," "shallow," or "barren" fashion[9] but rather active, working together with the Father and the Son to bring about our justification.

---

stands; if this article collapses, the church collapses" (McGrath, *Iustitia Dei*, 2:20).

3. "But no doctrinal dispute has ever been contested more fiercely or with such long-term consequences as the one over justification. There were other ancillary issues debated in the 16th century, but none [was] so central or so heated as this" (Sproul, "Reformation Rescued").

4. Sproul, *Faith Alone*.

5. Piper, *Counted Righteous in Christ*.

6. Gundry, "Why I Didn't Endorse," 6–9; "On Oden's 'Answer,'" 14–15, 39; "Nonimputation of Christ's Righteousness," 17–45.

7. Wright, *Paul* and *What Saint Paul Really Said*. Finally, Wright published a response to Piper's work in 2009, *Justification*.

8. Piper, *Future of Justification*.

9. Cf. Frank Macchia's extended contention of this point in his *Justified in the Spirit* and "Justification through New Creation," 205, 207, 216ff.

To accomplish this goal, we will explore some of the comments on justification in the work of a few representatives from the Reformation era and more recent church history. Specifically, we will briefly survey the history of justification, beginning with the traditional dating of Luther's initial Romans' lectures (May 1516) and concluding with the modern *Joint Declaration on Justification* between the Lutheran World Federation and representatives of the worldwide Roman Catholic Church on October 31, 1999. Of necessity, this will be only a cursory overview, nothing like Alister McGrath's wonderful two-volume *Iustitia Dei*[10] or Michael Horton's outstanding two-volume set *Justification*.[11] In other words, our historical survey will start with the beginning of the Protestant/Roman Catholic conflict and will run to its ostensible conclusion. This section will serve as both a historical background and a type of literature review, albeit one with significant gaps. After that, we will argue that the biblical expression "the word of the Lord" (*dābār YHWH*—דְּבַר־יְהוָה) is a normative expression of the Holy Spirit's activity within the Hebrew Bible.[12] In addition, we will draw upon resources gleaned from modern speech-act theory.[13] We will attempt to combine these results with concepts culled from modern (biblical) interpretative theory to develop our overall argument. Finally, we will attempt to draw all of these seemingly disparate lines of thought together to present our central thesis: in justification, the righteousness of Christ is imputed to the believer through a declaration of the Father, which is simply another way of saying that the Holy Spirit executes this justifying action. In short, the role of the Holy Spirit *is* the active speech of the Father, based on the work of the Son—hence, a genuinely trinitarian formulation of justification.

The title of this work, *Justification as the Speech of the Spirit*, originated from an essay by Frank D. Macchia, "Justification through New Creation: The Holy Spirit and the Doctrine by Which the Church Stands or Falls."[14] Macchia asks the important question: Since every act God performs is a

10. McGrath, *Iustitia*.

11. Horton, *Justification*. See also the recent monograph edited by Matthew Barrett, *Doctrine on Which the Church*.

12. This conclusion is drawn from the work of my former PhD classmate at Regent University, Steve Service. Steve's work on the *dābār YHWH* is what initially prompted my thinking on this subject. See Service, *Dabar YHWH Gospel Musterion*.

13. The literature on speech-act theory has become overwhelming. In the initial version of this project, I sought to include all the major contributors and participants. However, the corpus has become far too unwieldy. Thus, I only include representative works by perhaps the two best-known proponents, J. L. Austin and John Searle. For an introduction to the subject of speech-acts, see Austin, *How to Do Things,* and Searle, *Speech Acts*.

14. Macchia, "Justification through New Creation," 216.

trinitarian act, where, then, is the Holy Spirit in the classic Protestant formulation of justification? In this model, the *Father* declares the sinner to be righteous based on the work of the *Son*. "Where [then] is the Holy Spirit in this understanding of Christ's redemptive work for our justification?"[15] Macchia's question and subsequent proposal initially frustrated me and then later perplexed me, until I finally turned my full attention to the subject by writing an essay on the subject.[16]

In spite of the peaks and valleys of interest, the weight of history sides with Jaroslav Pelikan when he describes justification as "the chief doctrine of Christianity and the chief point of difference separating Protestantism and Roman Catholicism."[17] As such, it is a worthy enterprise to explore this important subject in an attempt to discover the differences and similarities in the Protestant and Roman Catholic Churches, as well as possible ways forward. Consequently, we will begin our examination of justification at the early stages of the Roman Catholic/Protestant split.

---

15. Macchia, "Justification through New Creation," 209. Macchia repeatedly demonstrates his hostility toward this view when he refers to it as "the shallow well of the forensic model" (205) and "the pneumatologically barren notion of forensic justification" (207), etc.

16. Anderson, "Holy Spirit and Justification," 292–305.

17. Pelikan, *Reformation of Church*, 139.

3.0

Methodology

The question of theological method plays a significant role in any theological enterprise, whether that role is recognized or not, acknowledged or not. Examining one's own method forces one to identify and acknowledge the underlying assumptions he/she brings to the theological task. Defining theological method is something I have struggled with over the years. I could try to explain it, but my explanations always seemed to be too lengthy or involved to be genuinely helpful. As a result, I developed three analogies to help describe it. The three analogies are *worldview*, the *distinction* (in philosophy) *between first- and second-order questions*, and *Aristotle's use of logic*.

WORLDVIEW

James Sire defines a worldview as "a set of assumptions (a fundamental orientation of heart), which may be true, partially true, or entirely false which we hold (consciously or subconsciously; consistently or inconsistently) about the basic fabric of reality, and that provides the foundation and meaning of our life."[1] While Sire's definition is helpful for those that are new to the subject, it is extremely dense unless someone unpacks the definition. Why?

---

1. Sire, *Universe Next Door*, 17.

Because *a worldview looks like a lot of other things*, even though it is not actually one of those things. When people first began to study worldview, they understandably notice a clear philosophical element. So they regularly ask, "Is this just another form of philosophy?" The answer is *no*, but worldview does incorporate philosophy, so the element of philosophy is frequently visible. Someone else might ask, "What about theology? Isn't it just another form of metaphysics? After all, it certainly affects our theology." Again, the answer is *no*, but it does affect the way we see things theologically. Actually, worldview incorporates ethics, biology, psychology, sociology, law, politics, economics, and history,[2] yet it is not exactly any of these. Instead, it is a complex of all of them. It is a grid. In fact, worldview is *the* grid through which we view the universe around us. We interpret all of reality through it. It influences how we interpret things. It determines what we value and what we do not. In many ways, it defines who we are. This is our first analogy to theological method.

FIRST- AND SECOND-ORDER QUESTIONS

The second analogy comes from the field of philosophy. As already noted, when we talk about theological method, some people understandably confuse it with theology. "Are you sure it's not a form of theology?" Yes, I'm sure, but it does determine our theology and is formed from our theology. "So, is it a hermeneutical approach?" No, but that is getting a little closer. The difference between hermeneutics and theological method is a little like the distinction made in philosophy between first-order questions and second-order questions. An example might be:

First-Order Question: "What is the meaning of X?"

Second-Order Question: "What is the meaning of the question, 'What is the meaning of X'?"

Second-order questions are more fundamental than first-order questions. A second-order question tends to focus on the unspoken assumptions behind the first order-question. So a first-order question in the field of hermeneutics might be, "What is the meaning of that text?" Second-order questions might be, "What events or influences led to the question, 'What is the meaning of that text?' What is the meaning of meaning? Is genuine meaning even possible?" In short, theological method is a kind of second-order function. It has to do with *how* we do our theology, what are the unquestioned assumptions—presuppositions—from which we operate. Theological method questions those presuppositions. Thus, our second analogy.

2. Myers and Noebel, *Understanding the Times*, chap. 1.

ARISTOTLE'S USE OF LOGIC

Our third analogy comes from the history of philosophy. By virtually all accounts, Aristotle was among the greatest minds in all human history. He was considered one of the few individuals to have achieved expert status in every known field of his day. This is something no-one today could accomplish; there are just too many disciplines today that didn't exist during Aristotle's time. Nevertheless, Aristotle was considered an expert in every known discipline and wrote on each. However, at one-point, Aristotle was questioned after someone read his works and noticed he had not included *logic* among the disciplines. The observer considered that to be a significant oversight. While logic may not be viewed as particularly vital today, in the ancient world, it was considered monumentally important. But, according to Aristotle, the absence of logic in his list of disciplines was *not* an oversight. In fact, he claimed that logic was *not* a discipline at all. Instead, he called it the *organon—the instrument* through which we access and use all the disciplines. Thus, while each discipline addressed a discrete field of knowledge, logic was the key to understanding that area of knowledge and how it should be researched.

This is very close to the idea of theological method. Theological method is not precisely our theology nor our philosophy, yet it influences both. It is generally not as concerned with the straightforward questions we ask in theology but instead questions our presuppositions. It is like logic, in that it is not among the normal disciplines. Rather, it has to do with *how* we go about those disciplines.

While the above analogies are intended to help grasp the idea of theological method, there is more to theological method than what is covered in these analogies. Theological method not only questions our theological presuppositions, it also prompts the questions we raise. It helps frame our inquiries. Every individual is also part of a larger community, and that community (be it evangelical, liberal, Anglican, Pentecostal, Presbyterian, Democrat, Republican, Caucasian, Asian, African-American, egalitarian, complementarian, or otherwise) shapes its own unique interpretive methods. These methods, in turn, influence and reshape the community. The point here is that methods are *not* neutral. They are rooted in concrete settings, in which specific beliefs are held and anchored into distinct epistemological backgrounds. Methods reflect what each community deems to be *true*, *valid*, and *valuable*. And it is here that every community is simultaneously strongest and most vulnerable. For example, as an evangelical, I was raised on an unspoken assumption of *a*historicity in interpretive methodology. That is, the objective of interpretation was to seek a neutral stance before the text of Scripture in order to ascertain its objective meaning. In other words, the goal was to eliminate all bias. Once subjectivity was removed, it was believed that the individual reader (i.e., the hermeneut) would be able to access the objective propositional content of the text and then apply it in the real world.[3]

Today, however, evangelicals in general freely acknowledge that such *neutrality* does not exist. We all have our biases, and even the most vigorous efforts of evangelicals to expel all such biases from our methodological practices do not result in a value-free method. We need to heed the admonition of John Goldingay, when he said that those who "pretend to be objective and critical and then find their own (Enlightenment or existential or feminist) concerns in the texts they study need to take a dose of self-suspicion."[4] The reality is that we all have traditions, whether we recognize them or not, and "the man who thinks he has none is the man who is the most enslaved to them."[5]

Yet it is precisely *because* we come to the text of Scripture in a biased state that our goal should be to identify those biases and discover how they influence us. For the more self-aware we become, the more insight we will gain from the text. It is one thing to say, "Complete objectivity can never be fully realized." It is another thing altogether to conclude that identifying our presuppositions in pointless. We *can* become more and more self-aware of our assumptions and thus make real progress in understanding the theological task. Although *complete* self-awareness (like *complete* objectivity) can never be fully realized, real progress toward such a goal is possible. We can,

---

3. It is easy to pick up on these kinds of assumptions when reading some of the older evangelicals like Hodge, *Systematic Theology*, 1:1. Nevertheless, we must be careful here. People from previous generations held different assumptions; they were not dumb (as they are so often portrayed). This means that it is relatively easy to notice disparities or inconsistencies in the work of earlier generations and unwittingly assume a superior attitude toward them and their work. This is what C. S. Lewis insightfully referred to as "chronological snobbery." He notes, "Every age has its own outlook. It is especially good at seeing certain truths and especially liable to make certain mistakes. . . . All contemporary writers share to some extent the contemporary outlook." The only remedy, says Lewis, against such period-bound assumptions "is to keep the clean sea breeze of the centuries blowing through our minds." And "this," he says, "can be done only by reading old books." Lewis notes, "If you join at eleven o'clock a conversation which began at eight you will often not see the real bearing of what is said. Remarks which seem to you very ordinary will produce laughter or irritation and you will not see why—the reason, of course, being that the earlier stages of the conversation have given them a special point. *It is far more challenging to spot the inconsistencies in our own generation or group*" (Lewis, "Introduction," 1; italics added). Thus, be careful at preemptively dismissing the claims of earlier periods.

4. Goldingay, *Models*, 45.

5. White in Hunt and White, *Debating Calvinism*, 173.

and should, make it our goal to see ever more clearly into the horizon of the text. This is one of many presuppositions with which I come to this project. The task of recognizing and stating our assumptions sometimes feels like an exercise in the obvious. Yet such self-conscious expression is necessary; what may seem perfectly obvious to one person may be completely opaque to another. Consequently, I beg the reader's indulgence for the next few moments as I state what seems almost childish.

I recognize at the outset that theology is a human intellectual enterprise, not divine revelation. To conflate theology with biblical revelation is to misunderstand the nature of both. Further, I write as an evangelical,[6] meaning, I hold to a very high view of Scripture (i.e., a high view of inspiration).[7] Although I am a self-conscious evangelical, my understanding of Scripture is perhaps best expressed by Kevin Vanhoozer[8] and Michael Horton[9] rather than, say, Carl F. H. Henry or Gordon Clark.[10] I am self-consciously *not* postmodern in an epistemological sense, but neither am I precisely modern in a Cartesian sense.[11] I believe that when we speak or write, we communicate meaningfully.[12] Likewise, when someone hears us speak or reads what we have written, there is (at least potentially) real, meaningful communication.[13] I am aware of the problems inherent within many epistemologies, and I am familiar with the problems which attend my own understanding of communication. Nevertheless, I believe these to be surmountable difficulties. Furthermore, I maintain the ongoing need for renewal theology.[14] Renewal theology is a distinct theological approach that attempts to foster and facilitate the reviving work of God, beginning in the church and then

---

6. For descriptions of evangelicalism see Knight, *Future for Truth*; Wells, *No Place for Truth*; McGrath, *Evangelicalism and the Future*; Grenz, *Revisioning Evangelical Theology*; and Bloesch, *New Handbook*.

7. Packer, *Truth and Power*; Packer, "Fundamentalism," 21; Packer, "Infallibility and Inerrancy"; and Moo and Naselli, "Problem of the New Testament's Use."

8. Vanhoozer, *Is There a Meaning*.

9. Horton, *Lord and Servant*; *People and Place*; *Covenant and Eschatology*.

10. Evangelical spokesmen from a previous generation. See, for example, Henry, *God, Revelation and Authority* and Clark, *Religion, Reason, and Revelation*.

11. If I had to decide between the one or the other, I would probably opt for the Cartesian category. Thankfully, however, it is a false dilemma.

12. Contra Derrida, *Michel Foucault*; and John D. Caputo, who is "arguably Jacques Derrida's most capable North American spokesman." See Vanhoozer et al., eds., *Hermeneutics at the Crossroads*, xiii.

13. See Gadamer, *Truth and Method*; Vanhoozer, "Discourse on Matter."

14. "Renewal theology" is a relatively new expression used mostly within Pentecostal/Charismatic circles. It stresses the need for the ever-renewing work of the Holy Spirit.

into the wider community.[15] Renewal itself is rooted in the idea that God alone is the source of all genuine reviving, and so *it seeks to foster within all people an inner experience of treasuring the beauty and worth of God in an ever-growing love for God and the Lordship of Christ over all of life*.[16] To this end, the Old and New Testaments are the primary means by which God makes known His nature, beauty, and will to humanity.[17] As such, the Old and New Testaments are God's self-disclosure through the many literary genres, like the many colors of the rainbow. No one literary type or device is preeminent (e.g., proposition, metaphor, etc.). Rather, God's renewing and reviving works are mediated through the multi-colored spectrum that constitute the palette of literary forms and expressions. The Spirit of God carries out his restoring and reviving work primarily through the Scriptures, by which he confronts, convicts, imparts faith, produces repentance, and creates life-sustaining joy in the heart, so that people begin to value and intentionally display his worth in their lives. These displays of his worth are expressed through our natural giftedness, as well as the spiritual gifts he grants for the purpose of building up the church—which is Christ's body—and to empower us as his witnesses, with the biblical text adjudicating these expressions, making it both the means and the standard of renewal.

---

15. While there have been a host of renewal theologians and authors over the past couple decades, for my part, the greatest renewal theologian was Jonathan Edwards. See especially Edwards, *Treatise Concerning Religious Affections*.

16. See Piper, *Desiring God*; Piper, "Inner Essence of Worship."

17. See Piper, *Reading the Bible Supernaturally*; Calvin, *Institutes* (Battles), 1.7.4.

4.0

A History of God's Righteousness

A Truncated Historical Overview of Justification— from the Protestant Reformation in 1517 to the Joint Declaration on Justification in 1999.

4.1. INTRODUCTION

In what follows, we will look briefly at a few pneumatological "movers and shakers." In early editions of this work, I identified more than fifty different contributors I planned to address. Almost immediately, it became clear that was far too many. I narrowed the list down to twenty-five, only to discover I was still tackling too much. Thus, I finally refined my criteria to only those that not only spoke meaningfully about justification, but also, in one way or another, addressed the subject of pneumatology. It is this narrowing of criteria that explains the incredible gaps between some contributors (e.g., John Calvin to Krister Stendahl). Each author, in one way or another, has contributed to the fields of soteriology and pneumatology. In some instances, the pneumatological contribution has been subtle or indirect, while in others it was obvious and direct. With this in mind, we will begin our examination of pneumatological justification with two of the best-known contributors: Martin Luther and John Calvin.

4.2. MARTIN LUTHER AND JOHN CALVIN: AN INTRODUCTION TO THEIR PNEUMATOLOGIES

John Calvin and Martin Luther are undoubtedly the two best-known leaders of the Protestant Reformation.[1] Yet, over the years, they have been labeled with a host of other appellations, each focusing on specific achievements. For example, Luther is not infrequently seen preeminently as the founder of the Protestant Reformation.[2] Others view him primarily as the founder of Lutheranism.[3] In Calvin's case, some understand him to be "the most important figure in the second generation of the Protestant Reformation,"[4] while others identify his *Institutes* as "the most famous book on Protestantism ever."[5] Still others insist that Calvin's importance transcends the parochial bounds of mere Protestantism and insist he produced the "most famous theological book ever published."[6] Some of these claims may or may not be true (it is difficult to objectively measure many of these claims). Yet, despite the Reformers' fame in many areas,[7] we will make our focus their work as "theologians of the Holy Spirit,"[8] along with a few of the soteriological implications. So, while Luther is frequently thought of as the "theologian of justification by faith alone,"[9] our attention will be specifically on his pneumatological contribution. In this vein, we note Benjamin Warfield's[10] claim that John Calvin should be thought of "preeminently" as "*the* theologian of the Holy Spirit."[11] This claim, in particular, is intriguing, given the heightened interest on the person and work of the Holy Spirit last century,

1. Tangelder, "Calvin and . . . Luther."
2. Pettinger, "Biography of Martin Luther."
3. "Martin Luther: Founder of Lutheranism," and Matheson, "Humanism and Reform Movements," 34.
4. A statement that is almost certainly true. See "John Calvin: Journalist, Theologian."
5. "English Bible History: John Calvin"; Bouwsma, *John Calvin*; Cottret, *Calvin*; and Wellman, *John Calvin*.
6. "John Calvin Biography."
7. One of Calvin's most deserved and celebrated titles is as "the theologian of the glory of God." Like the other labels we have mentioned, examples can be found passim. See McGoldrick, "John Calvin."
8. This particular label was given to Calvin by Warfield, "John Calvin the Theologian" (Warfield, *Calvin and Augustine*).
9. See Wriedt, "Luther's Theology," 88–94; Bouman, "Doctrine of Justification," 801; etc.
10. Warfield is perhaps best known for his role as professor of systematic theology at Princeton Seminary and for the many publications he authored during his years. He served for thirty-four years, until his death on February 16, 1921.
11. Warfield, *Calvin and Augustine*.

especially within the Pentecostal/Charismatic movements.¹² As a result, the validity of this title has been called into question. Warfield was acutely aware of the nascent Pentecostal movement.¹³ In fact, he is well-known for his opposition to the movement. In contrast, he insisted that Calvin was the pneumatological champion. Warfield notes that even though Calvin's name is most frequently associated with predestination,¹⁴ his contribution to that field was not truly "original."¹⁵ Rather, Calvin's creative genius is seen far more clearly in his pneumatology.¹⁶ Similarly, although Luther is widely considered the champion of justification by faith, it would be a mistake to limit his significance to that arena. Both theologians laid important theological groundwork for the pneumatologies that would follow. And although their pneumatologies were more latent than blatant—implied rather than stated—both men placed the white-hot sun of the Holy Spirit at the center of their theological solar systems. For example, according to

---

12. Warfield was not only aware of the nascent Pentecostal movement; he was staunchly opposed to it. There has been conjecture that Warfield's hostility was rooted not so much in theological concerns, as in the trauma of his wife's paralyzing injury and his disenchantment that God never healed her. "In 1876, at the age of twenty-five, he married Annie Pierce Kinkead and took a honeymoon to Germany. During a fierce storm Annie was struck by lightning and permanently paralyzed. After caring for her for thirty-nine years Warfield laid her to rest in 1915. Because of her extraordinary needs, Warfield seldom left his home for more than two hours at a time during all those years of marriage" (Nicole, "B. B. Warfield," 344).

Warfield himself records, "I recall saying to my wife the week before we married, 'If we have a car accident on our honeymoon, and you are disfigured or paralyzed, I will keep my vows, "for better or for worse."'" For Warfield, what had previously been little more than a theoretical event occurred. Annie was never healed. There was only the "spectacular patience and faithfulness of one man to one woman through thirty-eight years" (Warfield, *Faith and Life*, 204).

The notion that Warfield's hostility toward the embryonic Pentecostal movement was rooted in disappointment rather than theology was relatively common during my PhD work. I recall Vinson Synan regularly attributing Warfield's animosity toward the claims of contemporary miracles to this disappointment rather than to the theological rejection he later developed.

13. As noted above, Warfield was an outspoken opponent of the Pentecostal movement. See his *Counterfeit Miracles*.

14. Calvin did indeed write at length about predestination; but Calvin, by his own admission, was a recipient of this doctrine from Augustine and St. Paul before him. The doctrine did not originate with him.

15. Compare Calvin's work on predestination with Luther's book-length treatment in *Bondage of the Will*. Warfield makes this observation in his "Introduction," "Introduction," in *Work of the Holy Spirit*, xxxiv.

16. Warfield, "Introduction," xxxiv–v. Warfield notes that Calvin's contributions to Christology and Christian ethics was also original. However, as our focus is pneumatology, I have deliberately passed over those areas.

Warfield, Calvin was the first real systematizer of pneumatology: "[Calvin] himself gave [pneumatology] a very rich statement, developing it especially in the broad departments of 'Common Grace,' 'Regeneration,' and 'the Witness of the Spirit' . . . it is simply true that *these great topics received their first formulation at the hands of John Calvin*; and it is from him that the Church has derived them, and to him that it owes its thanks for them."[17] Yet, pneumatology in both Calvin and Luther is also elusive. Luther never published a work on systematics, and though Calvin did author such a work, he never produced a systematic statement on the Holy Spirit; there is no "Pneumatology" section in his *Institutes* or commentaries.[18] Instead, both theologians *presupposed* and seamlessly integrated pneumatology throughout their respective works so that it underlies, inspires, and informs the rest of their writing. Lutheran theologian Lauren Blatt writes, "The Holy Spirit lies at the *crux* of Martin Luther's theological framework and is essential [to] understanding his teachings."[19] Likewise, Lopes and DaConceicao state of Calvin, "There is practically no theological subject in which Calvin does not refer to the work of the Holy Spirit. . . . [He] fully integrated the doctrine of the Holy Spirit with other themes and areas of theology."[20] Thus, when these two theologians address virtually any subject, they treat it in a pneumatologically informed way. We should also note that neither Calvin nor Luther could be accused of being "ivory-tower theologians," somehow cut off from

---

17. Kuyper, *Work of the Holy Spirit*, xxxiv; italics added.

18. For that matter, neither is there a systematic discussion of the existence, nature, or the attributes of God in general—at least not in the traditional sense. For information on this, see Warfield, *Calvin and Calvinism*, 134.

19. Blatt, "Luther and the Holy Spirit."

20. Lopes and DaConceicao, "Calvin, Theologian of the Holy Spirit," 39. During the comprehensive exams for my PhD, one of the readers took issue with a statement I made concerning Calvin's pneumatology. During the oral critique, he handed me a two-volume set of Calvin's *Institutes* and asked me to show him a section on pneumatology. The question missed the genius of Calvin's pneumatology (as the above comment from Lopes and DaConceicao illustrates). I answered that Calvin did not address pneumatology in the same way he addressed the other subjects of systematics. For Calvin, pneumatology was a bit like the framing of a house. It was the skeleton upon which everything else hung. It is not usually seen, yet its presence is utterly essential. Even so, Calvin's pneumatology was not overt and obvious, but, without it, his theological construct would collapse. This is stated with clarity by Bernard Ramm, when he wrote, "To profess to know a great deal about the Spirit of God is contrary to the nature of the Spirit of God. There is a hiddenness to the Spirit that cannot be uncovered. There is an immediacy of the Spirit that cannot be shoved into vision. There is an invisibility of the Spirit that cannot be forced into visibility. There is a reticence of the Spirit that cannot be converted into openness. For these reasons one feels helpless, inadequate, and unworthy to write a line about the Spirit." See Ramm, *Rapping About the Spirit*, 7, on the challenges of studying the Spirit. Cf. Erickson, *Christian Theology*, 773–5.

the "real world." Rather, their publications were the natural overflow of their teaching[21] and preaching responsibilities.[22] Calvin was a pastor, Luther was a professor, but both men were driven by genuine pastoral concern. Calvin scholar Steven Lawson, writes, "First and foremost, Calvin was a pastor, the faithful shepherd of two churches for almost thirty years, and amid his many pastoral duties, he was primarily a preacher of the Word. For this magisterial Reformer, biblical preaching was job number one."[23] This observation is made again and again by Calvin biographers,[24] and both reformers believed preaching to be their highest and most sacred duty.[25] The twenty-two volumes of Calvin's *Commentaries* were merely the result of his expositional

---

21. Luther was a professor while Calvin was a pastor. Yet both were driven by pastoral concerns, and though Luther was not the town pastor, he regularly shared the preaching responsibilities with his friend Johannes Bugenhagen when he was in town. He often preached "twice on Sunday and once during the week." See Piper, "Martin Luther." Loewenich states that "Luther was one of the greatest preachers in the history of Christendom. . . . Between 1510 and 1546 Luther preached approximately 3,000 sermons. He frequently preached several times a week, sometimes twice (or more) a day." See Loewenich, *Luther*, 353; cf. Meuser, *Luther the Preacher*, 40–41.

22. Both Calvin and Luther produced a staggering number of publications. The editions of their collected works at Logos software currently shows one hundred eight volumes in the *Calvin 500 Collection* (not every volume in the collection is authored by Calvin, but the vast majority are) and fifty-five volumes in *Luther's Works* (with the three add-ins). Moreover, these are not slim volumes. They are substantial works. In Luther's collections, they average over four hundred pages each. In Calvin's collection, they average just under five hundred pages each. Parker observes that Calvin could scarcely have written more voluminously than he did if he "had been allowed his quiet life in Strassburg or Basel. In the thirty-two years (almost to a day) between the publication of his first book and his death, he created by himself an entire and complete literature" (Parker, *Portrait of Calvin*, 47).

23. Lawson, "Biblical Preaching of John Calvin." Compare the comments of Doumergue: "While [Calvin] has come to be remembered as a theologian who recovered the doctrinal landmarks, which had been buried under the debris of confused centuries, or as a powerful controversialist . . . the truth is that Calvin saw himself, first of all, as a pastor in the church of Christ and therefore as one whose chief duty must be to preach the Word" (Doumergue, *Calvin and the Reformation*, 38.)

24. See Parker, *Portrait of Calvin*; Doumergue, *Calvin and the Reformation*; Beza, *Life of John Calvin*; Torrance, *Hermeneutics of John Calvin*; Schaff, *History*, vol. 7; Sheldon, *History*, vol. 3; Piper, *John Calvin and His Passion*; Godfrey, *John Calvin*; Piper and Mathis, eds., *With Calvin in the Theater of God*; etc.

25. Lawson, "Biblical Preaching of John Calvin."

preaching ministry,[26] as were the thirty volumes of Luther's commentaries.[27] For his part, Calvin believed that the preacher had absolutely "nothing to say apart from Scripture."[28] Both men maintained that the central duty of a preacher/pastor was not to "get" a message, but to deliver one.[29] Preachers were not to offer up their own words but God's word—his message.[30] And this message included the work of God in justification. Thus, in these two initial segments, we will look at what Luther and Calvin had to say about the subject of justification and the work of the Holy Spirit. These sections will, of course, be brief and therefore selective.

4.3. MARTIN LUTHER: SOTERIOLOGY AND THE SPIRIT

4.3.A. Introduction to Luther

On a muggy day in early July 1505, a university student underwent a dramatic life-changing experience. Having recently completed a master's degree, this young man was considered to be one of the most promising young students of jurisprudence throughout Germany. He was on his way back to school following a short visit with his parents when the sky began to darken. The rain began to fall, and it quickly turned into a terrifying thunderstorm storm. Suddenly, a bolt of lightning tore across the sky and slammed into the ground next to where he was riding. The sheer power of the lightning bolt threw him from his saddle onto the ground. Trembling with fear he cried out, "Saint Anne, save me! I will become a monk." To his father's everlasting exasperation, the young man honored this vow. He attended a final going-away party with friends, and the following day he entered "the Black Monastery" in Erfurt in order to become an Augustinian monk. The young man was none other than Martin Luther.[31]

---

26. "For the duration of his ministry, Calvin's approach was to preach systematically through entire books of the Bible. . . . [He] preached from the New Testament on Sunday mornings, from the New Testament or the Psalms on Sunday afternoons, and from the Old Testament every morning of the week, every other week." In this way Calvin worked through most of the Bible. See Lawson, "Biblical Preaching of John Calvin." Adapted from Lawson, "Preacher of God's Word."

27. Vols. 1–30 of *Luther's Works* are devoted exclusively to biblical exposition.

28. Lawson, "Biblical Preaching of John Calvin."

29. Mayhue, "Rediscovering Expository Preaching."

30. Pae, *Study of John Piper's Sermon Preparation*.

31. See Bayer, *Martin Luthers Theologie*, ix; Bainton, *Here I Stand*, Kindle loc. 245–51; and "Martin Luther: Founder of Lutheranism." Luther's life is one of the most fascinating stories in church history. It has all the stuff you would hope to find in a good

4.3.B. Seeing the Power of the Spirit through the Seriousness of Sin

The emphasis of Luther's pneumatology was like several of his Reformation contemporaries, yet different than modern Charismatics/Pentecostals.[32] For Luther et al. the work of the Holy Spirit was focused salvifically. To understand Luther's pneumatology, we will need to take a step back and look at the larger brushstrokes of his theological canvas.

Like the other Reformers, Luther laid great stress on humanity's fallenness. Unlike the Orthodox tradition, where the fall is viewed less significantly, Luther insisted that the totality of every person was impaired by sin. He taught that sin debilitated a person morally and spiritually.[33] Although contemporary Lutheranism has not always been as consistent on this point,[34] Luther himself was unassailably clear. He delivered his most systematized statement on the subject in his book *The Bondage of the Will*, part of a protracted debate with Desiderius Erasmus (1466–1536).[35] Although Luther gives the subject of *original sin*[36] focused attention in this work, he

---

novel: parental conflict, spiritual agony, life-changing moments, near misses, princes, popes, emperors, castles, kidnapping, mobs, revolution, massacres, politics, courage, controversy, disguises, daring escapes, humor, and romance.

32. I am making a distinction here between Luther's conscious emphasis and what I am calling his unconscious emphasis. Luther's *conscious* pneumatological emphasis usually focused on the Holy Spirit's role in changing whatever is necessary in our relationship with God. So, for example, he writes, "You see very clearly that the Holy Spirit's office is not to write books nor to make laws, but freely to abrogate them; and that he is a God who writes only in the heart, who makes it burn, and creates new courage, so that man grows happy before God, filled with love toward him, and with a happy heart serves the people. When the office of the Holy Spirit is thus represented, it is rightly preached ... when he [the Holy Spirit] comes in this manner he abolishes the letter of the Law and desires to liberate the people from their sins and from the Law; the latter is no more needed, for he, himself, rules inwardly in the heart" (Luther, *Church Postil III*, 278). What I focus on above falls more under the category of Luther's unconscious pneumatological emphasis.

33. "Everyone must admit that one can do nothing until one has life. Therefore, all works, however precious and fine they may be, are absolutely nothing if performed before regeneration; they are nothing but sin and death" (Luther, *Sermons on the Gospel of St. John, Chap. 1—4*, 278).

34. I am thinking here of my experience as a non-denominational student attending a Lutheran seminary. I was astonished to find that I was frequently the only person that held Luther's view of sin. My Lutheran classmates (and Lutheran professor) again and again argued *against* the idea of total depravity. I repeatedly brought up Luther's *Bondage of the Will*, only to discover they rejected his teaching on the radical corruption of fallen humanity.

35. On the topic of Erasmus and his relationship with Luther, see Froude, *Life and Letters*, 214*ff*; Bainton, *Erasmus*, 151ff.

36. Luther's preferred expression for this was not *total depravity*, but *original sin*.

also addresses the topic throughout his corpus, describing, defending, and depicting the reality of our sinful condition.

Luther insists that *original sin* is the greatest of all sins. He writes, "Those who wish to . . . minimize *original sin* [should] consider that *original sin* surely appears both from the sins it produces and from the punishments it incurs. Thus, it is by far the greatest sin."[37] He says our pitiable situation is "the result of *original sin*," and "from it all the remaining creatures derive their shortcomings."[38] He contends that before Adam fell, "the sun was brighter, the water purer, the trees more fruitful, and the fields more fertile. But through sin and that awful fall not only our flesh is disfigured by the leprosy of sin, but *everything we use* in this life has *become corrupt*."[39] Luther had little sympathy for those that denied original sin,[40] or tried to describe it as nothing more than corruption.[41] He says that original sin "means that human nature has completely fallen; that the intellect has become darkened, so that we no longer know God and His will and no longer perceive the works of God; furthermore, that the will is extraordinarily depraved, so that we do not trust the mercy of God and do not fear God but are unconcerned, disregard the Word and will of God, and follow the desire and the impulses of the flesh."[42] It is something "planted in us through the sin of our first parents,"[43] and therefore it is as pervasive as it is inescapable.[44]

Although Erasmus is usually seen as a vocal opponent of Luther, it was not always so.[45] In the early days of his Protestant ministry, Luther expressed enthusiastic admiration for the Greek specialist. Erasmus had been a key figure in reviving interest in the biblical languages—which, according to Luther, was an essential precursor to any meaningful rediscovery of divine authority.[46] Erasmus produced the first Greek text of the NT since the days

---

37. Luther, *Lectures on Genesis*, 63.

38. Luther, *Lectures on Genesis*, 64.

39. Luther, *Lectures on Genesis*, 64; italics added.

40. Luther, *Lectures on Genesis*, 110. Luther writes, "Satan is making a great effort to deny original sin. And yet this is in truth the same as denying the suffering and resurrection of Christ."

41. Luther, *Lectures on Genesis*, 114. See Luther's criticism of monastic exegesis on this score in *Luther's Works*, 13:95nn32–33.

42. Luther, *Lectures on Genesis*, 114.

43. Luther, *Lectures on Genesis*, 171.

44. The above excerpts are merely representative and were limited to vol. 1 of Luther's fifty-five-volume *Works*.

45. Luther and Erasmus never actually met in person, but they did correspond occasionally. See Drewery, "Introduction," 33:11–12.

46. See Luther, *Letter to Eobanus Hessus*.

of the early church, *The Novum Instrumentum* (or, as it was more loosely referred to, *Erasmus's Greek New Testament*).⁴⁷ Luther made immediate use of the Greek translation, and this, in part, prompted much of Luther's early admiration. However, by March 1517, Luther was growing reticent of the Dutch scholar. He wrote to John Lang, saying, "I am reading our Erasmus but daily I dislike him more and more. . . . I am afraid . . . that he does not advance the cause of Christ and the grace of God sufficiently. . . . Human matters weigh more with him than the divine. . . . [So] I warn you not to . . . accept everything without scrutiny, for we live in perilous times."⁴⁸

As the Protestant Reformation continued to develop, Erasmus was under growing pressure to openly state his allegiance or opposition to Luther. As the "greatest scholar of his day,"⁴⁹ the support of Erasmus was earnestly sought by both sides in the controversy.⁵⁰ Eventually, Erasmus came out in opposition to Luther, publishing *On the Freedom of the Will*, frequently shortened to just the *Diatribe*.⁵¹ About a year later Luther responded with one of his greatest works,⁵² *The Bondage of the Will*.

Luther could not have been too surprised by Erasmus's response. Erasmus had "politely rejected" Luther's previous overtures of friendship and alliance. However, once Erasmus published the *Diatribe* and then *A Defense of the Diatribe* (*Hyperaspistes diatribae*),⁵³ Luther moved from being merely frustrated with Erasmus to embittered.⁵⁴ "He had always spoken less flatteringly *about* Erasmus than *to* him,"⁵⁵ and now that Erasmus had publicly ridiculed him, Luther responded with a visceral hostility. He called Erasmus a "heretic," a "heathen," and an "atheist." At one point, in the heat of anger, Luther wrote, "I hate Erasmus from the bottom of my heart,"⁵⁶ while at an-

47. Luther, *Bondage of the Will* (Lehmann), 11–12.
48. This letter can be found in Luther, *Letters I*, 12.
49. Graves, "Erasmus"; Drewery, "Introduction," 33:5.
50. Drewery, "Introduction," 33:5.
51. The full title of Erasmus's work was *De libero arbitrio diatribe sive collatio*. Philip S. Watson, a translator of Luther's *Bondage of the Will*, alternately translates the title as *Diatribe Concerning Free Choice*.
52. The question of *Bondage of the Will* (*De servo arbitrio*) being one of Luther's greatest works was his own evaluation. He believed it to be one of his two or three best works. See Drewery, "Introduction," 33:5.
53. The word *hyperaspistes* means "protector"—literally "one who holds a shield (*aspis*) over." Yet, the Greek *aspis* can also be translated as a *viper*. Thus, in a letter to Spalatin in March 1526, Luther referred to Erasmus's follow-up work as "that viper." See *Luther's Works*, 49:145.
54. Smith, *Erasmus*, 25.
55. Drewery, "Introduction," 33:12.
56. Luther, *No. 494: How to Preach*, 1.

other time, he said, "Erasmus is an eel . . . a double-dealing man."[57] Luther was nothing if not direct.

In the "Introduction" to Luther's *Bondage of the Will*, theologians J. I. Packer and O. R. Johnston note that, for Luther, the question of free-will was no mere academic question. "The whole Gospel . . . was bound up with it, and it stood or fell according to the way one decided it."[58] According to Luther, a "true theologian" could not be "unconcerned, or to pretend to be unconcerned, when the Gospel was in danger. . . . The doctrine of the bondage of the will was," he thought, "*the cornerstone of the Gospel* and the foundation of faith."[59]

Believing fallen humanity possessed "free-will" was the gravest of mistakes, in Luther's mind. He maintained that the Bible's uniform testimony concerning our fallen condition is not that we are *free* but that we are *enslaved*. We are told that sinful men and women are "*slaves* to sin" (Rom 6:6), "*blind* in their minds" (2 Cor 4:4), "*dead* in trespasses and sin" (Eph 2:1), "*incapable* of submitting to God's law" (Rom 8:7), and "*incapable* of understanding the things of God" (1 Cor 2:14). As such, claiming *free-will* while yet unregenerate was a complete reversal of reality. Moreover, Luther argued that our fallen condition renders us incapable of avoiding evil. "If man has lost his freedom, and is forced to serve sin, and cannot will good, what conclusion can more justly be drawn concerning him, than that *he sins and wills evil necessarily*?"[60] Erasmus had argued that the presence of divine commands implied the ability to obey those commands. In other words, the fact that God "commands all people everywhere to repent" (Acts 17:30) means that "all people everywhere" *must* be able to repent. To suggest otherwise (said Erasmus) was to make God a tyrant. Erasmus, like Pelagius before him, believed moral obligation implied moral ability. God would never command us to believe in Christ "if he had known that what he enjoined was beyond our achievement."[61] He believed "the issuance of a commandment implied an ability on the part of the hearer to obey the

---

57. Luther, *No. 131: Duplicity of Erasmus*, 19.

58. Packer and Johnston, in Luther's *Bondage of the Will*, 40–41.

59. Packer and Johnston, in Luther's *Bondage of the Will*, 41; italics added.

60. Luther, *Bondage of the Will* (Packer and Johnston), 149; italics added. Within *Bondage*, Luther develops a larger argument that involves God's absolute foreknowledge. If Luther lived in our own day, he would have been decidedly opposed to the Open Theism movement. He asks Erasmus whether it is "irreverent . . . to know whether God foreknows anything contingently?" He answers that "unless [events] are necessary and known with certainty, then neither God, nor Christ, nor gospel, nor faith, nor anything is left, not even of Judaism, much less of Christianity." See Luther, *Bondage of the Will* (Lehmann), 29–30.

61. As quoted in Pelikan, *Emergence of Catholic Tradition*, 1:313.

commandment."[62] Luther, however, demurred. He insisted that Erasmus was mistaken on virtually every level. For example, on the level of grammar alone, Erasmus's claim was fallacious.

> "If thou art willing . . . " is a verb in the subjunctive mood, which asserts nothing . . . a conditional statement asserts nothing indicatively. "If thou art willing . . . " "If thou hear . . . " "If thou do . . . " declares, *not* man's ability, but his duty.[63]

He further argued,

> the Diatribe persists in representing man to us as one who can either do what is commanded or at least knows that he cannot. *But such a man nowhere exists. . . . Scripture represents man as one who is not only bound, wretched, captive, sick, and dead, but in addition to his other miseries is afflicted, through the agency of Satan his prince, with this misery of blindness, so that he believes himself to be free, happy, unfettered, able, well, and alive.*[64]

Thus it is "Satan's work to prevent men from recognizing their plight and to keep them presuming that they can do everything they are told."[65] God's purpose in allowing us to labor under such an impossible state of affairs, says Luther, is to awaken us to our desperate need, turning us to the gospel. "The commandments are not . . . inappropriate or purposeless; they are given in order that blind, self-confident man may, through them, come to know his own diseased state of impotence if he attempts to do what is commanded."[66] And it is this impoverished condition that leads us to Luther's pneumatological emphasis.

For Luther, it was precisely because we are so morally and spiritually destitute—incapable of choosing Christ on our own—that the Holy Spirit is crucial. Jesus himself taught us, "No one can come to me unless the Father who sent me draws him" (John 6:44). Luther says of this, "[Jesus] is speaking *not* only to the Jews, but *all* who want to be Christians. . . . They must keep silent and not murmur but be satisfied. If you want to be saved, do not try to pry into this. Do not murmur. Do not undertake to fathom it, to measure it,

---

62. Pelikan, *Emergence of Catholic Tradition*, 1:313.
63. Luther, *Bondage of the Will* (Packer and Johnston), 157; italics added.
64. Luther, *Bondage of the Will* (Packer and Johnston), 157; italics added.
65. Luther, *Bondage of the Will* (Lehmann), 130.
66. Luther, *Bondage of the Will* (Lehmann), 128. Similarly, he writes, "By the law is the knowledge of sin [Rom 3:20], so the word of grace comes only to those who are distressed by a sense of sin and tempted to despair" (Luther, *Bondage of the Will* [Packer and Johnston], 168).

or to figure it out with your reason." He says the verse is "directed like a peal of thunder against all the works-righteous." He notes that there will always be those that *claim* fallen humanity possesses the ability to choose Christ of their own free-will. But, says Luther, this will only happen, "when a cow can crawl into a mousehole! For here it is written that this is 'impossible.' You cannot do it."[67]

If, then, it is a mistake to "attribute to free choice"[68] the moral ability to choose freely Christ, and if such an error "denigrates regeneration and renewal in the Holy Spirit,"[69] then it would seem we were at an impasse. If free-will is a sham, little more than an illusion (as Luther claims),[70] and yet it is absolutely essential that we be born-again, then how are we to resolve this problem? Luther rightly asks, "How can power to become children of God be given if there is no freedom in our will?"[71] How can one be born-again if the transformation is not the result of free-will? Luther answers: "[N]ew birth, renewal [and] regeneration" are "*wholly [and] entirely* the work of the Spirit."[72] He says he is "amazed and astounded that (Erasmus) could be so utterly ignorant of Holy Writ" concerning regeneration.[73] Regeneration, argues Luther, is the work of the Holy Spirit, not the will of a man. We believe *because* we have (first) been born-again by the Holy Spirit. "Everyone who believes that Jesus is the Christ has been born of God" (1 John 5:1 ESV). Moreover, Luther denies that any sort of "preparation" is necessary to become born-again. He writes that a person "does nothing and attempts nothing to prepare himself for this renewal,"[74] because regeneration is brought

---

67. Luther, *Sermons on Gospel of St. John, Chap. 6—8*, 85; italics added.
68. Luther, *Bondage of the Will* (Lehmann), 110.
69. Luther cites Titus 3:5 here (*Bondage of the Will* [Lehmann], 110).
70. Like Augustine before him, Luther is fully aware that all people possess a certain form of free-will. The concern of Augustine, Luther, Calvin et al. is that if man's will is fallen, so that "every inclination of the thoughts of his heart is only evil all the time" (Gen 6:5), then free-will does not solve the problem. It does not go deep enough, because if the heart is corrupt, then our every decision will always be to freely choose what is sinful. Unless something happens to change the basic nature and inclinations of our heart, free-will simply deepens the problem, because we desire what is forbidden. But, say Augustine, Luther, Calvin et al., this is precisely what regeneration does: God places a new principle of life within us at precisely the same moment he justifies us. Thus, we believe because we have been born-again.
71. Luther, *Bondage of the Will* (Lehmann), 157.
72. Luther, *Bondage of the Will* (Lehmann), 150-1; italics added.
73. Luther, *Bondage of the Will* (Lehmann), 150-1.
74. Luther, *Bondage of the Will* (Lehmann), 243. Luther is here responding to a medieval notion that preparation of the soul for regeneration was utterly indispensable. John of La Rochelle developed Alexander of Hales's idea of prevenient grace and insisted upon "the need for a disposition for justification in people, in that the recipients

about by the Holy Spirit. Luther concludes by stating that what John 6:44 and 6:65[75] have in view is "the very renewal and transformation of the old man."[76] In other words, we are spiritually brought to life through the agency of the Holy Spirit, who "ordains such persons as He wills to receive and partake of [God's] mercy."[77] All of this is simply another way of saying, "When you were dead . . . God made you alive with Christ" (Col 2:13). Or, "you were dead in your transgressions and sins . . . but . . . God . . . made us alive with Christ even when we were dead" (Eph 2:1, 4, 5).

One of the unavoidable implications of this view is what might be called a calvinistic view of election. However, we should be careful not to dismiss this idea in Luther's thought, for it is here that his pneumatology shines most brightly. Luther recognized that things can be only one way or the other: if we possess authentic free-will, then there can be no real divine election. Conversely, if God really does freely choose his elect, then there can be no autonomous free-will. He writes that "free choice in all men alike has the same limitations: it can will nothing good. In that case God will elect no one, nor is there any room left for election, but only the freedom of choice that accepts or rejects forbearance and wrath." And if free-will is defined in such a way as to deny God's sovereign election then "God is robbed of the power and wisdom to elect," and as a result he will be nothing more "than a false idol."[78] Luther claims that Erasmus's *Diatribe* "snores itself away and despises divine realities, so it also judges God, as if he snored away and exercised no wisdom, will, or present power in electing, discerning, and inspiring, but had handed over to men the busy and burdensome task of accepting or rejecting his forbearance and wrath."[79] Luther knew full well that such a view of things would grate against any human-centeredness within us, but he was convinced that anything else would belittle the majesty of God and denigrate the work of the Holy Spirit. So he says, "If flesh and blood are offended [by this doctrine] and murmur,[80] by all means let them murmur; it will achieve nothing; God will not change on that account. And

---

of uncreated grace—that is, of the Holy Spirit—are unable to receive it unless their souls have first been prepared for it" (McGrath, *Iustitia Dei*, 102).

75. "No one can come to me unless the Father who sent me draws him" and "no one can come to me unless the Father has enabled him" (John 6:44, 65).

76. Luther, *Bondage of the Will* (Lehmann), 157.

77. Luther, *Bondage of the Will* (Packer and Johnston), 169.

78. Luther, *Bondage of the Will* (Lehmann), 171.

79. Luther, *Bondage of the Will* (Lehmann), 171–72.

80. Luther cites John 6:61 here: "Jesus, being aware that his disciples were complaining about it, said to them, 'Does this offend you?'" (NRSV).

if the ungodly are scandalized and depart in great numbers,[81] yet the elect will remain." Luther says the same response could be given to those that perniciously ask why God "permitted Adam to fall, and why he creates us all infected with the same sin." Theoretically, God *could have* "preserved us or created us from another stock or from a seed which he had first purged." "But," says Luther, "He is God, and for his will there is no cause or reason that can be laid down as a rule or measure for it, since there is nothing equal or superior to it, but it is itself the rule of all things."[82]

The point we dare not miss here is the utter vulnerability of our condition before God. It is into this darkness that the Holy Spirit's work is seen, because the Spirit raises the dead, awakens the sleeping, and opens the eyes of the blind. Luther loved to quote Titus 3:4:

> But when the goodness and loving-kindness of God our Savior appeared, *He saved us*, not because of deeds done by us in righteousness, but in virtue of His own mercy, *by the washing of regeneration and renewal in the Holy Spirit*, which He poured out upon us richly through Jesus Christ our Savior, so *that we might be justified* by His grace and become heirs in hope of eternal life.[83]

Luther maintained that the Holy Spirit was the "effective agent behind the Word's encounter with humanity."[84] Moreover, he believed "the gospel brings the Holy Spirit."[85] And it is the Spirit that "preaches to us and brings us to Christ."[86] Thus, "the Spirit regenerates us, encourages and comforts,"[87] interceding for us "when we are at our weakest."[88] In short, "the Spirit is the antidote to the Law."[89]

Luther speaks of "the chief high articles of Christian doctrine established and set forth." Preeminent among these "chief high articles" are "the doctrine of the three distinct Persons in the Holy Trinity," and "the doctrine of justification by faith."[90] In fact, justification is "the *chief* article

---

81. Luther is referring here to John 6:66: "Because of this many of his disciples turned back and no longer went about with him" (NRSV).
82. Luther, *Bondage of the Will* (Lehmann), 180–1.
83. Titus 3:4 NIV; italics added.
84. Luther, *Large Catechism*, 436.
85. Bayer, *Martin Luthers Theologie*, 223; italics added.
86. Luther, *Large Catechism*, 436.
87. Bayer, *Martin Luthers Theologie*, 223.
88. Bayer, *Martin Luthers Theologie*, 223.
89. Bayer, *Martin Luthers Theologie*, 224.
90. Luther, *Sermons on Gospel of St. John, Chap. 14—16*, 7–8.

of Christian doctrine."[91] Interestingly, though, Luther also maintained that the doctrines of the Holy Trinity and justification were interconnected and mutually supportive of each other. He said their connection was "so clear and convincing" that they can "powerfully strike down all heretics and schismatic spirits."[92]

Finally, Luther maintained that the Holy Spirit was "sent forth" in two distinct ways. The first was the event of Pentecost, where the Spirit "was sent forth in a *manifest and visible form.*"[93] The second is when "the Holy Spirit, through the Word, is sent into the hearts of believers."[94] Here, Luther links the work of the Holy Spirit with the work of the Word. In fact, Luther goes so far as to say that without the bond between the Spirit and the Word, "it is impossible to form any sure judgments about anything."[95] Thus, for Luther, when we believe the gospel, *we are already involved in a pneumatological event.* Since the Word and the Spirit are inextricably bound up together in the gospel,[96] and the Spirit always functions as the "effective agent" in our encounter with the Word,[97] it is clear that regeneration and justification are at their core pneumatological events, even if they are not always overtly stated as such. Thus, Luther's pneumatology is seen in different places than contemporary Pentecostals or Charismatics. Although he believed the Spirit distributed gifts, he did not emphasize this role. Instead, Luther saw the

---

91. Luther, "Galatians 2:11," in *Lectures on Galatians, 1535, Chap. 1—4*, 106; italics added; cf. Luther, *What Luther Says*, 2:705.

92. Luther, *Sermons on Gospel of St. John, Chap. 14—16*, 7–8.

93. Luther, *Lectures on Galatians, 1535, Chap. 1—4*, 374, and Gal 4:6; italics added. Luther goes on to say, "Thus [the Holy Spirit] descended upon Christ at the Jordan in the form of a dove (Matt 3:16), and upon the apostles and other believers in the form of fire (Acts 2:3). This was the first sending forth of the Holy Spirit; it was necessary in the primitive church, which had to be established with visible signs on account of the unbelievers, as Paul testifies. 1 Cor 14:22: 'Tongues are a sign, not for believers but for unbelievers.' But later on, when the church had been gathered and confirmed by these signs, it was not necessary for this visible sending forth of the Holy Spirit to continue."

94. Luther, *Lectures on Galatians, 1535, Chap. 1—4*, 374–5. Luther says that this event "happens without a visible form, namely, when through the spoken Word we receive fire and light, by which we are made new and different, and by which a new judgment, new sensations, and new drives arise in us. This change and new judgment are not the work of human reason or power; they are the gift and accomplishment of the Holy Spirit, who comes with the preached Word, purifies our hearts by faith, and produces spiritual motivation in us."

95. Luther, *Lectures on Galatians, 1535, Chap. 1—4*, 374–5, and Gal 4:6. Luther believed this was what set him and the other Protestant Reformers apart from their Roman Catholic and more radical reforming opponents.

96. Bayer, *Martin Luthers Theologie*, 223; italics added.

97. Luther, *Large Catechism*, 436.

Spirit's work in breathing spiritual life into us "even when we were dead in trespasses and sins." Moreover, Luther seems to have viewed the entire salvific process as a pneumatological event, tying the Holy Spirit's work with the Word we encounter in the gospel and in the ongoing process of sanctification, as the Spirit and the Law cause "a holy life to arise spontaneously [in] the heart of a believer."[98]

4.4. CALVIN AND THE SPIRIT

4.4.A. Introduction: Calvin's Contribution

John Calvin is one of the best-known names of Church history. It is difficult to overstate Calvin's impact on both the secular and religious worlds. According to many sources, his *Institutes* is among the one hundred most influential writings of all human history.[99] Calvin's influence has been felt many ways. Among these were his pivotal roles as an expositor and theologian. Thomas Torrance writes, "If it fell to the lot of Martin Luther to transform the theological scene . . . it was certainly the destiny of John Calvin to be the father both of modern theology and of modern biblical exposition."[100] Calvin was far more than a simple theologian. As T. H. L. Parker points out, Calvin was "a man of encyclopedic mind, born . . . to grapple with libraries."[101] And while schooled in the Renaissance, Calvin did not adopt the pedantry so often associated with that school.[102] He tells us that his objective throughout his work was "lucid brevity."[103]

Calvin was born in Noyones, Picardy, on July 27, 1509, and later came to prominence as a Protestant reformer in the city of Geneva. Yet Calvin never set out to become a public reformer. One of the interesting events of his life was his decision to settle in the city of Geneva and work as a pastor and reformer. In August 1536, when he was twenty-seven years old (only two months after the Reformation had officially began),[104] Calvin began a

---

98. Godfrey, "Law and Gospel," 379.

99. See, for instance, even outside theological settings, its current listing in the thirty-fifth position in Wikipedia's "One Hundred Most Influential Books."

100. Torrance, *Hermeneutics of John Calvin*, 61.

101. Parker, *Portrait of Calvin*, 29.

102. For further information on Calvin's education and early life see Schaff, *History*, 8:266ff.

103. Calvin, "Epistle Dedication," in *Commentary on the Epistle of Paul*, xxiii.

104. Schaff, *History*, 8:348.

trip to the city of Strasbourg.[105] The journey required more than one day's travel, however, and Calvin was forced to stay the night in the city of Geneva, intending to continue his journey the following morning. However, a local pastor named Farel discovered Calvin was in Geneva and, thinking Calvin's talents would make him an invaluable alley in the Reformation effort, Farel located Calvin and urged him to remain in the city to help the Protestant cause. Calvin, though, was not inclined to the "harassing encounters of public ministry"[106] and instead sought a life of quiet retirement and academic research. Thus, Calvin refused Farel's invitation. But Farel was impetuous and frequently spoke "unadvisedly."[107] He thundered with prophetic authority, "You are only pursuing your own desires. I, therefore, declare to you in the name of Almighty God that if you refuse to take part in the Lord's work in this Church, God will curse the quiet life you seek for your studies."[108] Calvin later wrote of the incident, "Terrified by his words, and conscious of my own timidity and cowardice, I gave up my journey and attempted to apply whatever gift I had in defense of my faith."[109] Thus, Calvin remained in the city, pastoring and leading the congregation for many years to come.[110]

Calvin came to be known as "the king of commentators,"[111] a man whose reputation was recognized not only in later history but even during his own lifetime. For example, in a letter to Martin Bucer in 1539, Martin Luther said of Calvin, "Present my respectful greetings to Sturm and Calvin,

105. See Cottret, *Calvin*, 110, 114; Ganoczy, "Calvin's Life," 9ff.; and Parker, *John Calvin*, 52, 72.

106. Sheldon, *History*, 3:143.

107. Parker's expression for Farel. Parker, *Portrait of Calvin*, 37.

108. Parker, *Portrait of Calvin*, 37. Schaff recounts the same event in the following words (*History*, 8:348):

> His presence was made known to Farel through the imprudent zeal of Du Tillet, who had come from Basel via Neuchâtel, and remained in Geneva for more than a year. Farel instinctively felt that the providential man had come who was to complete and to save the Reformation of Geneva. He at once called on Calvin and held him fast, as by divine command. Calvin protested, pleading his youth, his inexperience, his need of further study, his natural timidity and bashfulness, which unfitted him for public action. But all in vain. Farel, "who burned of a marvellous (*sic*) zeal to advance the Gospel," threatened him with the curse of Almighty God if he preferred his studies to the work of the Lord, and his own interest to the cause of Christ. Calvin was terrified and shaken by these words of the fearless evangelist and felt "as if God from on high had stretched out his hand." He submitted, and accepted the call to the ministry, as teacher and pastor of the evangelical Church of Geneva.

109. Calvin, *Autobiographical Sketch*, 53.

110. Cf. Ramsay, *Church History*, 57.

111. Schaff, *History*, 7:524.

whose books I have pursued with singular pleasure."[112] Calvin's assistant and later biographer, Theodore Beza, stated, "I feel myself justly warranted to declare, that in him was presented to all men, one of the most beautiful and illustrious examples of the pious life and triumphant death of a real Christian . . . the most exalted virtue will find it difficult to imitate his conduct."[113] For his part, Philip Melanchthon referred to Calvin simply as "*The* Theologian." Philip Schaff said of Calvin's character, "All impartial writers admit the purity and integrity, if not the sanctity, of his character, and his absolute freedom from love of gain and notoriety."[114] Finally, we draw the readers' attention to two final statements from very unexpected sources. First, Jacobus Arminius, the man whose name has become virtually synonymous with opposition to Calvin's theology, stated, "Next to the study of the Scriptures which I earnestly inculcate, *I exhort my pupils to peruse Calvin's Commentaries*, which I extol in loftier terms than Helmich himself [a Dutch divine, 1551–1608]; for *I affirm that Calvin excels beyond comparison in the interpretation of Scripture.* . . . "[115] Second, Pope Pius IV (1559–65) begrudgingly said of Calvin, "The strength of that heretic consisted in this, that money never had the slightest charm for him. If I had such servants, my dominion would extend from sea to sea."[116] Such was the life of the Genevan Reformer.

4.4.B. Warfield's Insight into Calvin's Pneumatology

We noted earlier that Warfield labeled Calvin "*the* theologian of the Holy Spirit,"[117] and it is through this lens that we will approach Calvin's pneumatology. Warfield insists that the development of pneumatology is "*an exclusively Reformation doctrine, and more particularly a Reformed doctrine, and more particularly still a Puritan doctrine.*"[118] If we allow Warfield this premise (not all will), then we can begin to appreciate Warfield's insight into Calvin's pneumatological contribution. For example, Warfield notes that Calvin creates an inextricable connection between pneumatology and soteriology. For Warfield, it is this fundamental link that constitutes Calvin as "the theologian of the Holy Spirit." He writes,

---

112. Schaff, *History*, 7:272; italics added.
113. Beza, *Life of John Calvin*, 65.
114. Schaff, *History*, 7:271.
115. As quoted in Schaff, *History*, 7:280; italics added.
116. Pius IV, on the death of Calvin, as quoted in Durant, *Reformation*, 475.
117. Lopes and Da Conceicao, "Calvin, Theologian."
118. Kuyper, *Work of the Holy Spirit*, xxxiii.

Here then is probably Calvin's greatest contribution to theological development. In his hands, for the first time in the history of the Church, the doctrine of the Holy Spirit comes to its rights. Into the heart of none more than into his did the vision of the glory of God shine, and no one has been more determined than he not to give the glory of God to another. Who has been more devoted than he to the Saviour, by whose blood he has been bought? But, above everything else, it is the sense of the sovereign working of salvation by the almighty power of the Holy Spirit which characterizes all Calvin's thought of God. And above everything else he deserves, therefore, the great name of *the theologian of the Holy Spirit*.[119]

We should be wary of rushing past this statement, as it is the very crux of the matter for Warfield. It was Calvin's emphasis on the absolute necessity of the Holy Spirit as the sovereign soteriological agent that made Calvin unique in the eyes of Warfield. Like Calvin, Warfield believed that humanity is dead in trespasses and sins, and it is only through the direct and immediate interposition of the Holy Spirit that dead men and women are made alive. Both Warfield and Calvin were fond of noting that we were "dead in [our] transgressions and sins, in which [we] used to live" (Eph 2:1). Or that "When [we] were dead in [our] sins and in the uncircumcision of [our] sinful nature, God made [us] alive with Christ" (Col 2:13). For Calvin (and Warfield), such statements could not be reduced to merely figurative language. Rather, these statements describe the actual state of affairs, the very matrix that fallen humanity lives within—a kind of living death. Consequently, there can be no spiritual life apart from the Holy Spirit. When we are born again, we exercise saving faith precisely because of the work of the Spirit, who is "the initiator of faith, [and] who increases it by degrees until by it he leads us [the elect] to the kingdom of heaven."[120] In his commentary on Ephesians, Calvin states,

> [The apostle] does not mean simply that they were in danger of death; but he declares that it was a real and present death under which they labored. As spiritual death is nothing else than the alienation of the soul from God, we are all born as dead men, and we live as dead men, until we are made partakers of the life of Christ.[121]

---

119. Warfield, *Calvin and Augustine*, 485-6.
120. Calvin, *Institutes* (McNeill), 3.2.33.
121. Calvin, *Commentary on Epistle to Ephesians*, 27.

And, without doubt, the goal of becoming "partakers of the life of Christ" was paramount in Calvin's thought. He taught that "until our minds become intent upon the Spirit, Christ, so to speak, lies idle because we coldly contemplate him as outside ourselves—indeed, far from us."[122] The goal of the Holy Spirit in our lives, then, is union with Christ, both legally (justification) and practically (sanctification). To accomplish this, the Spirit illuminates the Scripture and bestows faith. "Union with Christ then leads to assurance of salvation and confidence in God."[123] In this way, the Holy Spirit leads believers to embrace sound doctrine, and "that doctrine must regulate all of life."[124] From this fountain, Calvin believed the life of Christ overflowed into the believer, leading to authentic holiness—holiness which required genuine repentance. Repentance brought the believer "under the government of [God's] Holy Spirit," who is "the fountain of all holiness, all righteousness, and, in short, all perfection."[125]

According to Calvin, then, fallen humanity can do no more to choose Christ or love God in their own power than Lazarus could choose to raise himself back to life. The Spirit's regenerating work is parallel to the raising of Lazarus, as it is a monergistic act in which dead persons are raised to life.[126] Apart from the Holy Spirit's decisive regenerating act, there is no hope for the spiritually dead. It is this "calvinistic"[127] understanding of spiritual death and rebirth that made Calvin preeminently the theologian of the Holy Spirit in Warfield's mind. Thus, Warfield argues that in the same way we have received from Augustine the doctrine of sin and grace, and from Anselm the doctrine of satisfaction, and from Luther the doctrine of justification by faith, so also "we must say that *the doctrine of the work of the Holy Spirit is a gift from Calvin to the Church.*"[128] Warfield goes further and states that, "What is special to [Calvin] is the clearness and emphasis of his reference of all that God brings to pass, especially in the processes of the new creation, to

---

122. Calvin, *Institutes* (McNeill), 3.1.3.

123. Calvin, *Institutes*, 3.2.33–35 (McNeill); cf. Evans, "John Calvin, Theologian of the Holy Spirit."

124. McGrath, *Spirituality*, 192.

125. Calvin, *Grace and Its Fruits*, 209–10.

126. On the topic of regeneration, see Piper, *Finally Alive*; Hoekema, *Saved By Grace*; Grudem, *Systematic Theology*, chap. 34; Murray, "Systematic Theology"; Packer, "Regeneration."

127. I place the term "calvinistic" in quotations here because, as Warfield argues, this was not unique to Calvin.

128. Warfield, "Calvin as a Theologian."

God the Holy Spirit, and the development from this point of view of a rich and full doctrine of the work of the Holy Spirit."[129]

This soteriological/pneumatological link in Calvin can be seen in other places in Warfield's work. In *Calvin and Calvinism,* he writes,

> The real difference between Calvin's and the ordinary Lutheran conception at this point lies in the greater profundity of Calvin's insight and the greater exactness of his analysis. The Lutheran is prone to begin with faith, which is naturally conceived at its apex, as faith in Jesus Christ our Redeemer; and to make everything else flow from this faith as its ultimate root. For what comes before faith, out of which faith itself flows, he has little impulse accurately to inquire. Calvin penetrates behind faith to the creative action of the Holy Spirit on the heart and the new creature which results therefrom. . . . The effect of this is that "efficacious grace"—what we call in modern speech "*regeneration*" . . . *takes the place of fundamental principle in Calvin's soteriology* and he becomes preeminently *the theologian of the Holy Spirit*. In point of fact it is from him accordingly that the effective study of the work of the Holy Spirit takes its rise, and it is only in the channels cut by him and at the hands of thinkers taught by him that the theology of the Holy Spirit has been richly developed.[130]

Additionally, Warfield notes how easy it is to lose sight of an essential element in our soteriological formulations—i.e., the noncontributory nature of saving faith. Simply affirming the necessity of "faith in Christ" may not be enough. Warfield suggests that Calvin's emphasis on the sovereignty of the Spirit in salvation places the emphasis in just the right place. For Calvin, "faith in Christ" was the *sine qua non* of justification. Obviously, faith is a *condition* of justification, but it is a condition that does not compromise the gracious nature of the gospel, but instead *arises from it*.[131] These conditions are the "noncontributory means by which we receive his grace."[132] "The important thing," says Warfield, "is not to deny conditions, but to underscore that it is *not* faith that saves, but Christ that saves *through* faith."[133] So, although faith is an essential element to our redemption, Warfield finds Calvin asking a deeper question: How does faith actually enter into the

---

129. Warfield, *Calvin and Augustine*, 485–6.

130. Warfield, *Calvin and Calvinism*, 62; italics added.

131. E.g., "Unless you repent, you too will all perish" (Luke 13:3). "It is only *if* we suffer with Christ that we will reign with him" (Rom 8:17). "*If* we confess our sins, he is faithful and just and will forgive us our sins" (1 John 1:9). Italics added.

132. Sinclair Ferguson, in Alexander, ed., *Christian Spirituality*, 34–35; italics added.

133. Warfield, *Works*, 2:504; italics added.

heart of the spiritually dead? How does one that is "by nature an object of wrath"[134] and "hostile to God"[135] somehow change his or her affections and become a friend of God? Calvin's answer is that the Spirit of God places a new principle of life within the sinner. This new life is what Jesus meant in John 3 when he said we must be born again (regenerated). "Everyone who believes that Jesus is the Christ *has been* born of God" (1 John 5:1; ESV). As a result of this new life, faith enters our heart, and this faith becomes the means of God's other redemptive gifts, including justification. Hence, Calvin states, "It is therefore the Spirit of God who regenerates us and makes us new creatures."[136] We do not cause new birth, God does. 1 Peter 1:3 states that "God . . . has caused us to be born again . . . " (ESV). This, according to Warfield, is the hinge upon which the whole pneumatological door turns. If we focus on other areas of pneumatology (e.g., spiritual gifts), yet neglect this, the weightiest and most essential element, we will miss the genius of Calvin's contribution to the field of pneumatology. This is why Warfield says our most interest in Calvin's pneumatology should be through his soteriology. He says that "within this broad field," Calvin's interest "was most intense in the application to the sinful soul of the salvation wrought out by Christ. . . . *The effect of [the Institutes] . . . has been to constitute Calvin preeminently the theologian of the Holy Spirit.*"[137] Although Warfield recognized that Calvin contributed more to the field of pneumatology than *just* soteriology, it was Calvin's soteriology that brought his pneumatology into its sharpest focus. That notwithstanding, Calvin did also develop his pneumatology in conjunction with his view of Scripture, a connection to which we now turn our attention.

Although Calvin's corpus is vast, the *Institutes* enables the interested reader to grasp his overall system, thereby succinctly consolidating the essentials of his theology. In fact, Calvin deliberately kept his *Institutes* small enough that a person could carry the work in the pocket of his cloak. The result is that one comes away from Calvin's magnum opus with a clear idea of what he taught on all the major subjects of biblical revelation, including justification.[138] For example, Calvin writes, "we simply interpret justification, as the acceptance with which God receives us into his favour as if we were righteous; and that this justification consists in the forgiveness of sins

---

134. Eph 2:3.
135. Rom 8:7.
136. Calvin, *Commentary on Epistle to Titus*, 50.
137. Warfield, "John Calvin the Theologian"; italics added.
138. See Shepherd, "Theology of John Calvin" and Shepherd, "Calvin on Justification." Calvin's exposition on justification is seen most predominantly in Calvin, *Institutes* (McNeill), 3.11.1–23.

and the imputation of the righteousness of Christ."¹³⁹ In a letter to Cardinal Sadoleto, Calvin says that justification by faith is "the first and keenest subject of controversy between" Protestants and Roman Catholics. Moreover, he insists, "Wherever the knowledge of [justification] is taken away, the glory of Christ is extinguished, religion abolished, the Church destroyed, and the hope of salvation utterly overthrown."¹⁴⁰ Yet, for Calvin, justification involved more than just the pardon of sins. It included what he called "the righteousness of faith."

> As all mankind are, in the sight of God, lost sinners, we hold that Christ is their only righteousness, since, by his obedience, he has wiped off our transgressions; by his sacrifice, appeased the divine anger; by his blood, washed away our stains; by his cross, borne our curse; and by his death, made satisfaction for us. We maintain that in this way man is reconciled in Christ to God the Father, by no merit of his own, by no value of works, but by gratuitous mercy. When we embrace Christ by faith, and come, as it were, into communion with him, this we term, after the manner of Scripture, the righteousness of faith.¹⁴¹

This righteousness of faith is the righteousness that Jesus Christ earned during his earthly life. Calvin believed that this positive righteousness was credited to the account of the sinner when he or she places his or her faith in Christ. For example, he writes, "To *justify*, therefore, is nothing else than to acquit from the charge of guilt, as if innocence were proved. [God does this] *by an imputation of righteousness*, so that though not righteous in ourselves, we are deemed righteous in Christ."¹⁴² Moreover, throughout the *Institutes*, Calvin sought to constructively set forth his doctrinal understanding and to respond to his many critics. One point of controversy was the distinction that Calvin made between regeneration, justification, and other aspects of redemption. Calvin's critics insisted that Calvin made illegitimate "separations." Calvin, however, insisted he made no "separation," only distinctions; for the elements of redemption are *always* and ineluctably together. "But it ought to be remembered . . . that the gift of justification is *not* separated from regeneration, though the two things are distinct."¹⁴³ That is, regeneration and justification are *always* together, yet they can be distinguished. Thus, Calvin (and the other magisterial reformers) insisted

---

139. Calvin, *Institutes* (Beveridge), 3.11.2; italics added.
140. Calvin, *Institutes* (Beveridge), 1:41.
141. Dillenberger, ed., *John Calvin*, 96.
142. Calvin, *Institutes* (Beveridge), 3.11.3; italics added.
143. Calvin, *Institutes* (Beveridge), 3.11:11; italics added.

that he was distinguishing between justification and regeneration; between justification and sanctification; between justification and good works. He did not *separate* them. Indeed, they cannot be separated. Nevertheless, they should be differentiated. Calvin stated the matter concisely when he wrote, "Thus it appears how true it is that we are justified not without, and yet not by works," insisting that genuine saving faith is never "devoid of good works," nor can "justification exist without them."[144]

4.5. KRISTER STENDAHL (1921–2008)

Krister Stendahl was a Swedish theologian and New Testament scholar who served the Churches of Sweden and the United States throughout his life. Born in 1921, Stendahl earned his PhD from Uppsala University, writing his dissertation on the Dead Sea Scrolls in 1947. He took a position at Harvard Divinity School in 1954,[145] where he taught until 1984, serving as dean of the school between 1968 and 1979.[146] Stendahl moved back to his homeland in 1984 to take a post within the Church of Sweden as bishop of Stockholm, a position he held until 1988. After four years, Stendahl returned to the US, where he actively participated in Jewish-Christian dialogue. In the early 1990s, however, Stendahl surprised everyone by coming out of retirement and taking a post at Brandeis University in Waltham, MA, where he taught various courses as his health permitted. During this period, he also served as Professor Emeritus for Harvard Divinity School. Stendahl died in Boston, MA, in 2008 at the age of 87.

Although Stendahl was raised Lutheran and was trained and ordained within that tradition, there was a clear disjunction between much of his thinking and traditional Lutheran theology. He is, perhaps, best known today for his two pioneering essays, "The Apostle Paul and the Introspective Conscience of the West" and "Paul among the Jews and Gentiles." As early as the first part of the 1960s, Stendahl began a series of lectures critiquing the Lutheran tradition, outlining his desires to understand the New Testament in its proper context and to correct what he believed to be a long-term fundamental misunderstanding of New Testament background. Although

---

144. Calvin, *Institutes* (Beveridge), 3.16.1.

145. There is a discrepancy on the precise year that Stendahl began teaching at Harvard. Douglas Martin, the author of the *New York Times* essay on Stendahl, states that he began teaching at Harvard in 1954. In contrast, Magnus Zetterholm lists Stendahl as beginning his time at Harvard in 1958. Since there is not the same amount of literature on Stendahl as on many within this section, it is difficult to verify the exact year. See Martin, "Krister Stendahl" and Zetterholm, *Approaches to Paul*, 97.

146. Martin, "Krister Stendahl."

there had been antecedents suggesting similar ideas,[147] these predecessors never produced an impact like Stendahl's "Paul among Jews and Gentiles," nor did the general atmosphere reach its tipping point until E. P. Sanders published his monograph *Paul and Palestinian Judaism* (see below).[148] Stendahl's work contains the seminal ideas which were later to flourish and grow through the so-called New Perspective on Paul.

One of the unique characteristics of Stendahl's interpretive methodology was the sharp distinction he made between *the original meaning of the biblical text along with the impact it had on society* (*Wirkungsgeschichte*) and *the meaning it* may *have in the here-and-now of the present day*. In effect, Stendahl cut the close tie between the exegetical task and the theological reflection that has traditionally characterized biblical studies. Instead, he related the problem to redemptive-historical (or salvation-historical) context, thus allowing for further theological development of Pauline ideas. One of the results of such a cleavage between two historically allied disciplines (exegesis and theological reflection) was that it provided Stendahl with considerably greater hermeneutical flexibility, as it did not push for complete unity between the historical meaning of the text of Scripture and the theology of the church.[149] "It is rather natural," Stendahl claims, "that the church emphasizes other aspects than the author originally stressed."[150] For those raised within the constraints of conservative evangelicalism, such statements are concerning. In his essay, "Paul and the Introspective Conscience of the West," Stendahl maintained there was potentially a vast difference between what the apostle originally intended and the meaning imputed to him by the leaders of the Protestant Reformation.

In his most famous essay, "Paul among Jews and Gentiles," originally written in Swedish and published later in English (1976),[151] Stendahl argued that the critical issue driving Paul's theology was quite different from what people have long thought. Based on a series of lectures delivered in the early 1960s, Stendahl argued that the primary impetus behind the apostle's letters

---

147. Some of the other first-century specialists include Claude G. Montefiore, Hans-Joachim Schoeps, Samuel Sandmel, George F. Moore, Wilhelm Bousset, Max Weber, and Emil Schürer. Obviously, not all these individuals had equal influence, and some fell out of favor later in time.

148. Sanders, *Paul and Palestinian Judaism*.

149. For support of these claims see Westerholm, *Perspectives*, 146; Stendahl, as quoted in Zetterholm, *Approaches to Paul*, 84–85; and Chester, "Justification, Ecclesiology."

150. As quoted in Zetterholm, *Approaches to Paul*, 97.

151. The same was true for Stendahl's other famous essay, "The Apostle Paul and the Introspective Conscience of the West." Cf. Hafemann, "Paul and His Interpreters," 675.

was his concern over the relationship between Jews and non-Jews and the aspects within the Mosaic law that highlighted Jewish distinctiveness over against the Gentiles' exclusion from the covenant. Even more basically, Stendahl argued for a radically different understanding of the law than Protestantism traditionally held. Whereas Protestants typically viewed the law as an instrument intended to bring people to a point of contrition, forcing them to discover their utter inability to obey its obligations,[152] Stendahl argued that such a view simply could not account for some of Paul's statements in Philippians where asserts that "in regard to the law," he considered himself "faultless" (Phil. 3:5–6). Consequently, Stendahl insisted that forgiveness of sins through justification could not be at the center of God's plan in the gospel message. The basic problem behind this error, he maintained, was that Luther was operating, and thus interpreting the biblical texts, on the basis of a medieval background, with its complex of problems and relationships. The result was that "the law" became a type of general principle where a form of "legalism" grew up. But, says Stendahl, a startling twist resulted from this: "Paul's argument that the Gentiles must not, and should not come to Christ *via* the Law, i.e., *via* circumcision etc., has turned into a statement according to which all men must come to Christ with consciences properly convicted by the Law and its insatiable requirements for righteousness. So drastic is the reinterpretation once the original framework of 'Jews and Gentiles' is lost, and the Western problems of conscience become its unchallenged and self-evident substitute."[153]

Finally, we briefly note Stendahl's understanding of Romans and Galatians. Stendahl argued that both letters must be understood in terms of the relationship between Jews and non-Jews which, he argued, had no bearing on the all-important question of whether humanity can be saved or how our deeds enter into the final judgment. Of course, both letters address the topic of race relations, and the apostle does not shy away from some potentially difficult topics.[154] According to Stendahl, however, justification is related to matters central to Rom 9–11, rather than 1–6. For those raised in the Protestant tradition, this is potentially confusing. According to Stendahl, the apostle addresses God's plan for ultimate salvation and how the Jew fits within this place in Rom 9–11, and thus this is where the question of

---

152. It was asserted by Stendahl and subsequently most of the proponents of the New Perspective on Paul that Protestants have historically understood the nature and purpose of the law through the lens of Luther's turbulent quest to find a merciful God. Thus, Luther and his emotionally tormented quest have ostensibly become the paradigm through which conversion is generally viewed within the Protestant tradition.

153. Stendahl, "Apostle Paul," 207; italics in original.

154. I am thinking here of passages in Rom 11 and Gal 2.

justification must be focused. Following God's promises to the nation in the beginning of Rom 9, Paul states that the Jews' rejection of the Messiah was what ultimately led to the offer of salvation to non-Jews. Stendahl insists that God anticipated the Jews' rejection of the gospel in order that non-Jews be included into the covenant. The result is that, in the end, "all Israel will be saved" (Rom 11:26-27). Moreover, there is no conflict between God's promise to Israel and the fact that Gentiles are also extended the offer of salvation. According to Stendahl, *this* is what the word *justification* means, namely, *victory* or *salvation*.[155] In the end, "God's righteousness will set everything right"[156] for both Jew and Gentile.

4.6. ERNST KÄSEMANN (1906–98)

Ernst Käsemann was heavily influenced by three of the greatest theological minds of the 20th century: Karl Barth, Adolf Schlatter, and his personal advisor, Rudolf Bultmann. Käsemann eventually broke with his intellectual mentors, blazing a unique scholarly path all his own. He sought to reignite the quest for the historical Jesus and to defend the doctrine of justification against those he perceived as a potential new threat, men like Krister Stendahl, E. P. Sanders, and the subsequent New Perspective on Paul.

Käsemann was born on July 12, 1906, in the Dahlhausen region of Bochum, Westphalia, Germany. He pursued a course in theological studies at the universities of Bonn, Tübingen, and Marburg, where he presented his dissertation in 1931 under the tutelage of Rudolf Bultmann, entitled *Leib und Leib Christi: Eine Untersuchung zur paulinischen Begrifflichkeit* (*Body and Christ's Body: A Study of Pauline Conceptuality*). Following his doctoral work, Käsemann served as pastor of a small congregation in Gelsenkirchen in the Ruhr Valley of North Rhine-Westphalia. However, as the Second World War developed, Käsemann found himself caught, like so many others, in a series of events that systematically forced him into a very difficult position, eventually resigning his position within the Westphalian church due to its implicit cooperation with the (German) state church. Looking back, Käsemann was ambivalent about the events taking place around him. His later publications allow us to see the way he progressively realized the severity of the political and theological affairs around him and how he reluctantly became a critic of the German state church, as well as of his own former congregation (and similar parishes) for their silent acquiescence to the Nazi programs. Käsemann was eventually arrested by the Gestapo in

---

155. See Stendahl, *Final Account*, 33–34.
156. Stendahl, *Final Account*, 34.

1937 for his open defiance of Hitler as the final authority. Specifically, it was Käsemann's use of Isaiah 26:13 in direct opposition to the German Führer: "O Lord our God, other lords besides thee have ruled over us, but thy name alone we acknowledge." The Nazis could not allow such blatant insolence to go unpunished and Käsemann was imprisoned.

While in prison, Käsemann began drafting his study on the Christian church as a "pilgrim people," based on the book of Hebrews.[157] When the war ended, Käsemann was released from prison, enabling his work to continue. He held short-term teaching positions at both Mainz (1946–51) and Göttingen (1951–9), but he eventually found his home as professor of New Testament at the University of Tübingen in 1959, a position he held until retirement in 1971.

Following the war, Käsemann became embroiled in other conflicts. Like his *Doktorvater* (doctoral advisor) Rudolf Bultmann, Käsemann sought to "demythologize" the biblical text. But, unlike Bultmann, Käsemann insisted that the "Christ of faith" must be rooted in genuine history. To do otherwise was to go down the road of docetism. Consequently, Käsemann was largely responsible for initiating the so-called "*new* quest of the historical Jesus,"[158] a movement that attempted to root the Christ-event in historical reality. Käsemann also differed from Bultmann (and later Stendahl and Sanders) on how best to define the righteousness of God.[159] According to Käsemann, Bultmann (like Luther) had claimed that righteousness was a status or an attribute that God gave to people. In contrast, Käsemann argued that the righteousness of God was his own "salvation-creating power."[160] He states that, for example, "the righteousness of God does not, in Paul's understanding, refer primarily to the individual and is not to be understood exclusively in the context of the doctrine of man; but it is impossible to avoid doing these two things if its character as gift is given first priority."[161] Closely related to

---

157. Käsemann, *Wandernde Gottesvolk*.

158. Wright, "Käsemann." According to the Bultmannian school, faith must not be based on history, otherwise it is reduced to a mere work.

159. As will be seen, this is a recurring question as it relates directly to the subject of justification. If the historic Protestant view of justification is accurate, then a definition of God's righteousness would appear to be at the very heart of the matter, since the believer is declared *righteous*.

160. Käsemann, *New Testament Questions*, 172.

161. Käsemann, *New Testament Questions*, 172–3. He goes on to say, "The apostle's present eschatology cannot be taken out of its context of future eschatology, any more than the gift of justification can be isolated from the context in which the righteousness of God is spoken of as a power which brings salvation to pass. Even when he became a Christian, Paul remained an apocalyptist. His doctrine of the *dikaiosyne theou* demonstrates this: God's power reaches out for the world, and the world's salvation lies in

the debate over God's righteousness, was his dispute over the "justification of the ungodly." Put simply, Käsemann maintained that the center of Paul's theology was the justification of the unrighteous.[162] He believed that justification should be understood as "applied Christology."[163] That is, justification and Christology, far from being two distinct categories, mutually interpret each other, each requiring the other to be properly understood. These two themes of *God's righteousness* and *justification as applied Christology* emerge repeatedly in his commentary on Romans—usually considered Käsemann's magnum opus—as well as within his publication on New Testament Questions of Today. For example, in an essay entitled "The Righteousness of God in Paul," he writes, "The epistle to the Romans subsumes the whole of the preaching and theology of Paul under the one head—*the self-revealing righteousness of God* . . . the central problem of Pauline theology is concentrated on this theme."[164] A few pages later, Käsemann attempts to clarify both what God's righteousness is and what it is not. He states,

> God's power becomes God's gift when it takes possession of us and, so to speak, enters into us. . . . This gives us a proper understanding of the double bearing of the genitive construction: the gift which is being bestowed here is never at any time separable from its Giver. It partakes of the character of power, in so far as God himself enters the arena and remains in the arena with it. Thus, personal address, obligation and service are indissolubly bound up with the gift. When God enters the arena, our experience is, that he maintains his lordship even in his giving; indeed, it is his gifts which are the very means by which he subordinates us to his lordship and makes us responsible beings. The widely held view that God's righteousness is simply a property of the divine nature can now be rejected as misleading. . . . *Dikaiosyne theou* is for Paul, as it is for the Old Testament and Judaism in general, a phrase expressing divine activity, treating not of the self-subsistent, but of the self-revealing God.[165]

---

its being recaptured for the sovereignty of God. For this very reason, it is the gift of God and the salvation of the individual human being when we become obedient to the divine righteousness."

162. He maintained this view over-against an immanent process of developing salvation-history (which he viewed, in seed form, in Luke's Gospel). Cf. Wright, "Käsemann."

163. Käsemann, *Commentary*, 96.

164. Käsemann, *New Testament Questions*, 168; italics added.

165. Käsemann, *New Testament Questions*, 170.

Käsemann refers here to the watershed passage of Rom 1:17[166] as "the fork in the road for all subsequent exposition." He insists that, "At least in the course of the last century we have freed ourselves from the Greek understanding of δικαιοσύνη as a norm of what is right for God and man.... In biblical usage righteousness, which is essentially forensic, denotes a relation in which one is set, namely, the 'recognition' in which one, for example, is acknowledged to be innocent. In Jewish apocalyptic literature this understanding is applied to the verdict of justification at the last judgment."[167] It is interesting to observe that Käsemann appears, *prima facie*, to be remaining faithful here to his Reformation/Lutheran background in continuing to see the declaration of righteousness made in justification as forensically tied to the last judgment. So the verdict of righteousness that God declares over the sinner in justification is none other than the verdict of forgiveness and righteousness destined for the last-day judgment, yet brought into the present. However, this is only an appearance. One gets the impression at times that although Käsemann *might* have held such views, it is clear that he charted a course all his own; he did not simply fall in lockstep behind anyone. Nevertheless, like the Reformers before him, Käsemann maintained that salvation and obedience were always connected.[168] He wrote, "Because of his christological connection and basis Paul must identify the righteousness of God with the righteousness of faith and let the stress fall on the conferred gift of salvation. On this account, however, standing in salvation is both here and everywhere standing in obedience, that is, in the presence and under the power of Christ. To this extent Paul's doctrine of justification is simply a precise theological variation of the primitive Christian proclamation of the kingdom of God as eschatological salvation."[169]

---

166. "For in it [the gospel] the righteousness of God is revealed through faith for faith; as it is written, 'The one who is righteous will live by faith'" (Rom 1:17 NRSV).

167. Käsemann, *Commentary*, 24.

168. For example, Luther said, "Works are not taken into consideration when the question respects justification. But *true faith will no more fail to produce them, than the sun can cease to give light.... Justification without subsequent sanctification is impossible*; sanctification confirms that justification has transpired. Conversely, if no works follow faith, that faith is dead; it is not a living faith in Christ." See Luther, *D. Martin Luthers Werke*, 27:69, 254. Calvin's position was virtually identical. In responding to one of the canons of the Council of Trent, he stated the matter succinctly in an open letter: "[I] wish the reader to understand that as often as we mention Faith alone in this question, we are not thinking of a dead faith, which worketh not by love, but holding faith to be the only cause of justification (Gal 5:6; Rom 3:22). It is therefore faith alone which justifies, and yet the faith which justifies is not alone ... we do not separate the whole grace of regeneration from faith but claim the power and faculty of justifying entirely for faith, as we ought" (Calvin and Beza, *Tracts Relating to the Reformation*, 3:152).

169. Käsemann, *Commentary*, 29.

As always, more could be said, but we must conclude our comments on Käsemann at this point. Käsemann spent much of his life attempting to refute Stendahl, Sanders, and Bultmann. He could be acerbic and caustic in his critiques, but he was also tremendously insightful. What is viewed as stubbornness by one may be perceived as steadfastness by another. Many that opposed the New Perspective on Paul saw in Käsemann not so much a sharp-tongued critic, but a virulent champion of the gospel and a defender of a Reformation view of justification.

4.7. E. P. SANDERS (1937-)

E. P. (Ed Parish) Sanders was born April 18, 1937, in Grand Prairie, TX, and is widely thought of as the father of the New Perspective on Paul. Sanders attended Wesleyan College in Fort Worth, TX (1955-9), and proceeded to the Perkins School of Theology at the Southern Methodist University in Dallas, TX (1959-62). He then spent an additional year studying at Göttingen, Oxford, and Jerusalem. Throughout these initial years of study, however, Sanders did not complete an academic doctoral degree. Thus, he matriculated to Union Theological Seminary in New York in 1963 and commenced work on a ThD, completing his studies in 1966. His thesis was entitled *The Tendencies of the Synoptic Tradition*.

Following his graduation, Sanders became a Professor at McMaster University in Hamilton, Ontario, where he taught for almost twenty years (1966-84). During those years, Sanders won a fellowship from the Canada Council and spent a year in Israel (in 1968) studying rabbinic Judaism. However, in 1984, he was offered the position of Dean Ireland Professor of Exegesis at the University of Oxford and as a Fellow of Queen's College. Sanders held these positions until he moved to Duke University in North Carolina in 1990. In addition to the above positions, Sanders also received several visiting professorships and lectureships (e.g., at Trinity College, Dublin, and University of Cambridge). Nevertheless, Sanders remained at Duke University until his retirement in 2005. In addition to his academic accomplishments, Sanders was also awarded a DLitt from the University of Oxford and a ThD from the University of Helsinki in 1990.

Stendahl's essay "Paul among the Jews and Gentiles" is often viewed as the forerunner to Sanders pivotal work, *Paul and Palestinian Judaism*, first published in 1977. The response to Sanders's work has been nothing short of tectonic. Many, perhaps most, have followed Sanders's conclusions in one way or another, thus forming what has become known as the "New Perspective on Paul." Even for those who have not followed Sanders's conclusions, there has also been a significant response denouncing his work and calling for a return to earlier ways of understanding Paul. More and more, however, Old and New Testament scholars have recognized that Sanders simply must be addressed. Tim Gallant correctly assessed the situation when he wrote, "Sanders' work has been significant enough that even those biblical scholars who disagree with his thesis must interact with it in order to be taken seriously."[170] The irony behind the present state of affairs is that Sanders's actual thesis was not genuinely revolutionary, although the response to it certainly has been. The fact is, other writers made the same basic point prior to Sanders. For example, Moisés Silva has expressed his surprise at the overwhelming response to Sanders's work, since its central point had been demonstrated in "not a few books and was readily accessible in standard works of reference."[171] Silva specifically identifies George Foot Moore's three-volume work on the Judaism of the first three centuries.[172] Moreover, we might include scholars such as Solomon Schechter,[173] R. Travers Herford,[174] Arthur Marmorstein,[175] and, of course, Claude Goldsmid Montefiore.[176] Tim Gallant observed this same sequence of authors addressing the topic prior to Sanders when he wrote, "Many Judaic specialists had quarreled with the accepted view for quite some time, at least as early as G. F. Moore, and numerous Jewish scholars had argued the same point in one fashion or another (e.g., Montefiore, Schoeps, Sandmel)."[177] None of this suggests that Sanders's work is any less significant, nor is this an attempt to downplay his pioneering role. Rather, it is merely to place the overall movement within its larger historical context. Sanders was not the first, nor will he be the last word on first-century Judaism and the apostle's place within it.

Regardless of its antecedents, Sanders's work jarred countless individuals into reexamining their assumptions regarding early Judaism. Yet how, one might fairly ask, did Sanders accomplish such a task? Sanders set for himself the task of reading a truly enormous body of primary source material, while asking one primary question: Did ancient Judaism teach or

170. Gallant, "Covenantal Nomism?"

171. Silva, "Law and Christianity," 348.

172. Moore, *Judaism in the First Centuries*. Silva calls attention to the adumbrating statements in Moore, 1:110–21, 520–45. Moore notes the same themes in Weber, Schürer, and Bousset ("Christian Writers on Judaism," 252).

173. Schechter, *Aspects of Rabbinic Theology*.

174. See especially Herford, *Judaism in the New Testament*.

175. Marmorstein, *Doctrine of Merits*.

176. See Montefiore, "On Some Misconceptions," "Jewish Scholarship and Christian Silence," and *Rabbinic Literature and Gospel Teaching*.

177. Gallant, "Covenantal Nomism?"

operate on a form of merit-based theology? That is, was first-century Judaism a works-righteousness religion? Sanders took the results of his intellectual labors and distilled them into a single monograph that was to have a far-reaching impact, initially within the academic community and later within the wider Christian world. The results have led to one of the most significant paradigm shifts in the modern world of biblical scholarship.

The most basic point Sanders sought to establish was that, contrary to popular belief, Judaism was *not* a religion whereby one ingratiated oneself with God through meritorious acts of righteousness; rather, rabbinic Judaism was a religion of grace. Sanders coined the expression "covenantal nomism" to describe the nature of Judaism he had in mind and described it in the following way: "Briefly put, covenantal nomism is the view that one's place in God's plan is established on the basis of the covenant and that the covenant requires as the proper response of man his obedience to its commandments, while providing means of atonement for transgression."[178]

Sanders went on to argue that ancient Judaism used the language of righteousness (using the Greek *dik* word group) differently than the NT authors, or, more accurately, differently than Paul. According to Sanders, Paul typically used the *dik* word group in its verb form; the words are then typically translated in English as *to justify*. Sanders argued that it was used as a "transfer term" by Paul, where it described the moment of salvation; yet, in Judaism, it was used predominantly as an adjective, referring to the right behavior of those already within the covenant.[179] The source material Sanders sifted through included Tannaitic literature, the Dead Sea scrolls, the Apocrypha, the Pseudepigrapha, the Jerusalem and the Babylonian Talmud, and, of course, the Hebrew Bible and the New Testament, among numerous other bodies of literature. His overall conclusion from this research was that, with the exception of 4 Ezra, Jewish literature presupposed election as the basis of the covenant. God chose Israel to be his own unique people; they have never needed to earn their way into the covenant.[180] Consequently, obedience to the law was never intended as a means of getting into the

---

178. Sanders, *Paul and Palestinian Judaism*, 75. The expression "covenantal nomism" will be covered more in the section on the New Perspective on Paul (see below).

179. Sanders, *Paul and Palestinian Judaism*, 544–5. According to Sanders, the exception to this general rule is the Qumran community, which also used "righteousness" language as a "transfer term." However, they apparently did not use it in the same way as Paul. Qumran employed it in reference to those who were already righteous, not in relation to those who were undeserving of justification.

180. 4 Ezra is unquestionably an exception to this rule. Sanders writes, "the human inability to avoid sin is considered to lead to damnation. It is this pessimistic view of the human plight which distinguishes the author from the rest of Judaism as it is revealed in the surviving literature." See Sanders, *Paul and Palestinian Judaism*, 420.

covenant; rather, obedience functioned more as an indicator that one was already a member of the covenant. Repudiation of obedience was, in effect, repudiation of the covenant.

Moreover, Sanders suggested that Judaism viewed the subjects of justice and mercy through two distinct lenses.

> God's mercy is greater than his justice. In the other literature, the usual formulation is that God punishes the wicked *for their deeds*, while bestowing *mercy on the righteous*.... The themes of *mercy* and *retribution* or justice are not actually in competition but serve different functions. Statements to the effect that God pays each man his just due serve to assert the justness of God and to assure both sinners and the righteous that what they do matters. God is not capricious. He will neither punish for obedience nor reward transgression. The theme of mercy . . . serves to assure that election and ultimately salvation cannot be earned but depend on God's grace. One can never be righteous enough to be worthy in God's sight of the ultimate gifts, which depend only on his mercy.[181]

Further, we should note that, when Sanders spoke of "works" (as in "good works"), he had in mind a very different idea than modern evangelicals when they discuss such matters. Sanders challenged the common meaning of the Hebrew word *zekut*. *Zekut* does not suggest or imply *works of supererogation*,[182] as one might find within Roman Catholicism. He pointed out that G. F. Moore had already established the point that *zekut* "cannot be so construed":[183]

---

181. Sanders, *Paul and Palestinian Judaism*, 421–2; italics added.

182. Late Latin, *supererogatio*: payment beyond what is due or asked, from the Latin words, *super* (beyond) and *erogare* (to pay out, expend). A work of supererogation is doing more than one's required duty. In the field of ethics, an act of supererogation would be considered morally good but not morally necessary. Thus, it is above and beyond what is necessary, and another work or act of less value or involving less would be perfectly acceptable. It differs from a duty in that refraining from one's duty would be morally wrong; in contrast, refraining from a work of supererogation would be morally neutral. Originally, the sale of indulgences was developed from the works of supererogation. Essentially, saints that have lived before us performed more good deeds (i.e., works of supererogation) than were necessary for their own lives. As a result, there was a kind of heavenly bank account in which their extra merit was deposited and from which present-day sinners could draw (with the sanction of the papal father). Hence, a person who had sinned could go to the church and, and for a fee, draw from this account of *extra* good works the necessary forgiveness for him/herself or for his/her needy family member. See Chisholm, "Supererogation," and Heyd, "Supererogation."

183. Sanders, *Paul and Palestinian Judaism*, 45.

> We should note here that *zekut* . . . does not necessarily bear the full meaning of the English word "merit." That is, one should not necessarily suppose that the appearance of *zekut* always implies the full doctrine of stored-up merits which some scholars have found in Rabbinic literature (and compared to the Roman Catholic "treasury of merits"). *Zekut* is closer to the English word "virtue" in one way: both can bear a full or a weak meaning.[184]

Finally, we must raise the question of how Sanders defines the concept of justification and/or the righteousness of God in the Bible and within the larger framework of Second Temple Judaism. In *Paul and Palestinian Judaism*, Sanders made the surprising move of conflating justification ("in the sense of acquitting judgment"[185]) and mercy.

> One of the most striking usages of the term ("righteousness") in relation to God is found in the comparisons of man with God. . . . [There is] the contrast of God's righteousness and man's wickedness. . . God is perfect, but man is sinful and inadequate . . . The second principal usage . . . the term ["righteousness"] can be paralleled with a term meaning "mercy." . . . ["Righteousness"] is frequently parallel to or set in sequence with the terms for mercy, lovingkindness and goodness. . . . *The primary meaning of ["righteousness"] is "mercy."* . . . *I do not see any difference between saying that one's justification* (in the sense of acquitting judgment) *is by ["righteousness"] and saying that it is by mercy.*[186]

In saying this, however, Sanders wants us to understand that God's righteousness should not be confused with his charity or leniency.[187] Rather, Sanders understands the righteousness of God as his justice—justice tempered by mercy. We must be careful here, however. The justice that Sanders has in view is neither simplistic nor theoretical understanding. He insists we must understand it as a concrete expression of God actively administering justice within the real world. Sanders writes, "It is a characteristic of the righteous to perceive and declare God's justice . . . the psalmist says that God has in fact made his judgment, and consequently his righteousness, manifest by punishing sinners. . . . This emphasis on the manifestation of the righteousness of God, which is evidenced in the destruction of sinners, serves not only to 'justify' God, but also the views of the pious, who were not

---

184. Sanders, *Paul and Palestinian Judaism*, 90.
185. Sanders, *Paul and Palestinian Judaism*, 307.
186. Sanders, *Paul and Palestinian Judaism*, 305–10; italics added.
187. See Sanders, *Paul and Palestinian Judaism*, 407–8.

totally destroyed and thus could hold themselves to have been chastised, but spared, by God."[188] Hence, God's justice is seen in concrete demonstrations, rather than theoretical explanations.[189]

Finally, when addressing the book of Romans, Sanders states that δικαιοσύνη never conveys a single meaning. Rather, the δικαιοσύνη θεοῦ[190] must be understood as God's power and/or actions, which are both manifestations of God's wrath and grace. "It is also his *rightness* and *fidelity* to what he promised and intended (3:1–7, where God's dikaiosyne is parallel to his *pistis* and *aletheia* and opposed to man's *adikia*). These definitions are no more incompatible than the different definitions of faith, but it seems unnecessary to beat them all into one meaning."[191] His conclusion is that the apostle simply does not use the language of righteousness with any single identifiable meaning. The Greek terms behind our English words may be used as equivalents for *salvation* or even possibly *life*. The Greek may even refer to the notion of *acquittal* in the present for past transgressions or to *vindication* in the future judgment (Rom 2:13), but, according to Sanders, one must never attempt to nail down the meaning to any one of these and make it normative.[192]

---

188. Sanders, *Paul and Palestinian Judaism*, 407–8.

189. Interestingly, Sanders's understanding of justice appears to be like the modern evangelical notion of God's justice or wrath. For example, Packer writes, "God's wrath is never the capricious, irritable and morally ignoble thing that human anger so often is. It is instead, the right and necessary reaction to objective moral evil. *The wrath of God in the Bible is always judicial—that is, it is administrating justice.* The man who experiences the fullness of God's wrath receives precisely what he deserves" (*Knowing God*, 176).

Cf. D. A. Carson's comments on the same topic (*Basics for Believers*, 37):

> In the Bible, God's justice or wrath is a function of His holiness. His wrath or anger is not the explosion of a bad temper or a chronic inability to restrain His irritability, but rather *a just and principled opposition to sin*. God's holiness is so spectacularly glorious that it demands that He be wrathful with those of His creatures who defy Him, slight His majesty, thumb their noses at his words and works, and insist on their own independence even though every breath they breathe, not to say their very existence, depends on His providential care. If God were to gaze at sin and rebellion, shrug His shoulders and mutter, 'Well, I'm not too bothered. I can forgive these people. I don't really care what they do,' surely there would be something morally deficient about Him.

John Stott echoes the same sentiments when he writes, "The justice (or wrath) of God is his steady, unrelenting, unremitting, uncompromising antagonism to evil in all its forms and manifestations. In short, God's anger is poles apart from ours. What provokes his anger (evil) seldom provokes ours" (*Cross of Christ*, 173).

190. Usually translated as *God's righteousness* or the *righteousness of God*.

191. Sanders, *Paul and Palestinian Judaism*, 491.

192. This, of course, also means that Käsemann and Stuhlmacher's attempt to

4.8. THE NEW PERSPECTIVE ON PAUL (1977–)

A little over thirty years ago,[193] a titanic "paradigm shift"[194] occurred in the area of Pauline studies. This new paradigm, or New Perspective, was the beginning of a "disparate family of perspectives"[195] that received its initial impetus from E. P. Sanders,[196] Krister Stendahl, and others.[197] These movements attempt to reinterpret the apostle Paul and his letters through a dramatically revised view of first-century Judaism, rather than the traditional understanding passed down from the Reformation (i.e., the Old Perspective). Traditionally, the Protestant Reformers viewed Paul battling a legalistic, Jewish religion wherein the participants were attempting to "earn" their way into salvation. In contrast, proponents of the New Perspective insist that such a conclusion is a misreading of the apostle and argue instead that the boastings of the Jews (of which Paul speaks) were not Jews bragging in their acts of righteousness, but rather misplaced pride in their election as God's chosen people.

---

uniformly derive the meaning of *righteousness* in Paul from the supposed technical term "righteousness of God" as God's saving power, ultimately fails, even though the phrase the "righteousness of God" in Rom 1 certainly bears the meaning Käsemann gives it. See Sanders, *Paul and Palestinian Judaism*, 495.

193. The origin of the New Perspective on Paul is typically tied to the release of Sanders's *Paul and Palestinian Judaism*. Cf. chap. 1 of Westerholm, *Israel's Law*.

194. Robert Jewett uses this expression to describe the new approach of the New Perspective on Paul in "Law and the Coexistence."

195. "There is no such thing as 'the new perspective' (despite the title of [James Dunn's] recent book!). There is only a disparate family of perspectives, some with more, some with less family likeness, and with fierce squabbles and sibling rivalries going on inside. There is no united front . . . pushing back the recalcitrant Westminster-Confession hordes with the ox-horns of liberal biblical scholarship. It doesn't work like that" (Wright, *Justification*, 244–5). Or, worded a bit differently, "[The New Perspective on Paul] is a bundle of interpretive approaches to Paul, some of which are mere differences in emphasis, and others of which compete rather antagonistically" (Carson, "Introduction," 1).

196. There is no question that Sanders was/is the pivotal figure in the New Perspective on Paul. Although others have made significant contributions, nevertheless, Sanders is the metaphorical Atlas upon whose shoulders everything rests. Atlas may not be the best analogy, however. Perhaps it would be more accurate to say that Sanders was the match that ignited the great conflagration that we now call the New Perspective on Paul. N. T. Wright said of him, "Sanders . . . dominates the landscape, and, until a major refutation of his central thesis is produced, honesty compels one to do business with him. I do not myself believe such a refutation can or will be offered; serious modifications are required, but I regard his basic point as established" (*What Saint Paul Really Said*, 20).

197. The major antecedents to the New Perspective on Paul were Claude G. Montefiore and George F. Moore (see above).

Although there is probably no way to accurately measure the overall influence of individual leaders, it is likely that the three most influential proponents of this/these New Perspective(s) on Paul are E. P. Sanders, James D. G. Dunn, and N. T. Wright.[198] The designation "the New Perspective on Paul" (henceforth, the NPP) was originally coined by N. T. Wright.[199] Regardless, the ideological pillars of the movement began long before its designation was established.

Proponents of the NPP argue that, out of all the peoples on earth, God chose the nation of Israel to be uniquely his own. This choice was entirely by grace,[200] and this was not based on anything the people had done to deserve God's kindness, much less earn his election. Nevertheless, God unilaterally chose the nation and established a relationship with them—a relationship based on a covenant. Rather than go into the details of covenantal structure here, we simply note that covenants usually contain promises, sanctions[201]

---

198. Dunn and Wright are "the best representatives of this 'new perspective,'" says Moo in his essay, "Israel and the Law," 185. Wright is "a remarkable blend of weighty academic scholarship, ecclesiastical leadership, ecumenical involvement, prophetic social engagement, popular Christian advocacy, musical talent, and family commitment" (Piper, *Future of Justification*, 15). The quantity of information on and by Wright is overwhelming, including audio and video materials by him available at http://www.ntwrightpage.com.

Obviously, we could have selected different individuals to examine the New Perspective on Paul rather than Wright, Dunn, and Sanders. Wright himself has expressed some bewilderment that he is the one so frequently called to task, when others could have written just as perceptively. "For some reason," says Wright, "[Ed Sanders, Jimmy Dunn and myself] are often mentioned as the chief culprits [i.e., proponents of the NPP]: why not Richard Hays or why not Douglas Campbell or Terry Donaldson or Bruce Longenecker?" (*Justification*, 247–8). In fairness, the emphasis on Wright, Dunn, and Sanders should not be too surprising. One need only look at the bibliography on The Paul Page (a well-known NPP web site) to see that nine of the twelve "Most Recommended" works are by Wright, Dunn, and Sanders (http://www.thepaulpage.com/new-perspective/bibliography/).

199. "There are times when I wish that the phrase 'the New Perspective on Paul' had never been invented. . . . I had quite forgotten that I had invented it myself (though even then it was borrowed from Krister Stendahl) until Dunn, who is normally credited with it, graciously pointed out that I had used it in my 1978 *Tyndale Lecture*, in which, as I well remember, he was sitting in the front row" (Wright, *Justification*, 28). See also Wright, "Paul of History" and Dunn, *New Perspective on Paul*, 7n24.

200. Note, for example, Gen 18:17, 19, "The Lord said, . . . 'I have chosen [Abraham], that he may charge his children and his household after him to keep the way of the Lord by doing righteousness and justice; so that the Lord may bring about for Abraham what he has promised him'" (NRSV) and Deut 4:37–8, "Because [the Lord God] loved your ancestors, he chose their descendants after them. He brought you out of Egypt with his own presence, by his great power, driving out before you nations greater and mightier than yourselves, to bring you in, giving you their land for a possession, as it is still today" (NRSV).

201. Typically, covenants contain both negative sanctions and positive sanctions;

(i.e., conditions), and a sign. In this case, God made a covenant with the nation of Israel through the person of Abraham. What followed, including first-century Judaism, can best be summed up, according to Sanders, in the expression "covenantal nomism."

While there are a host of additional issues that fall under the umbrella of the NPP, we will limit our analysis to that of early Judaism being a religion of grace (and not works) and thus examine the question of legalism (which falls under the heading of "covenantal nomism"); we will briefly observe what NPP advocates have to say about Judaism's boundary makers; and, finally, we will explore what advocates have to say about the soteriological issues of God's righteousness, justification, and the imputation of Christ's righteousness.

4.8.A. Legalism/"Covenantal Nomism"

As noted above, according to the NPP, first-century Judaism was *not* a legalistic religion; indeed, it could not have been, as it embraced grace in manifold ways. N. T. Wright, perhaps the most winsome and articulate exponent of the NPP, writes, "We have misjudged early Judaism, especially Pharisaism, if we have thought of it as an early version of Pelagianism."[202] Similarly, Sanders writes, "On the point at which many have found the decisive contrast between Paul and Judaism—grace and works—Paul is in agreement with Palestinian Judaism. . . . Salvation is by grace but judgment is according to works. . . . God saves by grace, but . . . within the framework established by grace he rewards good deeds and punishes transgression."[203]

Before we fully embrace these conclusions, however, we should reflect. Yes, first-century Judaism believed in grace. However, it is every bit as important to ask *why* early Judaism believed in grace as it is to assert the belief itself. Furthermore, it is important to understand *how* this grace was actually understood soteriologically in the day-to-day life of the early church.[204] "While one may enthusiastically endorse the 'new perspective' dictum that first-century Judaism was a religion of grace and acknowledge that it represents an important corrective of earlier caricatures, it is hardly pedantic to point out that more precision is needed before such a statement can

---

or, put differently, covenants contain curses and blessings. But such details need not detain us now.

202. Wright, *What Saint Paul Really Said*, 32.

203. Sanders, *Paul and Palestinian Judaism*, 543.

204. As Augustine discovered, *grace* can be understood in radically different ways. See Augustine, *St. Augustin: Anti-Pelagian Writings*.

illuminate a discussion of the "Lutheran" Paul. Pelagius and Augustine—to take the most obvious examples—both believed in human dependence on divine grace, but they construed that dependence very differently."[205] This, then, leads us back to covenantal nomism.

The topic of the covenant and the individual's appropriate response to it (that is, his or her obedience or disobedience to the terms of the covenant), is a pivotal question because, as both proponents and detractors of the NPP argue, how one understands this issue largely determines how one interprets Paul's interactions with his fellow Jews. If covenantal nomism was the primary category within which first-century Jews operated and interpreted the law, then expressions like "obeying the commandments" would have been understood to be the result of "keeping covenant." That is, it would have been the response of gratitude rather than of any sense of legalism.[206] The reason for this, we are told, is that the Jewish concept of righteousness "implies the maintenance of status among the group of the elect."[207] Dunn echoes this idea: "This covenant relationship was regulated by the law, not as a way of entering the covenant, or of gaining merit, but as the way of living *within* the covenant; and that included the provision of sacrifice and atonement for those who confessed their sins and thus repented."[208]

We are assured that obedience to the law was not the basis of one's entrance into the covenant—i.e., obedience did not merit God's favor or earn his grace.[209] Nevertheless, according to the NPP, obedience *is* the way

---

205. Westerholm, *Perspectives*, 261–2; italics added.

206. Even if we grant this claim, it still has insuperable internal problems. The Bible does not give *gratitude* or *thankfulness* as a motivation for obedience. Rather, the motivation that is given is *faith*. The difference is important because wrong motives ruin good acts. "If I give away all I have, and if I deliver my body to be burned, but have not love, I gain nothing" (1 Cor 13:3 ESV). So, the motivation to obey is the promise of grace—divine enablement (Ezek 36:27; Cor 1:8–9; Gal 5:22ff; Phil 2:13, 4:13; 1 Thess 3:12; Heb 13:21) or divine reward (Luke 9:24, 10:28, 12:33; Heb 11:24–6, 12:2, 13:5–6). Believers are called to do good works *by faith*—what Paul calls, "the obedience that comes from faith" (Rom 1:5, 16:26). That is, we perform good works (obey) confident that God will provide for or reward us through trusting him. For example, the apostle writes, "I worked harder than all of [the other apostles]—*yet not I, but the grace of God that was with me*" (1 Cor 15:10). We cannot legitimately serve God in any way that suggests we are somehow meeting His needs. Moreover, every act of obedience we do is itself a gift from God (e.g., Rom 11:35–6, 15:18). Thus, good works should *not* be thought of as a kind of repayment for God's goodness—the very thing Sanders is suggesting. Instead, good works put the believer ever deeper in debt to God's grace. It is the one kind of debt we should desire. Finally, this issue is both academic and pastoral. For an introduction to this topic see Piper, *Brothers*, chap. 5–6.

207. Sanders, *Paul and Palestinian Judaism*, 544.

208. Dunn, *New Perspective on Paul*, 132.

209. Prayson observes that Deut 6:25 could be used to argue that obedience to all

a person maintained his or her place within the covenant.²¹⁰ So, although obedience to the law was not viewed as the basis by which one gained entry into the covenant, it was a necessary element "if Israel's covenant status was to be maintained."²¹¹ Wright joins his voice to Dunn and Sanders when he states, "The Jew keeps the law out of gratitude, as the proper response to grace—not, in other words, in order to *get* into the covenant people, but to *stay* in. Being 'in' in the first place was God's gift."²¹²

4.8.B. Boundary Markers and Boasting

As we come to the topic of boundary markers, we find we are touching on one of the central issues of the NPP. Protestant theologians have historically understood Paul's concern in the book of Galatians to be that "false brothers" had infiltrated the congregation and corrupted the purity of the gospel by introducing foreign (legalistic) elements into it (Gal 2:4). In contrast, NPP advocates argue that the problem was not that the works in view were legalistic but ethnocentric. These ethnocentric works were used to create ethnic boundary markers to keep non-Jews out of distinctly Jewish matters. The result was a kind of national righteousness.²¹³ What were these boundary markers, if not works of legalism? They were distinct actions that set someone apart as Jewish. Examples of such works include observance of the Sabbath, the food laws of Leviticus and Deuteronomy, and, perhaps most importantly, circumcision. Each of these activities distinguished Jew from Gentile and, as a result, erected barriers that separated one from the

---

God's law is "righteousness" under this scheme. "If we diligently observe this entire commandment before the Lord our God, as he has commanded us, we will be in the right" (Deut 6:25 NRSV). See Prayson, "Works of the Law."

210. Sanders, *Paul and Palestinian Judaism*, 420.

211. Dunn, "Review of *Justification*," 111. In another place, Dunn goes on to say that for the typical first-century Palestinian Jew, "*it would be virtually impossible to conceive of participation in God's covenant, and so in God's covenant righteousness, apart from these observances, these works of the law*" (Dunn, *Jesus, Paul and the Law*, 193; italics in original).

212. Wright, *What Saint Paul Really Said*, 19.

213. We should note that this is not a question of whether such a problem existed in the first century (it did). In fact, it was a deeply rooted problem that was of grave concern to Jesus, John the Baptist, and the writer of Hebrews—all of whom addressed it. For example, Luke 3 states, "John said to the crowds that came out to be baptized by him, 'You brood of vipers! Who warned you to flee from the wrath to come? Bear fruits worthy of repentance. Do not begin to say to yourselves, "We have Abraham as our ancestor"; for I tell you, God is able from these stones to raise up children to Abraham'"(Luke 3:7–9 NRSV). The question then is, does the NPP provide the best accounting of these and other relevant texts?

other. Thus, when the apostle rebuked those within the church for relying on "works of the law," the real issue was these boundary markers, rather than the traditional notion of works-righteousness[214]—at least, as is usually understood in traditional Protestant interpretation.

Wright summarizes the point well: "If we ask how it is that Israel has missed her vocation, Paul's answer is that she is guilty not of 'legalism' or 'works-righteousness' but of what I call 'national righteousness,' the belief that fleshly Jewish descent guarantees membership of God's true covenant people."[215] Dunn agrees with Wright's assessment, stating, "Paul was reacting primarily against the exclusivism that he himself had previously fought to maintain."[216] He continues,

> "Works of law," "works of the righteousness" are nowhere understood here, either by his Jewish interlocutors or by Paul himself, as works which earn God's favor, as merit-amassing observances. *They are rather seen as badges*: they are simply what membership of the covenant people involves, what mark out the Jews as God's people . . . in other words, Paul has in view precisely what Sanders calls "covenantal nomism." And what he denies is that God's justification depends on "covenantal nomism," that God's grace extends only to those who wear the badge of the covenant.[217]

---

214. Wright recounts a pivotal experience that occurred sometime during the mid-seventies. He was reflecting on Rom 10:3, "For, being ignorant of the righteousness of God, and seeking to establish their own, they did not submit to God's righteousness" (ESV), and he was trying to make sense of it based on the "views passed down from the Reformation," but as far as he could tell, they could not be reconciled. So, he went on to say,

> I was reading C. E. B. Cranfield on Romans and trying to see how it would work with Galatians, and it simply doesn't work . . . It's very difficult. But I found then, and this was the mid-seventies before E. P. Sanders was published . . . that I came out with this reading of Romans 10:3 which is really the fulcrum for me around which everything else moved: 'Being ignorant of the righteousness of God and seeking to establish their own.' In other words, *what we have here is a covenant status which is for Jews and Jews only*. I have a vivid memory of going home that night, sitting up in bed, reading Galatians through in Greek and thinking, 'It works. It really works. This whole thing is going to fly.' And then all sorts of things just followed on from that.

See Tamerius, "Interview with N. T. Wright."

215. Wright, "Paul of History," 65.

216. Dunn, "Paul's Theology," 336. Cf. Dunn, *Epistle to Galatians*.

217. Dunn, *Jesus, Paul and the Law*, 194; italics added. For his part, Sanders goes in a different direction, and, in the process, makes a rather interesting admission. He states, "*this* is what Paul finds wrong in Judaism: it is not Christianity" (Sanders, *Paul*

In another place, Wright argues that the "boasting" the apostle refers to in Rom 2:17-24—the boasting Paul intends to exclude through the doctrine of justification—is not what we normally think. He offers,

> This "boasting" which is excluded is not the boasting of the successful moralist; it is the racial boast of the Jew, as in [Rom] 2:17-24. If this is not so, [Rom] 3:29 ("Or is God the God of the Jews only? Is he not of Gentiles also?") is a *non sequitur*. Paul has no thought in this passage of warding off a proto-Pelagianism, of which in any case his contemporaries were not guilty. He is here, as in Galatians and Philippians, declaring that there is no road into covenant membership on the grounds of Jewish racial privilege.[218]

4.8.C. God's Righteousness, Justification, and the Imputation of Christ's Righteousness

The third and lengthiest area of our analysis is in the understanding of God's righteousness, justification, and the imputation of Christ's righteousness. Obviously, each of these topics is closely related. Moreover, it is nearly impossible to think of one in isolation from the others. Nevertheless, the terms are distinguishable, as are the concepts behind them, so we will attempt to look at each in turn (albeit briefly). NPP authors are at some pains to impress upon their readers that the term *righteousness*, specifically God's righteousness, has a meaning quite distinct from what Protestants (as well

---

and Palestinian Judaism, 552).

218. Wright, *What Saint Paul Really Said*, 129. Additionally, although Wright and Dunn work independently and frequently have their disagreements, they nevertheless hold a great deal in common. On this issue, that agreement can be seen quite clearly. Wright states in "New Perspectives on Paul":

> [When] Jimmy Dunn added his stones to the growing pile I found myself in both agreement and disagreement with him. His proposal about the meaning of 'works of the law' in Paul—that they are not the moral works through which one gains merit but the works through which the Jew is defined over against the pagan—I regard as exactly right. It has proved itself again and again in the detailed exegesis; attempts to deny it have in my view failed. But Dunn, like Sanders (and like some other New Perspective writers such as John Ziesler) has not, I think, got to the heart of Paul. Again, much of my writing on Paul over the last twenty years at least has been in at least implicit dialogue with him, and I find his exposition of justification itself less than satisfying. For one thing, he never understands what I take to be Paul's fundamental covenant theology; for another, his typically protestant anti-sacramentalism leads him to miss the point of Romans 6.

as Catholics and the Orthodox) have historically understood. For example, Wright tells us that righteousness "denotes not so much the abstract idea of justice or virtue, as right standing and consequent right behaviour, within a community."[219] More to the point, he repeatedly asserts that God's righteousness is "*his covenant faithfulness.*"[220] This, Wright tells us, includes "his impartiality, his proper dealing with sin and his helping of the helpless." But, most fundamentally, God's righteousness is "his faithfulness to *his covenant promises* to Abraham."[221] Even when describing the death and resurrection of Christ, Wright casts these events in terms of God's covenantal faithfulness. He writes, "The death and resurrection of Jesus were themselves the great eschatological events, revealing *God's covenant faithfulness*, his way of putting the world to rights."[222] He maintains that when

> When the phrase [the righteousness of God] occurs in biblical and post-biblical Jewish texts, it always refers to God's own righteousness, not to the status people have from God . . . . In particular, the flow of thought through the letter as a whole makes far more sense if we understand the statement of the theme in 1:17 as being about God and God's covenant faithfulness and justice, rather than simply about 'justification.' It brings into focus chapters 9–11, not as an appendix to a more general treatment of sin and salvation, but as the intended major climax of the whole letter; and it allows for the significance of 15:1–13 as a final summing up of the subject.[223]

In a similar vein, yet also with a clear distinction, we find Dunn stating: "'The righteousness of God overlaps with that of God's faithfulness to Israel—righteousness as remaining true to his obligation to the people he had

---

219. Wright, "Righteousness," 591.

220. Italics added. For example, Wright states that in the context of Romans 3:1–8, "'God's righteousness' most naturally means 'God's covenant faithfulness'" (*What Saint Paul Really Said*, 106). See also, "The gospel—the announcement of the lordship of Jesus the Messiah—reveals God's righteousness, his covenant faithfulness "(*What Saint Paul Really Said*, 123). As will be clear, these are not the only places that Wright et al. make such statements, but they should demonstrate that the idea is clearly rooted in their work.

221. Wright, *Climax of Covenant*, 36; italics added.

222. Wright, *What Saint Paul Really Said*, 37; italics added. Additionally, Wright insists that "Romans [is] Paul's exposition of God's faithfulness to his covenant (in technical language, his righteousness')" (*What Saint Paul Really Said*, 48). Again, he says, "For a reader of the Septuagint, the Greek version of the Jewish scriptures, 'the righteousness of God' would have one obvious meaning: God's own faithfulness to his promises, to the covenant" (Wright, *What Saint Paul Really Said*).

223. Wright, "Letter to Romans," 10:405.

chosen as his own. Hence, the close link between God's 'faithfulness,' God's 'truth,' and God's 'righteousness' in Rom 3:3–7."[224] Lest we misunderstand Dunn's point, he clarifies: "The heart of Paul's theology of justification was *the dynamic interaction between 'the righteousness of God' as God's saving action for all who believe and 'the righteousness of God' as God's faithfulness to Israel*, his chosen people."[225] Perhaps most significantly, however, is Dunn's commentary on James. He delineates what righteousness is and is not.

> *Dikaiosyne* is a good example of the need to penetrate through Paul's Greek language in order to understand it in the light of his Jewish background and training. The concept which emerged from the Greco-Roman tradition to dominate Western thought was of righteousness/justice as an ideal or absolute ethical norm against which particular claims and duties could be measured. But since the fundamental study of H. Cremer[226] it has been recognized that in Hebrew thought ['righteousness'] is essentially a concept of relation. *Righteousness is not something which an individual has on his or her own, independently of anyone else; it is something which one has precisely in one's relationships as a social being.* People are righteous when they meet the claims which others have on them *by virtue of their relationship*. . . . So too when it is predicated of God—in this case the relationship being the covenant which God entered into with his people. . . . God is 'righteous' when he fulfills the obligations he took upon himself to be Israel's God. . . . It is with this sense that the phrase provides a key to his exposition in Romans, as elsewhere in his theology.[227]

One may rightly wonder at the turbulence of debate over something as seemingly innocuous as the term *righteousness*. The concern is that salvation itself is at stake. Since the time of the Reformation, Protestants have understood that God justifies the believer by imputing the righteousness of Christ at the moment of his or her conversion. However, with the rise of the NPP, this view is one of many things being challenged, along with many of its underlying assumptions, including the definition of righteousness. Since NPP advocates define righteousness in terms of covenantal faithfulness, they deny that such a trait can be given (imputed or imparted) to anyone. Covenantal faithfulness, they claim, is not an attribute or a virtue that can be

---

224. Dunn, *Theology of Paul*, 5742–4.
225. Dunn, *Theology of Paul*, 5745–6; italics added.
226. Cremer, *Paulinische Rechtfertigungslehre*.
227. Dunn, *Romans 1—8*, 40–41; italics added. Dunn has written substantially on God's righteousness and ours. See his *Romans*, 42–48, 97, and *Theology of Paul*, 340–44.

given to someone else. Consequently, it is viewed as a fundamental error—"a category mistake."[228] The result, we are told, is that *justification itself must be redefined.*[229] We can see this agenda in the work of N. T. Wright when he says,

> If we use the language of the law court, it makes no sense whatsoever to say that the judge imputes, imparts, bequeaths, conveys or otherwise transfers his righteousness to either the plaintiff or the defendant. Righteousness is not an object, a substance or a gas which can be passed across the courtroom. For the judge to be righteous does not mean that the court has found in his favor. For the plaintiff or defendant to be righteous does not mean that he or she has tried the case properly or impartially. To imagine the defendant somehow receiving the judge's righteousness is simply a category mistake. That is not how the language works.[230]

---

228. Wright, *What Saint Paul Really Said*, 98.

229. The claim that justification needs to be redefined is being sounded not only among NPP advocates, but also among numerous "renewal" theologians. There are other movements that also have sought to redefine justification (e.g., Auburn Avenue Theology et al.), but, due to limitations, we will not attempt to address them in this work.

230. Wright, *What Saint Paul Really Said*, 98. In *What Saint Paul Really Said*, Wright elaborates on this idea and thus clarifies his meaning. He writes:

"Part of the particular flavor of the term [*righteousness*], however, comes from the metaphor which it contains. 'Righteousness' is a forensic term that is taken from the law court. This needs to be unpacked just a bit.

"In the (biblical) Jewish law court there are three parties: the judge, the plaintiff and the defendant. There is no 'director of public prosecutions'; all cases take the form of one party versus the other party, with the judge deciding the issue.

"What does it mean to use the language of 'righteousness' in this context? It means something quite different when applied to the judge to what it means when applied to either the plaintiff or the defendant. Applied to the judge, it means (as is clear from the Old Testament) that the judge must try the case according to the law; that he must be impartial; that he must punish sin as it deserves; and that he must support and uphold those who are defenseless and who have no-one but him to plead their cause. For the judge to be 'righteous,' to have and practice 'righteousness' in this forensic setting, is therefore a complex matter to do with the way he handles the case.

"For the plaintiff and the defendant, however, to be 'righteous' has none of these connotations. They, after all, are not trying the case. Nor, less obviously to us because of the moral overtones the word 'righteous' now has in our language, does the word mean that they are, before the case starts, morally upright and so deserving to have the verdict go their way. No; for the plaintiff or defendant to be 'righteous' in the biblical sense *within the law-court setting* is for them to have that status *as a result of the decision of the court*. How does this work out? Let us take the plaintiff first. If and when the court upholds the plaintiff's accusation, he or she is 'righteous.' This doesn't necessarily mean that he or she is good, morally upright or virtuous; it simply means that in this case the court has vindicated him or her in the charge they have brought. It is the same with the defendant. If and when the court upholds the defendant, acquitting him or

This, of course, raises other interrelated issues.[231] We will address some of these questions later, but for now we merely acknowledge them and attempt to summarize some of the reactions to this "new" view.

4.8.D. Helps and Hazards of the NPP: An Initial Assessment

There is much to be grateful for in the NPP, even while we reject certain elements. Moisés Silva has helpfully identified areas where we should be grateful to the NPP,[232] first, for reminding us that it is inaccurate and unfair to portray the whole of postbiblical Judaism as legalistic and self-righteous. A hermeneutic of suspicion is rarely warranted and usually unhelpful. Elevating such "to the driving seat of interpretation is problematic."[233] We should instead adopt the Golden Rule of interpretation: to interpret others as we would have others interpret us. If such a charitable approach had been practiced all along, it seems unlikely that Sanders et al. would have needed to react so strongly.

Second, the NPP should be applauded for helping us see that Paul's primary concern in Galatians 2 and 3 was *not* to preach the Reformation doctrine of justification by faith alone. Instead, his goal was to address the Jewish/Gentile issues in the Church, thereby clarifying the genuine descendants of Abraham.

That said, we should be careful not to accept some of the exaggerated claims coming from the NPP, because "one exaggeration doesn't deserve another."[234] For example, we should reject the claim that seeking "right-standing with God by human effort was not much of a problem in Judaism (and therefore that such a thing was outside Paul's purview)."[235] It simply does not square with the biblical evidence. Similarly, we should abjure the claim that "the doctrine of justification by faith alone, as understood in Protestant theology, does not play a significant role in Galatians 3," or even

---

her of the charge, he or she is 'righteous.' This, again, doesn't necessarily mean that he or she is good, morally upright or virtuous; simply that he or she has, in this case, been vindicated against the accuser; in other words, acquitted." (Wright, *What Saint Paul Really Said*, 109–10)

Cf. Wright, *What Saint Paul Really Said*, 94–111. For additional comments from Wright on the righteousness of God, see his "Letter to Romans," 10:397–424 and *Justification*, 646–778.

231. The imputation of Christ's righteousness, the definition of justification, etc.
232. Silva, "Faith Versus Works," 217–48.
233. Parry, "Ideological Criticism," 315.
234. Taylor, "Gratitude for New Perspective."
235. Silva, "Faith Versus Works," 228.

that "it was foreign to Pauline thought!"[236] These types of claims should be concerning. Silva readily acknowledges the foolhardiness of denying "that (exclusivistic) national and sociological commitments on the part of Paul's Jewish contemporaries were an integral part of the attitudes the apostle was combatting." Such attitudes were, in fact, very much present. Yet, it would be equally naive to conclude that first-century Judaism was somehow "free from the universal human tendency to rely on one's own resources rather than on God's power."[237] Such sinful tendencies seem almost hardwired within us. In addition, "The NT *does* reflect certain sociological concerns not fully appreciated by the Reformers, but it hardly follows from this fact that other elements they saw in the text are false."[238] False dilemmas like this are, at best, misleading, and, at worse, they undermine and trivialize real concerns. And finally, we readily recognize that Protestants have frequently misrepresented rabbinic Judaism and thus painted an incomplete picture of Paul's thought.

However, it does not follow that the historic Protestant doctrine of justification should therefore be "overhauled."[239] Such abuses are not remedied by throwing out what is true and accurate. Rather, they are solved by correcting the inaccuracies and exaggerations and by clearly painting a more precise and complete picture. Thus, we will now turn our attention to a few authors who have attempted to do just that.

4.9. RESPONSES TO THE NEW PERSPECTIVE ON PAUL

The NPP has certainly revitalized theological dialogue on Paul and the question of justification.[240] It has gained an astonishing constituency and, at this point, it looks as though it may be the majority view in Pauline studies.[241] To be clear, the claim is not that the view is really new.[242] Nor is it fair

---

236. Silva, "Faith Versus Works," 228.

237. Silva, "Faith Versus Works" 246.

238. Silva, "Faith Versus Works," 247.

239. Silva, "Faith Versus Works," 247.

240. E.g., "It may not be an overstatement to suggest that the doctrine of justification is as widely discussed and challenged today as it was in the sixteenth century, within Protestantism as well as outside of it." Horton, "Traditional Reformed View," Kindle loc., 781–2.

241. See Horton, "Nine Points of Synod."

242. The 'new perspective' on Paul's teaching on justification by faith is not really 'new.' . . . It highlights a dimension of Paul's teaching that Paul himself regarded as central to his own understanding of justification. The reason why it has been called *new* is not because the aspects and emphases that it highlights have never before been

to depict the NPP as though it were a single uniform voice, expressing one monolithic idea—even though I have done so in places above.[243] It is rather a consortium of voices that share a number of commonalities, among the most important being the conviction that Protestants have misread Paul over the past five hundred years and, in turn, have misunderstood the nature of first-century Judaism. Yet not everyone has been willing to jump onto the proverbial bandwagon. There have, in fact, been a group of dissenting voices that, to varying degrees, have rejected different conclusions of the movement. Or perhaps it is more accurate to say that several authors have voiced concern that the NPP has taken their conclusions too far, even while applauding certain insights made by NPP writers. We will attempt to follow a few of these differing voices and analyze their concerns and counterclaims.

4.9.A. Mark Seifrid (1953–)

Among the growing group of dissenting voices is Mark Seifrid. Seifrid has been the Mildred and Ernest Hogan Professor of New Testament Interpretation at the Southern Baptist Theological Seminary in Louisville, KY, since 1992. During his academic ministry, he has authored or edited all or part of a number of works that speak directly or indirectly to the NPP. Some of his more relevant works include *Justification by Faith*, contributions to both volumes of *Justification and Variegated Nomism,* and, perhaps most helpfully, *Christ Our Righteousness: Paul's Theology of Justification*. On the subject of God's righteousness, Seifrid has written considerably. He notes:

> In appealing to this Scripture [Hab 2:4] Paul is clarifying the meaning of the "righteousness of God," which is revealed in the gospel. Implicitly, therefore this "righteousness of God" is nothing other than the "life" which is given to the one who believes. Because "life" and "righteousness" are contingent upon faith, *Paul speaks in a twofold manner of the righteousness of God* as

given such attention. Rather it is 'new' because the dimension of Paul's teaching that it highlights has been largely lost to sight in more contemporary expositions, even though it was so central to Paul's own formulation of the doctrine. It is 'new' because it gives a renewed emphasis to aspects of the historical situation that gave rise to Paul's formulation of the doctrine, which were fundamental to that formulation and which should remain fundamental for our understanding of Paul's gospel for today" (Dunn, "New Perspective View," Kindle loc., 1904–5, 1906–10).

243. This is a challenge with any multifaceted movement or set of movements. Accuracy would seem to dictate that each branch or facet be addressed separately. Yet such an approach quickly becomes unwieldy and thus unhelpful. Consequently, like many of the NPP proponents, I have frequently addressed the ideas as though the NPP were a singular movement. This caveat should be kept in mind while reading.

revealed "from faith unto faith." Faith is both the source and goal of the righteousness of God, the means of "seeing" it and the demand which it lays upon us.[244]

Seifrid denies the claim made by Wright, Dunn, and others that God's righteousness should be defined as covenantal faithfulness. After surveying the many pertinent texts, he concludes that, in the OT, "*the 'righteousness of God' clearly signifies an act of God in which his saving righteousness is displayed.*"[245] The psalmist, says Seifrid, pictures God intervening "on behalf of his people against unnamed enemies before the eyes of all the nations. . . . In revealing his righteousness, God was not only delivering his people, but establishing his own cause against those who contend against him."[246] Although such a statement could be construed as an implicit admission of God's righteousness as covenantal faithfulness, Seifrid clarifies precisely what he does and does not mean:

> It is currently *quite common for scholars to interpret 'God's righteousness' as his covenant-faithfulness* toward Israel. In other words, God is "righteous" in that he fulfills his promises to save his people. *Despite its initial appeal, this interpretation does not fit.* . . . Although the Lord might be said to act out of covenant-faithfulness to his people, his action itself cannot properly be called covenantal. It rather represents the judgment of the King, who establishes justice in his creation . . . his deliverance of Israel anticipates his "coming" to judge savingly on behalf of the entire earth. The nations themselves expect to receive his saving justice (verses 7–9). For this reason, the very elements of creation—the sea, the rivers and the hills—celebrate his coming. The fidelity which God displayed toward Israel is only one manifestation of the saving righteousness which he exercises as ruler of all.[247]

---

244. Seifrid, *Christ Our Righteousness*, 38; italics added.

245. Seifrid, *Christ Our Righteousness*, 39; italics added. Although this differs from Wright's "covenantal faithfulness," it does sound similar to Dunn's "righteousness" as "something which one has precisely in one's relationships as a social being." See Dunn, *Romans 1—8*, 40–41.

246. Seifrid, *Christ Our Righteousness*, 39; italics added.

247. Seifrid, *Christ Our Righteousness*, 38. Seifrid goes on to say (41):

> The 'creational' context of 'God's righteousness' which appears in Psalm 98 is characteristic of biblical usage. The language of 'righteousness' appears with remarkable frequency in association with the vocabulary of 'ruling and judging.' . . . This activity of 'ruling and judging' extends well beyond God's relationship with Israel, as, for example, in the Genesis account of Abraham's intercession for Sodom and Gomorrah. Upon hearing of the coming destruction which God will bring upon these cities,

Seifrid points out, as have others, the surprising infrequency of *righteous/righteousness* in the same context as *covenant*.²⁴⁸ If God's righteousness is in fact his covenantal faithfulness, one would reasonably expect to find these terms close together, perhaps even an inordinately high proportion of such occurrences. Yet we find exactly the opposite. What we discover instead is that the OT rarely uses the terms בְּרִת (*berith*—*covenant*) and צדקה (*Sedaqa*—*righteousness*) in the same immediate context. Seifrid summarizes this point: "*All 'covenant-keeping' is righteous behavior, but not all righteous behavior is 'covenant-keeping.'* It is misleading, therefore, to speak of 'God's righteousness' as his 'covenant-faithfulness.' *It would be closer to the biblical language to speak of 'faithfulness' as 'covenant-righteousness.'*"²⁴⁹

Seifrid argues that the OT texts offer a different definition of the righteousness of God than the current trend of covenant faithfulness. In keeping with a previous generation of scholars, Seifrid suggests that righteousness

---

Abraham raises the objection that there might be righteous persons who would be slain along with the wicked. For God to allow such an inequity is out of the question: 'Shall not the judge of all the earth render just judgment?' The narrative suggests that God might indeed find some 'righteous ones' among the pagans of these two cities (although he did not), and that they would deserve justice from him. God is expected to render judgment in favor of the righteous, whatever their national descent. The title given to God in the text, the 'judge of all the earth,' is itself indicative of the context of biblical conception of righteousness. In the broader biblical witness, God repeatedly intervenes as the good and gracious ruler of all the earth to 'do justice and righteousness' for the weak and oppressed, who are unable to obtain justice for themselves. Since evil prevails in the world which he made, God must again and again act to restore the right order of his good creation.

248. Seifrid notes in "Righteousness Language" (416–17):

Interpreters often render references to "God's righteousness" in biblical contexts as God's "covenant-faithfulness," expressed in his saving acts on behalf of his people. This way of understanding the biblical language presupposes that the idea of a promissory covenant is both fundamental and pervasive within the Hebrew Scriptures, a matter which is highly debated. . . . Here, [however], we can speak only in the most general way: when one examines word-usage, it becomes clear that to speak of "righteousness" as "covenant-faithfulness" is to invert the actual semantic relation between the terms. Only rarely do [covenant] and [righteousness] terms appear in any proximity to one another, despite their considerable frequency in the Hebrew Scriptures. "Covenant" occurs 283 times, [righteousness] terminology some 524 times, and yet in only seven passages do the terms come into any significant semantic contact. This lack of convergence in usage is all the more striking when we take into account that both [covenant] and the [righteousness] word-group have fields of meaning having to do with relationships, and both have ethical and juridicial dimensions.

249. Seifrid, "Righteousness Language," 417; italics added.

(God's and humanity's) must be defined as *conformity to a particular norm or standard*.[250] What this specific norm might be is hotly debated,[251] yet over the past century and a half (perhaps a little less), the debate in OT circles seems to have shifted from mutually exclusive concepts of righteousness to views that stress a particular emphasis.[252] Yet even while suggesting righteousness as conformity to a norm, Seifrid is careful not to circumscribe it to *only* this concept.[253] In other words, while proposing that righteous-

---

250. "This usage of 'righteousness' terminology quite clearly includes the concept of a 'norm,' an order within the world, which God graciously acts (again and again) to restore. 'Righteousness' therefore cannot be reduced to the idea of a 'proper relation,' as often has been done in recent interpretation"(Seifrid, *Christ Our Righteousness*, 41). In "Righteousness Language" (416), Seifrid writes,

> In a related way, there has been a continuing debate as to whether it is proper to speak of the vocabulary of righteousness in the Hebrew Bible as generally bearing the sense of 'accordance with a norm' or, alternatively, "fidelity to a relationship." Obviously, theological issues related to the first question are present here. If "righteousness" involves correspondence to a standard, we may readily account for passages in which a punitive righteousness appears. If "righteousness" is regarded solely as descriptive of a "right relation," the way is open to interpreting divine righteousness in purely salvific terms: God's righteousness consists in his fidelity to his people in saving them.

251. Moo, *Epistle to Romans*, 83.

252. Snaith, *Distinctive Ideas*, 77ff. Hill argued that, "*Tsedeq*, with its kindred words, signifies that standard which God maintains in the world. It is the norm by which all must be judged" (*Greek Words and Hebrew Meanings*, 84). Similarly, "צדק basically connotes conformity to a norm" (Schmid, *Gerechtigkeit als Weltordnung*, 183). For a fuller bibliography of scholars who stress the norm-character of righteousness, see Piper, *Justification of God*, 82–85.

253. Seifrid maintains that virtually all "righteousness" language is "creational" in nature ("Righteousness Language," 418):

> The common inversion of the biblical word-relations is not without its misleading effects. Once the further step is taken to reduce biblical usage of "covenant" to a simple promissory covenant, the characterization of God's saving action as "righteousness" is fully explicable in a syllogistic manner. God is "righteous" because he has promised to save, a promise which he has fulfilled or yet will fulfill. . . . [But if] righteousness language in the Hebrew Scriptures has to do in the first instance with God's ordering of creation, its relative distance from covenantal contexts is entirely explicable. In favor of this conclusion, we may point not only to the infrequent collocation of "righteousness" with "covenant," but also to the remarkable frequency with which "righteousness" is associated with the vocabulary of "ruling and judging" . . . found in close proximity (i.e. within five words of one another) in 142 contexts, a dramatic contrast with the usage of [covenant]. Since kingship obviously includes the making of "covenants," it is not surprising that "ruling and judging" sometimes has to do with a covenant with Israel (and with David, in particular): occasionally "righteousness" and "covenant" appear together

ness means conformity to a norm, he recognizes there is—indeed, there must be—more to the concept than *simply* conformity to a norm (at least in certain texts). Moreover, what the norm is or is not, is not always clear. He writes:

> It is simply not the case that *righteousness* terminology in the Hebrew Scriptures does not include the idea of normativity within its semantic range. If we may venture a generalization: *biblical usage of righteousness language* is distinct from Greek thought not in the lack of the idea of a norm, but in that it *does not define the norm it presupposes* in terms of the idea of the good: particularly not in terms of an idea of the good derived from [nature] or formulated in [law]. The Hebrew Scriptures operate with the simple but profound assumption that "righteousness" in its various expressions is ultimately bound up with God and his working. As a state of affairs in the world, "righteousness" cannot be accomplished or even rightly conceived apart from its enactment by God. That the world and its history have (and are yet to be given) a comprehensive moral order is everywhere presupposed, even (or, rather, especially) in the biblical laments. But precisely what that order is and when and how it is to come about, is left for God to enact, reveal and make known. The biblical writers expect, moreover, that this order shall be effected not in a mere educative sense, but in judgments upon human rebellion. The ultimate hope of the Hebrew Scriptures, we may suggest, is that "righteousness"—presently still unseen—shall be realized finally by God himself through is Anointed, not through a philosopher-king, a [moralist], or a [wise man].[254]

Finally, Seifrid correctly notes that all definitions of God's righteousness are ultimately "untenable" if they are limited to *only* the saving acts of God. He observes that there are just too many instances where God's righteousness is manifested through his punishment/wrath,[255] whether that

---

in larger literary units (e.g. Ps 50; Ps 89). At root, however, the biblical conception of kingship bears a universal dimension, as is apparent in its various aspects and developments: in the connection between ruling and wisdom, in the hope for all-embracing justice by means of God's rule, and in the messianic ideal. The frequent association of "righteousness" language with "ruling and judging" therefore strongly supports Schmid's claim that in biblical thought "righteousness" has to do with creational theology.

254. Seifrid, "Righteousness Language," 55; italics added.
255. Seifrid observes ("Righteousness Language," 428):

Despite the inevitable exegetical debates associated with some of these texts, in my judgment there are approximately 15 instances in the Hebrew

wrath is focused against Israel's enemies or directed against the nation itself. The fact remains, the only event one can point to as a full and vivid portrayal of God's righteousness—both in his wrath and salvation—is "the Christ-event."[256] Mark Seifrid is certainly not the only critic of the NPP, yet he is one of the most incisive and helpful. We now turn our attention to another remarkably articulate critic of the NPP, Stephen Westerholm.

4.9.B. Stephen Westerholm (1949–)

Stephen Westerholm is the professor of New Testament and Pauline studies in the department of Religious Studies at McMaster University (Hamilton, Ontario). He has written, co-written, translated, and/or edited voluminously in the area of Pauline and Synoptic studies, as well as in Septuagint studies and the history of biblical interpretation.[257] In so doing, Westerholm has also addressed many of the subjects inherent within the NPP, including God's righteousness and justification of the unrighteous. In addressing how to define the righteousness of God, Westerholm assesses the various

> Scriptures in which God's righteousness is conceived in retributive or punitive terms (Exod 9:27; Ps 7:10, 7:12, 11:5–7, 50:6, Isa 1:27, 5:15–6, 10:22, 28:17, Lam 1:18, 2 Chr 12:1–6, Neh 9:33, Dan 9:7, 9:14, 9:16). Not surprisingly, all these occurrences appear in juridicial contexts. Nine of these 15 examples involve confessions in which God is described with the adjective [righteous]. Six of these nine have basically the same form: a guilty party who has suffered divine punishment confesses, "Yahweh is righteous."... We find then a lexical distinction: the biblical writers often uses [the noun 'righteousness'] when speaking of a vindicating act of God (probably a nominalization of the verb), and the adjective ['righteous'] (derived from the abstract) when signifying a retributive justice of God.... The difference in meaning between the noun and the adjective should not be unexpected: in the Hebrew Scriptures in all but one instance (the word 'righteous') is used of persons, while, as we have observed, the use of ('righteousness') is weighted toward description of action.

256. "It is also important to observe that Paul's language obviously includes the idea of retribution.... Any interpretation of God's righteousness or justification in purely salvific terms is forced into the untenable position of ignoring a significant element of Paul's language and argument as it appears in Romans.... For Paul, God's righteousness is revealed in the event of Christ's cross and resurrection. Here the contention between the Creator and the fallen creature is decided in God's favor and yet savingly resolved.... There is no definition of 'righteousness,' not even in narrative terms, which adequately accounts for the simultaneity of righteous wrath and the gift of righteousness of which Paul speaks (Rom 3:4–5, 21–6). The Christ-event itself supplies the final definition of the language" (Seifrid, "Righteousness Language," 58–59).

257. Representative examples include Westerholm's *Israel's Law and Church's Faith*; *Perspectives Old and New*; *Understanding Paul*; and Westerholm, ed., *Blackwell Companion to Paul*.

options, e.g., reference to a moral attribute within God (Luther's early view); God's covenantal faithfulness to his promise to Abraham and/or the nation of Israel (*à la* New Perspective); conformity to a norm; etc. Westerholm defines the righteousness of God as his "dynamic activity in history to set His good yet marred creation right, through Jesus' saving death and resurrection, through which the wicked are judged and the faith-filled people of God are vindicated."[258] This definition takes into account the widespread expectation of God's redemptive purpose, which was fulfilled in response to his promise to the patriarchs and understood within the books of Psalms and Isaiah. He picks up the subject of God's righteousness and offers a helpful analysis of the "divine goodness" (i.e., righteousness) as conceived in Hebrew. He writes:

> Divine goodness cannot . . . fail in the end, nor remain ambiguous forever: divine *tzedakah* will see to that. This Hebrew word is commonly translated "righteousness," a term that captures part of what the psalmists mean to convey: God keeps his word and lives up to his obligations, which included enforcing the moral order, seeing to it that both righteous and wicked receive their due recompense. But the term righteousness has fallen into disuse and does not in any case sufficiently suggest the element of goodness so obviously present in the psalmic texts that summon the universe to celebrate God's *tzedakah*. In such verses *tzedakah* refers to the faithfulness of God toward his creation or his people, a faithfulness that moves him to intervene, to set things wonderfully right when they have gone disastrously awry. It is the reassertion of God's goodness seen in the restoration of just order to a disturbed creation, of peace and prosperity to a distressed people. In this sense *tzedakah* is close in meaning to salvation. What *tzedakah* adds to the "reassertion of goodness" and even "salvation" is the implication that God, in the process, is living up to his responsibility and role as God. He is proving himself loyal to the commitments he undertook when he first made the world good or adopted Israel as his people.[259]

In addition to his analysis of the Hebrew concept of righteousness, Westerholm also examines its Greek usage. He notes that,[260]

---

258. Westerholm, *Understanding Paul*, 34.

259. Westerholm, *Understanding Paul*, 34.

260. Throughout this work, Westerholm uses the Greek *dikaiosness* instead of the English word *righteousness*. Within the context of the book, it makes sense and flows easily. However, for the sake of smoother reading in this quotation, I have adjusted the language back to English.

> In Romans 3:5 God's righteousness is his rightness, his truthfulness (cf. v. 4), as demonstrated in his faithfulness to his commitments (cf. v. 3): a rightness that is vindicated whenever called in question by (sinful, lying, unfaithful) human beings (cf. v. 4) and by which he (rightly) judges the world (cf. vv. 5–7). . . . The same divine righteousness appears to be referred to in 3:25 and 26 as well: God's advocacy of what is right and good seemed silent when he "passed over sins committed in the past, at the time of God's forbearance." What proves God to be righteous after all is his putting forward of Christ Jesus as the atoning sacrifice for sins: far from overlooking human wrongdoing, God had merely postponed its decisive condemnation until it could be channeled onto the crucified Christ rather than onto the wrongdoers themselves. In this way he proved righteous himself (his rightness and commitment to goodness were never more apparent) at the same time he justifies (acquits) sinners who have faith in Jesus (3:26).[261]

In a final citation from Westerholm, we note his distinction between the ways *God's righteousness* is used by the NT authors generally and Paul more specifically. He says:

> Elsewhere, too, God's righteousness is explicitly tied to the (extraordinary) righteousness of faith. What is not always clear is whether the reference is to his own salvific act in justifying (acquitting) sinners or whether it is to the "gift of righteousness (acquittal)" that he gives them. . . . On the other hand, since God's righteousness is used as a parallel to his salvation in a number of Septuagintal texts, many scholars read it the same way in Romans 1:17. . . . This makes good sense—as far as it goes. Still, righteousness, though at times parallel to "salvation," necessarily means something more. A salvation that is also designated God's righteousness is one in which the divine endorsement of good and hostility to evil are given triumphant expression: what is right, and God's commitment to uphold the right, must be vindicated in the process. Since Romans 3:25–26 indicates clearly that for Paul such a vindication is involved in God's display of righteousness in Christ, we must assume that it is to be understood in 1:17 as well. But even that is not all. To render righteousness "salvation" in 1:17 is to obscure Paul's play on words between the revelation of God's righteousness in the gospel and the reference (quoted from Habakkuk) to the human being who is righteous through faith; the life of the latter

---

261. Westerholm, *Perspectives*, 284–6.

must somehow illustrate the former. Hence, if righteousness is not simply God's gift of acquittal here, we must say it is that salvific activity by which God's commitment to uphold the right is vindicated at the same time as sinners (those guilty of the *un*-righteousness of 1:18) who believe the gospel become righteous (in accordance with Habakkuk's dictum).... Paul clearly means 1:17 to serve as a heading for his subsequent argument.[262]

4.9.C. Douglas Moo (1950–)

Douglas Moo has been the Kenneth T. Wessner Chair of New Testament at Wheaton College since 2000, where he works with students in the biblical exegesis and PhD programs. Prior to his appointment at Wheaton, Moo served for twenty-three years at Trinity Evangelical Divinity School in Deerfield, IL, teaching and writing in NT studies, with a focus in Pauline theology. Like the above authors, Moo has written considerably in the areas of NT and Pauline studies.[263] Within the scope of his work, Moo has addressed the topics of *God's righteousness, justification,* and related subjects repeatedly, yet he is careful never to simply parrot his previous conclusions or those of others. For example, Moo surveys and assesses the different possibilities of how best to define the expression, *the righteousness of God.* Moo summarizes the three ways in which the expression has traditionally been rendered. These include: "(1) The expression might refer to an attribute of God.... (2) 'Righteousness of God' in 1:17 might refer to a status given by God.... (3) 'Righteousness of God' might denote an activity of God."[264] He then proceeds to unpack and explicate the differences between the Greek δικαιοσύνη (*dikaiosyne*) and the English *righteousness*. He notes:

> The English word "righteousness" naturally designates an abstract quality, but the use of the equivalent Greek term (*dikaiosyne*) in the LXX has a much broader range of meaning—including the dynamic sense of "establishing right." Especially significant are the many places in the Psalms and Isaiah where God's "righteousness" refers to his salvific intervention on

---

262. Westerholm, *Perspectives*, 284–6. In the original version of this work, I included five additional excerpts from Westerholm. These have been cut in an attempt to make this volume more manageable.

263. Representative examples include *Letters to the Colossians and to Philemon; Encountering the Book of Romans; Romans; Letter of James; 2 Peter, Jude; Commentary on the Epistle to the Romans;* along with dozens of other monographs and articles.

264. Moo, *Epistle to Romans,* 74.

behalf of his people. If Paul is using this "biblical" meaning of the word, then his point here would be that the gospel manifests "the saving action of God."[265]

These three options are neither exhaustive nor mutually exclusive, and it is not unusual to find authors who have combined two or more of the meanings, particularly when they interpret Rom 1:17. In fact, Moo says, "every possible combination of the three basic interpretations is found in the [scholarly] literature. . . ."[266] According to Moo, though, there are three considerations that should influence our decision on the matter. These factors include: 1) the background and use of the term in the OT; 2) the way in which the word is generally used throughout Romans; and 3) the immediate context of the term. "Whereas the OT provides warrant for each of the main alternatives, there is no doubt that the third—God's saving activity—receives strongest support. When 'righteousness' is attributed to God [in the OT], it has this meaning more than any other; and it is God's 'righteousness' in this sense—a saving, vindicating intervention of God—that the prophets say will characterize the eschatological deliverance of God's people. . . ."[267] If we recognize the OT influence on the word, "we would expect this notion of saving activity to be included when he announces the revelation of 'the righteousness of God.'"[268] Moo then notes that, although Paul uses the *dik-* word group in several ways, there is, nevertheless, one striking characteristic of his usage that marks his work throughout: the connection the apostle makes between faith and righteousness.[269]

Confusion over how to best understand the expression is understandable. There is no question that it is used in different ways, thus making it appear to be polysemous.[270] Whatever the case, most interpreters usually

265. Moo, *Epistle to Romans*, 74–75.
266. Moo, *Epistle to Romans*, 75.
267. Moo, *Epistle to Romans*, 69.
268. Moo, *Epistle to Romans*, 70.

269. Moo, *Epistle to Romans*, 70. Moo states that it is no "exaggeration to call this a *leitmotif* of the letter." He says, "*Paul links 'righteousness of God' closely with the response of faith in 1:17, in 3:21–2,* and (cf. 10:6) in 10:3. *This ties the idea of 'righteousness' in the phrase 'righteousness of God' to Paul's use of the word generally in Romans*, where it is typically linked to faith. And 'righteousness' is used most often in Romans to denote the 'gift of righteousness' (5:17)—a righteous status that God bestows on the one who believes. . . . Paul's use of 'righteousness' language in Romans, then, strongly suggests that 'righteousness of God' in 1:17; 3:21, 22; and 10:3 includes reference to the status of righteousness 'given' to the believer by God" (*Epistle to Romans*, 70–71; italics added).

270. Moo writes (*Epistle to Romans*, 72):

If these first two factors point in two different directions, the consideration of the context only confuses matters further by giving some support

make a decision on Rom 1:17, choosing to understand the expression as either an activity or as a status. This conclusion, then, tends to wield significant influence as the interpreter proceeds. But, Moo asks, must we make such a decision? "Do we have to choose between theology (God acting) and anthropology (the human being who receives)—as some have stated the dilemma? Could we not take 'righteousness of God' here to include both God's activity of 'making right'—saving, vindicating—and the status of those who are so made right, in a relational sense that bridges the divine and the human?"[271] After all, the Septuagint "makes it likely that 'the righteousness of God' is first of all the saving intervention of God in history, predicted by the prophets, manifested on the cross, and constantly made effective in the preaching of the gospel. But God's righteousness never operates in a vacuum, and the OT occurrences often allude also to the situation or status of those who experience God's saving intervention."[272] From this, Moo draws a conclusion and a definition: "For Paul, as in the OT, [the] 'righteousness of God' is a relational concept. Bringing together the aspects of activity and status, *we can define it as the act by which God brings people into right relationship with himself.*"[273] After devoting close to two dozen pages to analysis of righteousness and its uses, Moo concludes, "To summarize, then, we find that God's *dikaiosyne* in the OT can denote God's character as that of a God who will always do what is right, God's activity of establishing right, and even, as a product of this activity, the state of those who have been, or hope to be, put right. While the expectation that God would act to put his people in the right is usually founded on the covenant commitment, some texts,

---

to each possibility. On the one hand, Paul's use of "reveal"—particularly if it has the dynamic meaning we have suggested—makes better sense if "righteousness of God" denotes a divine activity than if it refers to a divine gift. Furthermore, the "revelation of God's wrath" in 1:18 appears to parallel v. 17, and "wrath" in v. 18 is clearly a divine activity. On the other hand, the "gift" character of "righteousness" receives support from the prepositional addition "on the basis of faith" and from the quotation of Hab 2:4 at the end of the verse, where the cognate word "righteous" designates human status. And this stress on faith as the means by which the righteousness of God is received binds this verse closely to those many others in Romans in which righteousness is clearly a status given to the one who believes. The contexts in which the related occurrences of "righteousness of God" are found evidence the same ambiguity: God's righteousness is "manifested" (3:21), and people are to "submit" to it (10:3)—suggesting activity; and yet it is also "based on" faith-suggesting gift or status.

271. Moo, *Epistle to Romans*, 72–73.

272. Moo, *Epistle to Romans*, 73. "[T]he dual aspect of God's righteousness as both divine activity and human status [has] its antecedents in the OT."

273. Moo, *Epistle to Romans*, 73–74; italics added.

such as Ps 143, Dan 9, and probably Isa 46 and 50, anticipate an irruption of God's righteousness that cannot be tied to the covenant as such. . . ."²⁷⁴ So where does this leave us? According to Moo, when *all* the relevant material is taken into consideration, we are left with a unique tension in Paul.

> Despite his debt to the OT and Judaism in his use of *dikaioo*, Paul differs from the normal OT/Jewish usage in . . . important respects. First, the verdict pronounced by a judge, according to the OT, was required to be in accordance with facts (cf. especially Exod 23:7; 1 Kgs 8:32). It is a keystone of Paul's doctrine, however, that "God justifies the ungodly" (Rom 4:5). His realization of the seriousness of sin and concern to maintain the absolute grace of God manifested in Christ led him to see that God's justifying verdict could never be forthcoming if the human being were regarded in himself. *It is not that God acts "unjustly" against the facts; but his justifying takes into account a larger set of facts,* including the atoning character of Jesus' death and the righteousness he thereby acquired.²⁷⁵

More recently, Moo notes an interesting features of *righteousness* language in both Romans and Galatians. He observes, "Of course, as is well known, Paul can use the noun, reflecting the common Old Testament use of צדקה (usually δικαιοσύνη in the LXX), to mean 'the behavior that God deems to be right.' But more often δικαιοσύνη in Paul echoes the basic semantic force of the verb, referring to the status of righteousness that the action, or verdict, of 'justify' confers."²⁷⁶ Forty years ago, one could practically assume, at least within evangelical circles, that the meaning of justification was entirely forensic. Today, however, such a consensus is not shared, as a growing number of NT scholars—scholars from a wide variety

274. Moo, *Epistle to Romans*, 79–87, 91.

275. Moo, *Epistle to Romans*, 86–87; italics added. In a footnote to the above, Moo suggests an illustration from C. S. Lewis's *The Lion, the Witch, and the Wardrobe* (Lewis, 163). Toward the end of the book, Aslan, the great lion that rules the land of Narnia, remarks that "though the White Witch knew the Deep Magic" of absolute justice,

> there is a magic deeper still which she did not know. Her knowledge goes back only to the dawn of time. But if she could have looked a little further back, into the stillness and the darkness before Time dawned, she would have read there a different incantation. She would have known that when a willing victim who had committed no treachery was killed in a traitor's stead, the [Stone] Table would crack and Death itself would start working backward.

276. Moo, "Justification in Galatians," 163. In line with this, Westerholm perceptively notes that "Paul's use of δικαιοσύνη is derived from his use of the verb δικαιόω and that it is the verb that stands in continuity with the Old Testament" (Westerholm, *Perspectives*, 276–7).

of theological traditions—argue for a view of justification that entails a distinctly transformative element.[277]

4.9.D. John Piper (1946–)

John Stephen Piper was born January 11, 1946, in Chattanooga, TN, to Bill and Ruth Piper. Piper's father, a traveling fundamentalist evangelist,[278] made a deep and lasting impression upon his son—one which would be reflected throughout his written work.[279] Piper attended Wheaton College (BA), Fuller Theological Seminary (BD), and the University of Munich (DTh), conducting his research under Leonard Goppelt with a dissertation entitled *Love Your Enemies*. After completing his doctoral work, Piper moved to St. Paul, MN, where he accepted the position of professor of biblical studies at Bethel College, a post he held for six years. In 1980, however, Piper left Bethel to become the senior pastor of Bethlehem Baptist Church in Minneapolis, a position he filled for thirty-three years. In early 2013, Piper stepped down from his role at Bethlehem Baptist in order to take on "a more visionary role" within the organization he started, Desiring God.[280] He is currently the chancellor of Bethlehem College and Seminary (founded in 2009). He has authored or coauthored nearly a hundred books, as well as hundreds of articles and essays. His major academic works include *Desiring God: Meditations of Christian Hedonist*; *Counted Righteous in Christ: Should We Abandon the Imputation of Christ*; *Finally Alive: What Happens When We Are Born Again*; *The Future of Justification: A Response to N. T. Wright*; and *The Justification of God: An Exegetical and Theological Study of Romans 9:1–23*.

With Piper, we begin by noting the unique way he defines the nettlesome expression "the righteousness of God." In his monograph on Rom 9:1–23 (*The Justification of God*), Piper says that "the righteousness of God consists most basically in [His] unswerving commitment to preserve the

---

277. Cf. Moo, "Justification in Galatians," 163. Moo adds, "A certain element of transformation in justification is implied in the significant ecumenical agreement between the Roman Catholic Church and the Lutheran World Federation. Among those arguing for a transformative view are the so-called "Finnish School" (e.g., Tuomo Mannermaa), and . . . also Michael Gorman."

278. Piper, "Evangelist Bill Piper" and "Honoring Biblical Call of Motherhood."

279. One need only read a brief sample of both men's work to discover the striking similarity, both in style and content, between father and son. See Bill Piper, *Greatest Menace*, 30ff; *A Good Time*, 65ff; *Stones Out of the Rubbish*, 63–64; *Tyranny of Tolerance*, 28ff; and *Dead Men Made Alive*.

280. www.desiringgod.org.

honor of his name and display his glory."[281] This way of describing God's righteousness is not unique to this particular work. Rather, we find it repeatedly throughout Piper's collected works, and it is at the very heart of his theological program. Thus we see it emerge again and again.[282] For example, a few pages later, in the same book just mentioned, he states: "The righteousness of God [is] his unswerving commitment to preserve the honor of his name and display his glory."[283] In one of his earliest works, Piper states: "[Rom 3:21–26] demonstrates the righteousness of God because *God's righteousness is His unswerving allegiance to uphold the value of His glory*."[284] And again, "*God's righteousness is his unwavering commitment to uphold and display the infinite worth of his glory in all that he does*, which would seem to require punishment for all who have 'fallen short of the glory of God' (Rom 3:23). But since God's righteousness *(his commitment to his glory)* and his mercy (his commitment to our joy) are not ultimately at odds, he made a way to 'be both just and the justifier of him who has faith in Jesus' (Rom 3:26)."[285] A practical upshot of this understanding is that "Every sin flows from the failure to treasure the glory of God above all things."[286] Piper explains the origins of this idea. In particular, he points to two essays by Jonathan Edwards which were profoundly influential on his own theological understanding. He notes that he finds himself often returning "to the friend of my soul, Jonathan Edwards. [No one] has come close to shaking the biblical foundations of divine righteousness demonstrated so magnificently in Edwards's two works, *The End for Which God Created the World* and *Concerning the Necessity and Reasonableness of the Christian Doctrine of Satisfaction for* Sin."[287] The reason for emphasizing Edwards's influence on Piper's thought is that it impacts Piper's understanding not only of God's righteousness, but of God's purpose in all things.[288] As previously

281. Piper, *Justification of God*, 119. "Thus, if God ever abandoned this commitment and no longer sought in all things the magnifying of his own glory, then there indeed would be unrighteousness with God." See his expansion of this idea, 135–50.

282. See Piper, *God's Passion for His Glory*, 31–38; *Pleasures of God*, 165–76; *Brothers*, 50–51.

283. Piper, *Future of Justification*, 121.

284. Piper, *Desiring God*, 320; italics added.

285. Piper, *God's Passion for His Glory*, 33n37; italics added.

286. Piper, "Preaching as Expository Exultation."

287. Piper, *Pleasures of God*, 74–75. Both the works listed by Edwards are found in *Works of Jonathan Edwards*.

288. Although Piper notes other authors that have influenced him (e.g., Daniel Fuller, C. S. Lewis, E. D. Hirsch, George Ladd et al.), it is clear from his corpus that Edwards takes the pride of place. However, Edwards is not always cited directly. Rather, it is more that "Edwards' . . . ghost walks through most of Piper's pages. . . . [Edwards]

noted, Piper defines God's righteousness as his "unwavering commitment to uphold and display the honor of his own glory."[289] Part of this idea is rooted in a critical quotation from Edwards. Edwards states,

> The moral rectitude of God must consist in a due respect to things that are objects of moral respect; that is, to intelligent beings capable of moral actions and relations. And therefore, it must chiefly consist in giving due respect to that Being to whom most is due; for God is infinitely the most worthy of regard. The worthiness of others is as nothing to his; so that to him belongs all possible respect. To him belongs the whole of the respect that any intelligent being is capable of.[290]

This insight pervades Edwards's writing, and its implications are legion.

One of the more practical consequences of this statement is the way God glorifies himself. It is here that we come to the crux of Piper's understanding of Edwards and thus Piper's entire theological enterprise. When God glorifies himself toward humanity, he does so in two ways:

> 1. By appearing to . . . their understanding. [And], 2. In communicating Himself to their hearts, and in their rejoicing and delighting in, and enjoying, the manifestations which He makes of Himself . . . *God is glorified not only by His glory's being seen, but by its being rejoiced in.* When those that see it delight in it, "God is more glorified than if they only see it."[291]

This is probably the most important quotation in all of Edwards's corpus for Piper; it represents the very center of Piper's theological system, that "God is most glorified in us when we are most satisfied in him."[292] This pervades virtually everything he has published, coloring his entire approach to life, mission, ministry, and everything else within the Christian life. As a result, it is easy to misunderstand some ideas in Piper's work until this one

---

would be delighted with his disciple." See J. I. Packer's endorsement in Piper, *Desiring God*, vii.

289. Piper, *God's Passion for His Glory*, 33.

290. Edwards, *Dissertation*, 98. Cf. Piper, *God's Passion for His Glory*, 31–38.

291. Edwards, "Miscellanies," 13:495, Miscellany 448; italics added. See also Miscellanies 87, 251–2; 332, 410; 679. These Miscellanies were the private notebooks of Edwards from which he built his books, like *A Dissertation Concerning the End for Which God Created the World*. See Piper's book-length review of that work in Piper, *God's Passion for His Glory*, 31–38.

292. Piper, *Desiring God*, 10, 288, 309, 313; Piper, *Supremacy of God in Preaching*; Piper, *Let the Nations Be Glad!*, Kindle loc., 853, 855, 861, 874, 968, 2424, 4817; and many more.

essential concept is first understood. However, once this is grasped, everything else follows.

The above comments are more a sketch of Piper's central convictions than an outline of his response to the NPP. We will look at how Piper has contributed to a couple of the discussions on justification later on. For now, we simply note that, more than anyone else, Piper has made God's glory—and God's love for his own glory—the very center of all his work.

4.10. PENTECOSTAL CONTRIBUTIONS TO JUSTIFICATION

One arena in which the topic of justification has experienced considerable reassessment is the world of Pentecostal/Charismatic (a.k.a. P/C) scholarship.[293] Not only have P/C theologians closely examined the theological and historical developments of justification, in several instances they have been among the leading voices in attempting to renew and rework this doctrine. Although a long list of P/C representatives could be produced as possible candidates for examination, for our purposes we will limit our focus to only two theologians:[294] Frank Macchia and Veli-Matti Kärkkäinen.[295]

4.10.A. Frank Macchia

Frank Macchia is a Pentecostal theologian and ecumenicist who serves as professor of systematic theology at Vanguard University in Costa Mesa, CA. Macchia completed his BA at Southern California College; an MA at the Wheaton College Graduate School; an MDiv from Union Theological Seminary in New York City; and his DTh at the University of Basel, Switzerland. He is past president of the Society for Pentecostal Studies and served as the editor of *Pneuma: The Journal of the Society for Pentecostal Studies* for more

---

293. Going forward, I will use the shorthand abbreviation "P/C" for the Pentecostal/Charismatic movements. Likewise, I will use the term "renewal" as a descriptive for P/C Christians.

294. The original version of this work incorporated five prominent "renewal" theologians: D. Lyle Dabney, Steven M. Studebaker, Frank Macchia, Amos Yong, and Veli-Matti Kärkkäinen. However, it simply became too unwieldy. Thus, I have limited myself to Macchia and Kärkkäinen.

295. See Kärkkäinen's *One with God*; "Justification as Forgiveness," 32–45; and "Salvation as Justification," 74–82.

than a decade. Macchia is a prolific author[296] with an astonishing intellect, specializing in systematic, ecumenical, and Pentecostal theology.

In an article entitled "Justification through New Creation," Frank Macchia calls into question some of the most basic assumptions held by evangelicals regarding justification.[297] Macchia begins his work by recounting Luther's now famous definition of justification, yet it is clear that he is very unhappy with this formulation. He states with palpable frustration, "Protestant theology has tended . . . to confine justification to the cross as the event in which God's justice and wrath were satisfied and the basis of justification of the sinner *objectively* established. [But] where is the Holy Spirit in this understanding of Christ's redemptive work for our justification?"[298] Macchia infers that the absence of a pneumatological understanding of justification indicates that the Reformers did not believe the Spirit played an active part in justification.[299] Macchia's exasperation with the traditional Protestant view of justification is evident when he describes it as "the shallow well of the forensic model"[300] and a "pneumatologically barren notion."[301] Macchia's fear is that a forensic view is "one-sided,"[302] "narrowly Christological,"[303] "distant,"[304] without "the eschatological reach of the Spirit,"[305] and, perhaps

---

296. The primary works of Macchia that I used for this volume were, "Justification through New Creation" and *Justified in the Spirit*.

297. Macchia, "Justification through New Creation," 216.

298. Macchia, "Justification through New Creation," 209.

299. Arguments from silence are universally recognized to be invalid. It would be a bit like assuming that the participants of Nicea did not believe the Holy Spirit was a full member of the Godhead because they were nearly silent regarding the Spirit, even though they spoke at length about the Father and the Son. This illustrates the danger of drawing conclusions from silence. The leaders of Nicea said almost nothing about the Holy Spirit in 325 because it was the doctrine of Christ and the Trinity that were being assailed—not the person and work of the Spirit. Thus, when there was no direct attack, there was silence. An omission does not imply a denial. Further, to suggest that Luther's silence on the Spirit's role in justification implies a doctrinal position, trivializes the debate that *was* taking place.

300. Macchia, "Justification through New Creation," 205.

301. Macchia, "Justification through New Creation," 207. In *Justified in the Spirit*, Macchia cites with approval Osiander's statement that forensic justification is a "thing colder than ice" (207), calling it "one-sided" (7, 40), and claims that such a view is "narrowly Christological" (40). He says that "such a view of justification is not Pauline, or even biblical for that matter. . . " (206–7).

302. Macchia, *Justified in the Spirit*, 7, 40, 67; Macchia, "Justification through New Creation," 205–6.

303. Macchia, *Justified in the Spirit*, 40.

304. Macchia, *Justified in the Spirit*, 7.

305. Macchia, *Justified in the Spirit*, 8, 67; Macchia, "Justification through New

most concerning of all, is isolated[306]—separate from the other aspects of redemption[307] and the Spirit[308]—and, consequently, neglects the role of faith.[309] Thus, he approvingly cites Osiander's sentiment that forensic justification is a "thing colder than ice,"[310] concluding that "such a view of justification is not Pauline, or even biblical for that matter . . . . "[311] To try to summarize, two contentions seem to dominate Macchia's work: 1. Justification is *more* than an external legal declaration, but participatory and internal; and 2. Justification *must* be understood pneumatologically. Although Macchia's antipathy toward the forensic view is regularly apparent, it is not his only concern. In fact, Macchia even affirms a forensic element to justification—at least in a qualified sense.[312] Nevertheless, the routine absence of the pneumatological is a significant concern for Macchia,[313] as well as his insistence that justification must not be separated from regeneration or sanctification.

The background to Macchia's pneumatological concerns is that since the time of Augustine (and probably before him), the Christian church has believed that "the external works of the Trinity are undivided" (i.e., *opera trinitatis ad extra sunt indivisa*).[314] Put differently, every action of God

Creation," 207–8, 212–3.

306. Macchia, *Justified in the Spirit*, 50, 67; Macchia, "Justification through New Creation," 213.

307. Macchia, *Justified in the Spirit*, 8, 61, 67, 73, 104.

308. Macchia, *Justified in the Spirit*, 61, 67.

309. Macchia, *Justified in the Spirit*, 51; Macchia, "Justification through New Creation," 202, 204, 207.

310. Originally, "Kelter ding dan das eyes." Osiander, "Disputation von der Rechtfertigung," in *Schriften and Briefe 1549 bis August 1551*, 73, as quoted in Macchia, *Justified in the Spirit*, 207.

311. Macchia, *Justified in the Spirit*, 206–7.

312. For example, Macchia says, "I would go so far as to say that justification in the Spirit for Paul has legal or forensic overtones" (*Justified in the Spirit*, 206). Similarly, "the sense of forensic judgment is not absent from the Old Testament " (Macchia, "Justification through New Creation," 207).

313. He repeatedly asks questions like, "Where is the Holy Spirit in this forensic model of justification" (209) and, "Where is the Holy Spirit in this understanding of Christ's redemptive work for our Justification?" (205). He insists that, "What is needed . . . is a fresh focus on the . . . role of the Holy Spirit . . . in . . . justification" (206). Macchia, "Justification through New Creation."

314. See Augustine, *Sermon 52*, and Gregory of Nyssa, *On "Not Three Gods."* However, Augustine more regularly uses the expressions *inseparabilia sunt opera Trinitatis* (the works of the Trinity are inseparable), or *neque enim separata sunt dona vel opera inseparabilis Trinitatis* (neither the gifts nor the Trinity are separable). The idea is repeated throughout the Latin West in various forms. It seems likely that Augustine took the idea that was already prevalent in the tradition and transformed it into the basic formula of the above phrase. I am indebted to Dale Coulter (professor of historical

is effected by all three members of the Godhead, even though each may perform a unique role.[315] Thus, there is a unity between Father, Son, and Holy Spirit, and all three are involved in every act that God decrees. This idea has significant implications when considering the doctrine of justification. Protestants have almost universally claimed that justification is a legal declaration made by the Father about the believer, based on the work of the Son. The question then is: where is the Holy Spirit in this formulation? If the ancient church was correct in its belief that the actions of the Trinity are "undivided" (and we have no reason to believe they were mistaken), then it appears there is a serious gap in the classic Protestant articulation. For we have the activity of the Father (decreeing our justification) and the Son (purchasing our justification through his death and resurrection), but the Holy Spirit is absent. It is this pneumatological absence that has elicited the concerns of Macchia and others.

After outlining the key points of the forensic model, Macchia concludes, "This forensic theory that came to dominate later Lutheran confessions and subsequent evangelical theology needs to be questioned. The picture it supports is of an impartial judge who must regard us as guilty but whose wrath is turned away by the work of Christ, which merits favor in our stead."[316] From here, he raises a series of rhetorical questions, all of which imply a non-biblical origin to forensic justification.

> [A.] Where in this doctrine of forensic justification is the God of Scripture who functions as an injured party pursuing us relentlessly in love? [B.] Where is the biblical sense of justice that is not fundamentally punitive but redemptive? [C.] *Most of all, where is the Holy Spirit in this forensic model of justification, the Spirit who serves as the agent by which God makes things right for, and with, fallen creation?* [D.] Does Jesus satisfy God's righteousness through meritorious deeds, or does he inaugurate it for all of creation in the power of the Spirit?[317]

---

theology at Pentecostal Theological Seminary and former associate professor of church history at Regent University, School of Divinity) for his help in tracing the roots of these expressions.

315. The standard evangelical explanation of this idea is that the Father decrees our salvation, the Son procures and purchases it, and the Holy Spirit applies and seals it in our life. There are, of course, almost unlimited ways of saying this, but the basic idea is that there is an economic distinction between members of the Godhead, even while they are coequal and coeternal. See Eric Alexander, "Basis of Christian Salvation."

316. Macchia, "Justification through New Creation," 205.

317. Macchia, "Justification through New Creation," 205; italics added. I inserted the A, B, C, and D lettering as reference points for below.

The problem with such questions, and particularly the final question (D), is that they commit the informal fallacy of the complex question (*plurium interrogationum*). This type of question cannot be answered in the kind of straight-forward, honest way that the question appears to require. The questioner implies he is looking for simple answers: either *yes* or *no*. The question is like asking, "Have you stopped beating your wife yet?" or "Did your sales increase as a result of your misleading advertising?"[318] A simple *yes* or *no* answer falls into a trap. The question itself is phrased so that a simple answer will not work. Thus, when Macchia asks, "Where is the biblical sense of justice that is not fundamentally punitive but redemptive? . . . Does Jesus satisfy God's righteousness through meritorious deeds, or does he inaugurate it for all of creation in the power of the Spirit?"[319] he is forcing false dilemmas, as if the only two options are either, "Jesus satisfied God's righteousness," or, "he inaugurated it for all creation." His questions are more complex than his initial formulation might suggest.

Nevertheless, we should be careful not to throw out the insight of Macchia's reflection—i.e., the Holy Spirit's absence in the classic Protestant view of justification. The very fact that such a theological lacuna could continue for so long is itself a telling point. It calls attention to the church's lack of attention to the person and work of the Spirit in all areas of soteriology for, perhaps, centuries.

Macchia's expanded work *Justified in the Spirit* begins with a basic summary of Protestant, Catholic, and Pentecostal teaching on justification, a summary that includes current trends and an analysis of "Spirit baptism" for Pentecostals. He then provides an overview of Old and New Testament teaching on the subject, as well as topical overviews of creation, redemption, the Trinity, and other subjects. Macchia argues for an "effective" understanding of justification. However, a number of pieces in his explanation do not quite fit. For example, Macchia devotes considerable space to the notion of creation's healing and related ideas. Here, he has in mind more than a simple eschatological consummation, where the "wolf will live with the lamb, the leopard will lie down with the goat, the calf and the lion and the yearling together; and a little child will lead them" (Is 11:6). Rather, Macchia takes the increasingly popular position that understands divine judgment (and the various related expressions, particularly those found in the Old Testament) as essentially the natural result of human sin.[320] Yet, Macchia does not

---

318. See Copi, *Introduction to Logic*, 72–73; Watts, *Logic*; Copi, *Improvement of the Mind*.

319. Macchia, "Justification through New Creation," 205.

320. Perhaps the most common illustration of this idea is through the imagery of war—war being the natural result of nations acting sinfully or exclusively in their

devote his attention to the nature of God's judgment, but instead addresses the question of how the Spirit is bound up with God's word of promise and how the giving of the Spirit is fulfilled in Christ's resurrection. When all is said and done, we discover that Macchia's proposal is strikingly similar to that of Andreas Osiander's.[321] For that very reason, we will now take a few moments to look at the life and work of Andreas Osiander[322] and use it as a lens through which to examine Macchia.

4.10.B. Andreas Osiander (1498–1552)[323]

Andreas Osiander (1498–1552), was born on December 19, 1498, in Gunzenhausen (near Nuremberg), Germany, and was, perhaps the greatest man "among the men of second rank in the Reformation period."[324] He died on October 17, 1552, in Königsberg. Osiander participated in some of the most significant assemblies of Protestant Reformation history. For example, he was present at the Colloquy of Marburg in 1529, where he met Luther personally; he contributed to the discussions at the Diet of Augsburg in 1530; in 1537, he participated in the initial draft of the Smalcald Articles, later voting for their adoption; and, finally, in 1540, Osiander was also present for the famous Diet of Worms.

Osiander's theological concerns began when he was appointed parish priest of St. Lawrence's Church in the free city of Nürnberg, having become an advocate of the Reformation cause by 1522. Although Osiander labored energetically in Nürnberg, he did not remain in the city. When the Catholic church began imposing restrictions on Luther's followers in late 1548, Osiander eventually capitulated and moved to Königsberg in January 1549, where he was warmly received by Count Albrecht of Prussia. Albrecht regarded Osiander as a kind of spiritual father, appointing him to pastor the Old City Church and later to become professor of theology at the university. Although Osiander had studied Hebrew at the University of Ingolstadt and

---

own self-interest. The "violent" book of Joshua is often held up as the exemplar. See Fretheim, "God and Violence," 23–24, and Tollington, "Ethics of Warfare," 86–87.

321. See Seifrid, Review of *Justified in the Spirit*.

322. Within *Justified in the Spirit*, Macchia not only holds an essentially Osiandrian position, but he also self-consciously reproduces his position (see 55–61, 84, 321, 345).

323. I realize that Osiander should probably be situated further up, between Luther and Calvin. However, I placed him immediately after Macchia, because Macchia's view of justification is essentially that of Osiander's.

324. Seeberg, *Textbook of History of Doctrines*, 2:369–74. See also Hirsch, *Theologie des Andreas Osiander*. Most of the content in this section was taken from these two volumes. See also Seebass, *Bibliographia Osiandrica*.

"became an accomplished Hebraist,"[325] he never completed a single academic degree, thus inciting the ire of his colleagues. Ultimately, Albrecht's favor toward Osiander only intensified the animus of his peers, as they felt the sting of jealously.

All this was exacerbated by Osiander's personality. By nature, he seems to have had a prickly, overbearing personality, going about his daily affairs with what appeared to be an almost scheming methodology. He had a knack for turning potential allies into real enemies. Wherever Osiander went, he seems to have left a legacy of rancor in his wake. Even when his efforts proved to be helpful, when he left, few were sorry to see him go.[326] The atmosphere around the university became so volatile that professors started to carry weapons to their classes. Yet despite Osiander's difficult personality, the controversy surrounding his name was not the result of his truculent temperament. Instead, it was the result of Osiander's speculative and sometimes "mystical" views of justification and what it meant for humanity to be genuinely *imago Dei*. Whether Osiander reverted to a more Roman Catholic understanding (as some Lutheran opponents suggested), or simply had never fully embraced Luther's teaching on justification (as other adversaries offered), the result was Osiander's rejection of forensic justification. He said, "[The Reformers] teach . . . that we are accounted righteous only on account of the remission of sins, and not also on account of the righteousness of the Christ dwelling in us by faith. God is not indeed so unjust as to regard him as righteous in whom there is really nothing of true righteousness."[327] Although Osiander's thinking on justification was initially unclear (as the above citation indicates), he eventually clarified his understanding of it in several theological treatises: *Whether the Son of God Would Have Had to Be Incarnated if Sin Had Not Entered the World* (1550), *Concerning the Only Mediator Jesus Christ and Justification of Faith* (1551), *Disputation on Justification* (1550).[328] The final two works, in particular, are where we find Osiander's clearest statements on justification, as well as some of his more novel concepts.

---

325. Steinmetz, *Reformers in the Wings*, 63.

326. Steinmetz, *Reformers in the Wings*, 63.

327. Osiander, "Disputatio de Iustificatione"(1550), thesis 73ff, with the assistance of an online translator. It is clear that this statement by Osiander could be understood in a couple of ways. On the surface, it sounds as though he is suggesting that the reformers taught a form of justification that included forgiveness but not Christ's righteousness "dwelling in us by faith"; but, as we will see, this was *not* the teaching of the Reformers. Moreover, Osiander himself had an unusual view of what it meant for "the righteousness of Christ to dwell in us by faith."

328. See also Niesel, *Theology of Calvin*, 133ff.

The two most able and determined opponents of Osiander were Joachim Mörlin and Matthias Flacius.[329] Mörlin noted that Osiander's doctrine taught that faith rests upon a righteous condition within the individual, while Flacius observed that Osiander's denial of the imputation of Christ's righteousness had unintentionally divorced Christ's satisfaction from the believer's justification, thereby obscuring the centrality of that satisfaction. Men like Mörlin and Flacius believed that it was not possible to possess a genuine assurance of God's acceptance unless the believer's faith rested squarely upon the objective (or alien) righteousness of Christ.

Furthermore, Osiander claimed that redemption and justification were not the same and thus should not be equated. Such a claim will not seem odd to contemporary evangelicals. For their part, Mörlin and Flacius agreed that redemption and justification should not be conflated, but, unlike Osiander, they denied that they were unrelated or separable. In short, Flacius argued that the connection between redemption and justification was much closer than Osiander allowed. The function of redemption was not simply to make justification possible. The act of redemption, Flacius contended, was in a fundamental way the same as the act of justification, for when we are justified, God considers us as righteous by virtue of Christ's redemption. Moreover, Flacius insisted that his distinction was important, because Osiander's position tended to place the emphasis on the eternal Word of God, by virtue of whose very presence it/he justified sinners. But, he argued, *if this is the case, the sacrificial act of the incarnate Word cannot be made sense of*. Consequently, Mörlin and Flacius insisted that God justifies us, not because of the eternal Word in us, but because of Christ's obedience *for* us.[330]

The conflict between the two sides eventually captured the attention of the larger church within Germany. The dispute that followed concluded with the rejection of Osiander's doctrinal formula and the reaffirmation of Melanchthon's statement on the imputation of Christ's righteousness. Osiander, however, refused to concede defeat. In the words of Steinmetz, "The sound of battle stirred the old veteran to buckle on his armor and sharpen his sword. He loved nothing so much as a good fight, and he launched a counterattack with all the pugnacity and fervor he could muster. The pages of his anti-Melanchthonian polemic were hot to the touch."[331]

---

329. Seeberg, *Textbook of History of Doctrines*, 2:370, and Hirsch, *Theologie des Andreas Osiander*. Flacius was perhaps the "greatest Lutheran theologian of the second generation" (Ritschl, *Dogmengeschichte*, 4:475).

330. González, *History*, 3:104.

331. Steinmetz, *Reformers in the Wings*, 66.

Osiander continued to publish works defending his position against any and all comers;[332] yet other adversaries besides Mörlin arose and also denounced Osiander's teaching,[333] which finally brought the conflict to its zenith. And it was just then that Osiander abruptly died. Although the conflicts continued through some of Osiander's followers, in principle the battle was over and finally concluded when the *Corpus doctrinae Pruthenicum*, or *Borussicum* (composed by Mörlin and Martin Chemnitz),[334] was officially adopted at Königsberg in 1567, in which the teaching of Osiander was officially repudiated for his insistence that forensic justification simply "could not be correct,"[335] because God "could never *declare* sinners to be just; they must actually be *intrinsically* just."[336] Hence, Königsberg rejected the idea that justification involved "an infusion of the divine nature, and on that basis men are declared to be just."[337] Following the above events, Melanchthon declared that Osiander had "departed from the clear teaching of the gospel, and that by claiming that God justifies us by virtue of the righteousness of [the divine nature of] Christ in the sinner the professor at Königsberg was abandoning the doctrine of imputed righteousness and coming precariously close to Roman Catholicism."[338] In the Reformation age, such a charge was indeed serious.

When we assess both what Osiander's critics had to say and what he himself said, we discover that his opponents represented him fairly evenhandedly. In the examples that follow, note the way Osiander either conflates or confuses justification and regeneration. For example, in his most articulate work on justification, *A Defense of Justification*, Osiander states that *justification* of the ungodly refers to "bringing the dead to life."[339] The new life that results can be experienced now as "a movement of the Spirit, which *God awakens in our hearts* by his Spirit through the preaching of the

332. See Osiander, *Beweisung*.

333. E.g., the "Philippists," such as Gallus, Amsdorf, and Wigand, were each prominently arraigned against Osiander.

334. The "second Martin" of the Reformation (Pelikan, *Riddle of Roman Catholicism*, 50).

335. Osiander, as quoted in Seeberg, *Textbook of History of Doctrines*, 2:369.

336. Osiander, as quoted in Seeberg, *Textbook of History of Doctrines*, 2:369-74; italics added.

337. Osiander, *Von dem einigen Mittler*, thesis 26, with the assistance of an online translator. Calvin also rejected Osiander's teaching. See Calvin, *Institutes*, 3:11:5-21 (McNeill).

338. Manschreck, ed., *Melanchthon*, 179.

339. Osiander, *Defense of Justification*, §4, as quoted in Macchia, *Justified in the Spirit*, 55. Cf. Macchia's statement that justification "can [be] regenerative without being anthropocentric" (*Justified in the Spirit*, 85).

Word."³⁴⁰ Osiander insists that the apostle's rejection of the law as a path of justification was preeminently (according to Gal 3:21) because *it could not give life*,³⁴¹ not because the law was unable to justify the wicked. That difference is significant. All blessings, says Osiander, come to us through Christ's glorified presence *within, including justification*.³⁴² But how does this justification take place? He tells us that it is not faith as a virtue or quality that justifies us, but "only that faith that grasps and is united to Christ, which is its object."³⁴³ As to imputation, he does maintain a form of "reckoning" righteousness, but this righteousness comes about through a mystical union with the divine Christ.³⁴⁴ Again, *it is not the human righteousness of Christ that faith grasps hold of that saves us, but rather the divine righteousness of Christ that is present to us in faith*.³⁴⁵ Thus "*we are justified by his essential righteousness.*"³⁴⁶ Moreover, the righteousness that we enjoy in justification is the righteousness that is shared by the Father and the Son, as well as by *the Spirit, who makes the godless righteous*.³⁴⁷

Osiander makes an interesting claim when he states that "only the Lord Jesus Christ who has fulfilled the law and all righteousness is righteous."³⁴⁸ On the surface, this might simply be an affirmation of the active obedience of Christ. That is, that Jesus actively obeyed all the Law of Moses and all his Father's will *perfectly*, thereby earning positive righteousness. But before we

---

340. Osiander, *Defense of Justification*, 10, as quoted in Macchia, *Justified in the Spirit*, 55; italics added. Cf. Macchia's statement that justifcation "is the pardon and liberation experienced in the embrace of the Spirit" (*Justified in the Spirit*, 85). Justification also includes "empowered witness, healing, and divine vindication through signs and wonders and, ultimately, resurrection" (*Justified in the Spirit*, 85).

341. Osiander, *Defense of Justification*, 1–2, as quoted in Macchia, *Justified in the Spirit*, 55. That is, because the law could not regenerate.

342. Osiander, *Defense of Justification*, 52, as quoted in Macchia, *Justified in the Spirit*, 56; italics added.

343. Osiander, *Defense of Justification*, 19, as quoted in Macchia, *Justified in the Spirit*, 56. Likewise, Macchia says that "*the justified relationship is* not primarily legal or moral but rather *involves mutual indwelling*" (*Justified in the Spirit*, 99; italics added.)

344. Osiander, *Defense of Justification*, 76, as quoted in Macchia, *Justified in the Spirit*, 56.

345. Osiander, *Defense of Justification*, 21, as quoted in Macchia, *Justified in the Spirit*, 56; italics added.

346. Osiander, *Defense of Justification*, 53, as quoted in Macchia, *Justified in the Spirit*, 56; italics added.

347. Osiander, *Defense of Justification*, 28, as quoted in Macchia, *Justified in the Spirit*, 56. Osiander says, "This is the righteousness of all three persons of the Trinity that came into the world when the Son became flesh" (*Defense of Justification*, 54).

348. Osiander, *Defense of Justification*, 26, as quoted in Macchia, *Justified in the Spirit*, 56.

conclude this, we should note that he immediately follows up with, "Christ was *not* righteous *because* he fulfilled the law." Rather, says Osiander, Christ was righteous "because he was born from the righteous Father from all eternity as the righteous Son."[349] He goes on to say that the righteousness that comes to us through "the Christ within" is still very much a part of the overall picture, because of "Christ's death and resurrection, which brings pardon for sin, and without which no one can receive righteousness and life from Christ.[350] He concludes that "justification thus consists of pardon for sin and reconciliation. But this reconciliation with Christ through the Spirit within is not comparable to human reconciliation but is to be understood theologically as a union with deity through spiritual rebirth. After all, Christ in us is the object of reconciliation and not another human being."[351]

The main point here is that it is the divine nature of Christ himself that indwells the believer by faith. Thus he maintains that it is the Holy Spirit indwelling the believer that makes him or her righteous, rather than any external legal declaration of righteousness.[352] Moreover, it is through "this indwelling that man becomes righteous. Righteousness is no work, no act, no endurance . . . but it is the character which makes him who receives and possesses it righteous and moves him to act and endure aright."[353] In examining Osiander's view of righteousness, one modern historian/theologian observes,

---

349. Osiander, *Defense of Justification*, 27, as quoted in Macchia, *Justified in the Spirit*, 56; italics added. It is interesting to note the contrast with Calvin. Calvin says that since Osiander is "not contented with that *righteousness, which was procured for us by the obedience and sacrificial death of Christ*, [Osiander] maintains that we are substantially righteous in God by an infused essence as well as quality. For this is the reason why he so vehemently contends that not only Christ but the Father and the Spirit dwell in us" (Calvin, *Institutes*, 3:11:5 [Beveridge]; italics added).

350. Osiander, *Defense of Justification*, 29, as quoted in Macchia, *Justified in the Spirit*, 56.

351. Osiander, *Defense of Justification*, 31, as quoted in Macchia, *Justified in the Spirit*, 56.

352. "'That righteousness is granted because sin has been before forgiven.' We are righteous only in so far as we become alive; but we become alive, or righteous, only through the indwelling of Christ. Justification is therefore not to be conceived forensically, but as a making righteous. *Justificare* is 'from an ungodly to make a righteous man, i. e., to recall the dead to life.' This indwelling of the divine nature of Christ, with which at the same time the Triune God dwells in us, is our righteousness before God. Still more precisely, 'his divine nature is our righteousness.' It is therefore perfectly clear, that justification is the renewal of man wrought by the presence of Christ" (Osiander, as quoted in Seeberg, *Textbook of History of Doctrines*, 25202–8).

353. Osiander, *Concerning the Only Mediator*, 8:4; cf. Seeberg, *Textbook of History of Doctrines*, 25172–7.

In order for this righteousness to be true of an individual, however, one must be justified. This Christ does by dwelling in that person. *Thus, justification is not*, as for Luther, *imputed by God out of loving grace, but is rather something that God finds in us because Christ is in us. The righteousness of the believer is the indwelling God.* . . . Osiander affirms that what actually happens when Christ comes to dwell in the believer is that *the ocean of his divine righteousness engulfs the small drop of our sinfulness, and that God then looks at that vast ocean of purity rather than at the small drop of sinfulness and declares us to be righteous*.[354]

What then is the difference between Osiander's understanding of righteousness and that of the reformers? The difference was essentially this: for Luther et al., righteousness consisted in God's forgiveness of the believer *and* the gift of Christ's righteousness by faith. The believer's righteousness was something external — something outside of him or her. Though we remain unworthy of this gift throughout our lives, the gospel remains for us a word of comfort and joy, a promise of grace that gives what it promises to whomever believes.[355] As Luther described it in his treatise *The Freedom of a Christian*, the gospel is like a wedding vow that gives us a divine bridegroom, God's own son, together with all that is his: the righteousness of God, blessing, and eternal life.[356] The fact that this alien righteousness was outside the believer was, in Luther's mind, good news, for it meant that the doubts and uncertainties which so frequently assail Christians could not actually touch the righteousness God had given. Since it was bestowed by God and external, believers could not subjectively contaminate or destroy it. Hence,

354. González, *History*, 3:103-4; italics added. Osiander himself writes, "If the Scriptures make righteousness dependent upon faith, faith is thus mentioned by them because its content is Christ, i. e., 'Jesus Christ, true God and man, who dwells in our hearts by faith. . . .' When we are united with Christ by faith, we are 'overwhelmed and filled' with divine righteousness. And although sin indeed still clings to us, yet *it is only as an impure drop compared with a whole pure ocean, and, on account of Christ's righteousness which is within us*" (as quoted in Seeberg, *Textbook of History of Doctrines*, 25208-13; italics added). One can see that the authors of "The Formula of Concord" were addressing themselves to this issue when they wrote, "The question has arisen: *According to which nature is Christ our Righteousness?* and thus two contrary errors have arisen in some churches. For the one side has held that Christ according to His divinity alone is our Righteousness, if He dwell in us by faith; contrasted with this divinity, dwelling in us by faith, the sins of all men must be regarded *as a drop of water compared to the great ocean*. Others, on the contrary, have held that Christ is our Righteousness before God according to the human nature alone " ("Righteousness of Faith").

355. See Luther, *Bondage of the Will* (Packer and Johnston), 132, 135-6.

356. Luther, *Freedom of a Christian*, 343-58; cf. Cary, *Luther*, Lecture 5, 12:00. See also Luther, "Excerpt on the Mass," 595-610; Althaus, *Theology of Martin Luther*, chap. 18—19; and Rupp, *Righteousness of God*, 5-6.

it was insulated from our own corruption. For Osiander, however, it was the actual presence of the divine within the believer that made a man or woman righteous. It was *not* "union with Christ" that made the sinner righteous in Osiander's eyes, but only union with the divine nature of Christ that made him or her righteous.[357] The difference between the two is significant.

Similarly, Osiander and Macchia reverse the order of things in the classic *ordo salutis*. Historically, Protestants have understood the gift of the Spirit as logically preceding sanctification. In contrast, Macchia notes with approval that sanctification was a kind of preparation for receiving the Spirit in early Pentecostalism. Instead of the Spirit as the means of sanctification, early Pentecostals understood sanctification to be the precondition for receiving the Spirit. A believer was sanctified and *then* filled with the Spirit. The focus shifted from the *effects* of the Spirit's indwelling to the *indwelling itself* as the chief end.[358] This is in stark contrast to the traditional order of salvation, and the order is extremely important. John Murray notes that there are "conclusive reasons" for the order of events in the application of redemption. They "take place in a certain order, and that order has been established by divine appointment."[359]

Yet, despite the worries over Macchia's (and Osiander's) soteriology, Macchia does raise a number of legitimate issues. Although I do not share his conclusions, the question of the Holy Spirit's role in justification is appropriate. Nevertheless, discarding the classic Reformation understanding of justification seems like a gross overreaction, as does his attempt to change the meaning of the word *justification*.[360] Yet Macchia should be commended for his quest to press the borders of pneumatology beyond the parochial bounds of personal experience into all areas of soteriology. By his own admission, he discovered that most Pentecostal testimonies were narrowly focused on personal struggles. While such an emphasis may be understandable, Macchia has attempted to move beyond such narrow foci to embrace a much broader, more socially aware background and take these

---

357. Seeberg, *Textbook of History of Doctrines*, 25174–81. Calvin compares Osiander to a cuttlefish, "which by the ejection of dark and inky blood, conceals its many tails" (*Institutes*, 3.11.6 [McNeill]). This comparison seems apropos, for in a number of places, Osiander makes statements that are unassailably true, yet he infuses his words with a meaning different than normal, thus making an articulate response a challenge. For example, he claims that "we are one with Christ," as if Christians would contest this. However, in saying this, Osiander actually conflates the essence of Christ with ours. See Calvin, *Institutes*, 3.11.5.

358. See Macchia, *Spirit-Baptized Church*.

359. Murray, *Redemption*, 80.

360. One of my initial attempts to address some of Macchia's concerns can be found in Anderson, "Holy Spirit and Justification."

pressing questions of the present into "the even more encompassing arms of the inter-Trinitarian communion."[361] Thus, I applaud Macchia's attempts at creating a pneumatologically informed understanding of justification.

4.10.C. Veli-Matti Kärkkäinen (1958–)

Veli-Matti Kärkkäinen is professor of systematic theology at Fuller Theological Seminary's School of Theology[362] and docent of ecumenics at the University of Helsinki. Prior to his arrival at Fuller, Kärkkäinen also served at Iso Kirja College in Keuruu, Finland. He has taught and lived with his family on three continents: Europe, Asia (Thailand), and North America (US). Kärkkäinen has authored numerous theological works,[363] particularly in the field of systematic theology, and has worked tirelessly for ecumenical unity, particularly within the World Council of Churches. Such are just a few of the labors of Veli-Matti Kärkkäinen.

As we turn our attention more specifically to his work on justification, we discover that Kärkkäinen leverages both the tried and tested, as well as the new and the novel. His understanding of salvation is a blend of the old and new. He is a product of the modern Finnish reinterpretation of Martin Luther's theology, combined with the Orthodox understanding of *theosis* (or *divinization*). The result is a blend of theological ideas presented by a capable author. Put differently, Kärkkäinen does not offer one simple (i.e., traditional) view of justification that can be easily illustrated from a historical example. Instead, his thinking represents a combination of currents that usually keep within their own self-contained systems.

Kärkkäinen rejects the traditional Protestant approach to justification. Like the Eastern church, Kärkkäinen does not put an emphasis on justification. Instead, he adopts an Orthodox understanding of salvation, rejecting the typical "Western lens" of salvation. One of the implications of this is that Kärkkäinen's view is essentially that of the Orthodox Church. This means he frequently cites Orthodox authors to illustrate or support his claims. As a result, we will use those same authors to illustrate and support our claims of Kärkkäinen.

As noted, Kärkkäinen does not advocate a western approach to salvation. Instead, he approaches it through the lens of 2 Pet 1:4, "[God] has given us . . . his precious and very great promises, so that through them

361. Macchia, "Baptized in the Spirit," 15.
362. Kärkkäinen came to Fuller in 2000 and received full professorship in 2003.
363. E.g., *One with God*; "Justification"; "Justification as Forgiveness"; "Holy Spirit and Justification"; "Salvation as Justification."

you . . . may become participants of the divine nature" (NRSV; italics added). At its simplest, the goal of salvation for Kärkkäinen is participation in the divine nature. This idea is most commonly expressed through the terms of *deification, divinization,* or *theosis*.[364]

Kallistos Ware unpacks these expressions, stating, "Various facets of the meaning of deification are highlighted by the rich vocabulary of Eastern theology with regard to salvation. Terms such as *transformation, union, participation, partaking, intermingling, elevation, interpenetration, transmutation, commingling, assimilation, reintegration, adoption, recreation* are used to refer to the same reality."[365] Similarly, Vladimir Lossky captured the concept of *theosis* when he wrote, "Divine life has manifested itself in Christ. In the church as the body of Christ, man has a share in this life. Man partakes thereby of 'the divine nature.' This 'nature,' or divine life, permeates the being of man like a leaven in order to restore it to its original condition as *imago Dei*."[366]

It is *theosis* that theologians like Kärkkäinen and Tuomo Mannermaa have in mind when they discuss salvation. They are working with categories found primarily in Eastern Christianity, rather than the soteriological ideas found in Western Christianity. Hence, the concepts and groupings are unfamiliar to many modern Western Christians. Nor is Kärkkäinen's methodology typical of the individualistic approach so often found in the West. He simply does not adopt the same lens of distinct logical distinctions, where one begins at the logical starting point of God's foreknowledge and then works through the logical progressions (i.e., steps of salvation) to its consummation (i.e., glorification).

Instead, Kärkkäinen understands salvation to have one primary goal: union with God. He states, "*salvation involves some form of union with God.*"[367] He claims that the Christian faith has always

> offered an answer to the world and its followers in the form of the doctrine of *deification* and/or union with God. Even though the Eastern wing of the church has been the major champion of this doctrine through the patristic era to our own day, never has it been the sole treasure of one part of Christendom. The

---

364. See Zizioulas, *Being as Communion*, 68, and Zizioulas, "Preserving God's Creation" (*King's Review* 12), 2.

365. Ware, *Orthodox Way*, 168.

366. Lossky, *Mystical Theology*, 134; cf. Mantzaridis, *Deification of Man*, 105.

367. Kärkkäinen, *One with God*, 1; italics added.

Western church has approached the idea of union with the help of different vocabulary.[368]

We should not make the mistake of thinking this is merely a semantic difference, or that it is simply a peculiarity of Kärkkäinen's thought. Rather, it is a foundational idea within Orthodoxy. For example, Christoforos Stavropoulos states, "*This* is the purpose of life: that we be participants, sharers in the nature of God and in the life of Christ, communicants of divine grace and energy—to become just like God, true gods."[369] The Orthodox Church traces this notion into the early days of the church, and thereby roots the idea into the tradition of the fathers as well as the Bible.[370] According to Basil the Great (329/330–79), "Man is a creature that has received the command to become a god."[371] Likewise, Gregory of Nazianzus (330–390) said, "[Man] has been ordered to become God."[372] Later, Simeon the New Theologian (949–1022) stated somewhat tersely, "God is not united except with gods,"[373] while Anastasius of Sinai wrote that, "*Theosis* is elevation to what is better, but not the reduction of our nature to something less, nor is it an essential change of our human nature. A divine plan, it is the willing condescension of tremendous dimension by God, which he did for the salvation of others. That which is of God is that which has been lifted up

---

368. Kärkkäinen, *One with God*, 1.

369. Stavropoulos, *Partakers of Divine Nature*, 17. Kärkkäinen quotes "Doxastikon at the Praises," a Feast of the Annunciation poem from the Eastern tradition, that captures several prominent ideas of Orthodoxy (*One with God*, 2):
Adam of old was deceived:
Wanting to be God he failed to be God.
God becomes man,
So that He may make Adam god.

370. See the Cappadocian Fathers Gregory of Nyssa (335–394), Basil of Caesarea, or Basil the Great (329/330–379), Gregory of Nazianzus (330–390), and the frequently overlooked sister of Basil and Gregory, Macrina (327–379). See González, *History*, 1:302–8.

371. Basil the Great, as quoted in Stavropoulos, "Partakers of Divine Nature," 184. Kärkkäinen also quotes with approval F. W. Norris with approval when Norris writes in "Deification" (413):

Conforming to the world is not our goal. Yet by allowing our minds to be transformed, we may be prepared to contextualize the Gospel for this new wave of spirituality. To do that while still being true to Christian tradition, we must recapture one great spiritual vision of Christian salvation which twentieth-century Protestants have largely ignored. Koinonia, fellowship with God, is actually deification, participation in God.

372. Gregory of Nazianzus, *Oration 43*.

373. Simeon the New Theologian, as quoted in Stavropoulos, in "Partakers of Divine Nature," 184.

to a greater glory, without its own nature being changed."³⁷⁴ As we might expect, Kärkkäinen includes Irenaeus' epigrammatic dictum, "God became man that we might become gods."³⁷⁵ For Kärkkäinen, deification is "the very essence of Christianity," for it describes the "ineffable descent of God to the ultimate limit of our fallen human condition, even unto death—a descent of God which opens to men a path of ascent, the unlimited vistas of the union of created beings with the Divinity."³⁷⁶ This deification is brought about through the purification of the mind and body—*theoria (contemplation of the divine)*.³⁷⁷ Yet the ultimate goal in Orthodoxy—whether now or in the age to come—is always the same: participation in the divine life.³⁷⁸ The purpose of our present earthly life is growth and development for this eternal communion. Thus Kärkkäinen insists that God originally intended us to enter into *theosis through a natural process of development and growth*. This natural process would have involved growing in the knowledge and experience of love (i.e., an education in love), and a free collaboration with God.³⁷⁹ To summarize, when the Son became incarnate, "he opened the way for people to ascend to him, assume divinity, and become in-godded."³⁸⁰ In its very definition of the gospel, then, Eastern Christianity presupposes the idea of deification. Even when the term is not explicitly mentioned, it is implicitly present "as the content of the salvation proclaimed by the gospel."³⁸¹ This is why Kärkkäinen can so frequently cite Orthodox authors

---

374. Anastasius of Sinai, *Concerning the Word*, 77, as quoted in Stavropoulos, *Partakers of Divine Nature*, 19. More recently, Stavropoulos defined theosis like this ("Partakers of Divine Nature," 184): "Theosis! What does this deep and profound word mean? It means the elevation of the human being to the divine sphere, to the atmosphere of God. It means the union of the human with the divine. That, in its essence, is the meaning of theosis. Thus, human nature ought to be moving toward spiritualization, and in the process, its heavy materialism is to be broken down and dissolved."

375. In this particular instance, however, Kärkkäinen is citing Arthur Peacocke's work *Theology for a Scientific Age*, 189. A more modernized translation might be something like the following: "God became human that we might become divine."

376. Kärkkäinen citing Lossky's *In the Image*, 97.

377. Bartos, *Deification*, 253, and Archimandrite George of Mount Athos, *Theosis*.

378. The idea is very similar to an exchange recounted by Packer (*Knowing God*, 24): "I walked in the sunshine with a scholar who had effectively forfeited his prospects of academic advancement by clashing with church dignitaries over the gospel of grace. 'But it doesn't matter,' he said at length, 'for I've known God and they haven't.'"

379. Irenaeus, *Against Heresies*, 1–3.

380. Athanasius, *Letter 60*, 1337. Like many others before him, Psellus (died c. 1078) also declared, "God became man that man might become God." As quoted in Lossky, *Vision of God*, 98.

381. Pelikan, *Spirit of Eastern Christianity*, 11, cf. 46; cf. also Mantzaridis, *Deification*, 13.

like Georgios I. Mantzaridis when he says, "The idea of deification, oneness with God, God-likeness, is that which from the beginning has constituted the innermost longing of man's existence."[382]

Kärkkäinen summarizes his view when he writes, "*Union with God: both the Eastern understanding of theosis and the Western idea of justification have union as the ultimate goal.*"[383] This statement captures the essence not only of Kärkkäinen's soteriology, but of the biblical message. The ultimate goal for evangelicals is not justification but to know God. Justification is the means to that end. "One thing I ask of the Lord, this is what I seek: that I may dwell in the house of the Lord all the days of my life, to gaze upon the beauty of the Lord and to seek him in his temple" (Ps 27:4). Or, to use the words of Jesus, "Now this is eternal life: that they may know you, the only true God, and Jesus Christ, whom you have sent" (John 17:3). Again, the goal of union with God and savoring his goodness is not the sole property of the Eastern church. "This is the all-encompassing gift of God's love through the gospel—to see and savor the glory of Christ forever."[384] Thus, we can say with the *Westminster Shorter Catechism* that our "chief end is to glorify know God and enjoy him forever."[385]

What then is justification for Kärkkäinen? It is *theosis*. In other words, it is not so much a particular understanding of justification as it is a different way of approaching salvation altogether. Kärkkäinen states that his desire is to differentiate "the Protestant idea of salvation as justification and the Eastern Church's notion of salvation as *theosis*."[386] These kinds of statements, in my estimation, are unhelpful. Protestants do not view "salvation as justification." Rather, we understand justification as one of the many facets of salvation. There is also regeneration, faith, repentance, sanctification, etc. The word "salvation" is an umbrella term, incorporating all of Christ's redemptive work, not simply justification. Protestants no more equate justification and salvation than they do adoption and glorification. While Protestants do distinguish between the elements of salvation, generally they are careful not to separate them. This was true even during the Reformation

---

382. Mantzaridis, as quoted in Kärkkäinen, *One with God*, 2.

383. Kärkkäinen, *One with God*, 4; italics added.

384. Piper, *God Is the Gospel*, 11. Richard Daniels summarizes the theology of John Owen, stating: "There is one motif so important to John Owen, so often and so broadly cited by him, that the writer would go so far as to call it the focal point of Owen's theology . . . namely, the doctrine that *in the gospel we behold, by the Christ-given Holy Spirit, the glory of God 'in the face of Christ' and are thereby changed into his image*" (*Christology of John Owen*, 92; italics added).

385. *Westminster Shorter Catechism*, answer 1.

386. Kärkkäinen, "Deification View," Kindle loc. 2433–4.

era. For "as Christ cannot be divided into parts, so the two things, justification and sanctification, which we perceive to be united together in him, are inseparable."[387]

4.11. THE JOINT DECLARATION ON THE DOCTRINE OF JUSTIFICATION

As we approach the present, it becomes ever more difficult to choose which individuals or movements to assess and which to leave out. In the original edition of this work, I touched briefly on Joseph Fitzmyer, C. E. B. Cranfield, Vincent Taylor, J. Christiaan Beker, Colin Kruse, Arland Hultgren, Francis Watson, and others. However, as noted previously, it is simply not realistic to address all the contributors in the ongoing discussion on and about justification and the apostle to the Gentiles. There are, however, a few instances where I felt I must comment. One of those is the *Joint Declaration on the Doctrine of Justification* (henceforth, *JDDJ*) between the Lutheran World Federation (henceforth LWF) and the worldwide Roman Catholic Church (henceforth RCC). The document in question was signed on Reformation Sunday, October 31, 1999 (All Saints Day Eve). The signing occurred in the city of Augsburg, Germany, where the original Augsburg Confession had been drafted and presented in 1530 by the Lutheran reformers in their attempt to diffuse the growing tensions between the burgeoning Reformation movement and the Roman Catholic Church of the sixteenth century.[388] Four hundred and sixty-nine years later, official representatives from both the Lutheran and the Roman Catholic churches signed a document that obviated the anathemas each body had placed on the other, offsetting the condemnations with statements of "guarded fellowship." Before we examine the document itself, however, it is worth noting a few of the developments that led to its publication.

Since Vatican II,[389] the ecumenical climate for dialogue had improved drastically. Protestant denominations were no longer viewed as "heretics,"[390] but as "separated brethren."[391] This shift in attitude made conversations with Protestant denominations possible—conversations which were previously impossible. In 1972, several Catholic and Lutheran groups began working

---

387. Calvin, *Institutes* (Beveridge), 3.11.6.

388. See Stuckenberg, *History of Augsburg Confession*.

389. Vatican II ran a little over three years, from October 11, 1962, until December 8, 1965.

390. See the condemnations of the Council of Trent.

391. See Vatican II, "Decree on Ecumenism," and Kroll, "Church History Corner."

collaboratively on potential joint statements on justification. As drafts were formulated, clarified, and refined, official representatives of both the LWF and the RCC began to circulate these drafts to gain support from their respective bodies. The final document was finalized in 1997 and *appeared* to be ratified on June 16, 1998. However, in a surprising turn of events, the Vatican suddenly withdrew its support, announcing that it would soon release a response document addressing the matter. The document was published on June 25 of the same year,[392] and although it did not overtly reject the joint endeavor, it was a strong statement of the RCC's reservations. Father James Akin notes, "This [document] was an embarrassment. The drafting of *The Joint Declaration* had been a years-long process, and the text had already been finalized. The concerns that were announced on June 25 [1998] should have been brought up and the corresponding clarifications given *before* the Lutherans went out on a limb by voting to approve the declaration."[393] Lutheran representatives were understandably frustrated by this sudden withdrawal and reluctance on the part of the Roman church. Yet the ecumenical motive that drove the process seems to have been authentic, because the two groups worked through the clarifications of the response with "admirable tact" and ultimately produced the *Annex to the Joint Declaration*.[394]

The document acknowledges the importance of justification, and the turbulent history between the Lutheran and Roman Catholic churches. It then points to previous ecumenical endeavors already completed between Roman Catholics and Lutherans.[395] Their point was to underscore the previous labors upon which the *JDDJ* was built and that the *JDDJ* did not appear *ex nihilo*. Ultimately, the authors were attempting to answer the question of whether the mutual condemnations of the sixteenth century were still binding, or had the two bodies arrived at a consensus, thereby allowing them to move beyond the historical impasse? In short, their answer was that they had found sufficient agreement around the doctrine of justification and that they were no longer enemies but allies.[396] "A common understanding

---

392. Congregation for the Doctrine of the Faith and the Pontifical Council for Promoting Christian Unity, *Response of the Catholic Church to the Joint Declaration of the Catholic Church and the Lutheran World Federation on the Doctrine of Justification*.

393. Akin, "Setting the Record Straight." Akin is a senior apologist at *Catholic Answers* and contributing editor to *This Rock*, San Diego, CA.

394. Released on June 11, 1999. Sometimes referred to as simply "The Annex."

395. Joint Lutheran-Roman Catholic Study Commission: "The Gospel and the Church"; *Church and Justification*; *Justification by Faith*.

396. Section 5 states, "The present Joint Declaration has this intention: namely, to show that on the basis of their dialogue the subscribing Lutheran churches and the

of justification is therefore fundamental and indispensable to overcoming that division. By appropriating insights of recent biblical studies and drawing on modern investigations of the history of theology and dogma, the post-Vatican II ecumenical dialogue has led to a notable convergence concerning justification. . . . In light of this consensus, the corresponding doctrinal condemnations of the sixteenth century do not apply to today's partner."[397] The creators of the document are strikingly clear on several points—points that are most frequently censured by critics. For example, the authors state that although the document "does encompass a consensus on basic truths of the doctrine of justification and shows that the remaining differences in its explication are no longer the occasion for doctrinal condemnations," it does *not*, however, "cover all that either church teaches about justification."[398] Moreover, reflecting on their history, the contributors seem eager to point out that they do not "take the condemnations lightly nor do they disavow their own past"; nevertheless, both bodies have "have come to new insights."[399] Among these new insights is that justification can occur only "by God's grace through faith."[400] Note also how both bodies define justification. First, justification involves the forgiveness of sins.[401] Second, it is the "liberation from the dominating power of sin and death."[402] Third, it entails freedom "from the curse of the law."[403] Fourth, it includes "acceptance into communion with God," in part now, and later with the coming of God's kingdom in its fullness.[404] Fifth, it unites the believer "with Christ and with his death and resurrection."[405] Sixth, it "occurs in the reception of the Holy Spirit in baptism and incorporation into the one body."[406] Seventh, and finally, we are told that all of the above actions are incorporated into justification, which is "from God alone, for Christ's sake, by grace, through faith

---

Roman Catholic Church are now able to articulate a common understanding of our justification by God's grace through faith in Christ." Section 14 states that the two bodies have reached "a consensus in the basic truths" about the doctrine.

397. Lutheran World Federation and the Roman Catholic Chuch, *JDDJ*, §13.

398. LWF and RCC, *JDDJ*, §5.

399. LWF and RCC, *JDDJ*, §7.

400. LWF and RCC, *JDDJ*, §9. I am not entirely sure what is "new" about this insight, but it is listed among the new developments which allowed such ecumenical endeavors.

401. LWF and RCC, *JDDJ*, §11; Rom 3:23-5, Acts 13:39, and Luke 18:14.

402. LWF and RCC, *JDDJ*, §11; Rom 5:12-21.

403. LWF and RCC, *JDDJ*, §11; Gal 3:10-14.

404. LWF and RCC, *JDDJ*, §11; Rom 5:1ff.

405. LWF and RCC, *JDDJ*, §11; Rom 6:5.

406. LWF and RCC, *JDDJ*, §11; Rom 8:1ff, 9ff; 1 Cor 12:12ff.

in 'the gospel of God's Son.'"⁴⁰⁷ The final result is that justification "means that Christ himself is our righteousness, in which we share through the Holy Spirit in accord with the will of the Father."⁴⁰⁸ The result is that both bodies believe: "By grace alone, in faith in Christ's saving work and not because of any merit on our part, we are accepted by God and receive the Holy Spirit, who renews our hearts while equipping and calling us to good works."⁴⁰⁹

The *JDDJ* takes some pains to present, and then balance, views that are typically thought of as exclusive to either the LWF or the RCC. For example, Section 20 states, "When Catholics say that persons 'cooperate' in preparing for and accepting justification by consenting to God's justifying action, they see such personal consent as itself an effect of grace, not as an action arising from innate human abilities." Similarly, although it is well known that "Lutherans emphasize that the righteousness of Christ is *our* righteousness," we are told that the driving force behind this emphasis is to "insist that the sinner is granted righteousness before God in Christ through the declaration of forgiveness and that only in union with Christ is one's life renewed."⁴¹⁰ Furthermore, Lutherans do not deny that "God's gift of grace in justification remains independent of human cooperation" when they accentuate Christ's righteousness as our own.⁴¹¹ Nor should we conclude that the Lutheran emphasis on Christ's righteousness in some way abrogates human cooperation with God's grace.⁴¹² Lutherans and Roman Catholics believe that "God's [justifying] act . . . affects *all* dimensions of the person."⁴¹³ Both churches maintain that justification not only "frees human beings from sin's enslaving power," but it also "imparts the gift of new life."⁴¹⁴

A major focus of the document's authors was the relationship of good works to justification. Historically, Lutheranism has eschewed any doctrinal

---

407. LWF and RCC, *JDDJ*, §11; Rom 1:1-3.

408. LWF and RCC, *JDDJ*, §15.

409. LWF and RCC, *JDDJ*, §15, citing paragraph 14 of the *Report of the Joint Lutheran-Roman Catholic Study Commission*, as quoted in *JDDJ*.

410. LWF and RCC, *JDDJ*, §23.

411. LWF and RCC, *JDDJ*, §24.

412. LWF and RCC, *JDDJ*, §24.

413. LWF and RCC, *JDDJ*, §26.

414. LWF and RCC, *JDDJ*, §26. According to §26, these two aspects of justification, although distinguished, must never be separated: "God's act . . . affects all dimensions of the person. . . . In the doctrine of "justification by faith alone," a distinction but not a separation is made between justification itself and the renewal of one's way of life that necessarily follows from justification and without which faith does not exist. . . . Justification and renewal are joined in Christ, who is present in faith. While Catholic teaching emphasizes the renewal of life . . . is always dependent on God's unfathomable grace and contributes nothing to justification."

formulation of justification that might suggest good works were necessary for salvation.[415] For clarification, it is not that Lutheranism has historically denied the necessity of good works for salvation; rather, the concern has been in viewing good works as an essential element of justification. In contrast, Roman Catholicism has historically taught that the individual is justified by faith *and* the internal renovation of the soul[416]—that is, by faith *and* regeneration and sanctification (good works).[417] So it is no surprise to read in the *Joint Declaration,* "According to Catholic understanding, good works, made possible by grace and the working of the Holy Spirit, contribute to growth in grace, so that the righteousness that comes from God is preserved and communion with Christ is deepened."[418] They continue: When "Catholics affirm the 'meritorious' character of good works, they wish to say that, according to the biblical witness, a reward in heaven is promised to these works. Their intention is to emphasize the responsibility of persons for their actions, not to contest *the character of those works as gifts,* or far less to deny that justification always remains the unmerited gift of grace."[419] The ultimate conclusion of *JDDJ* is that, "the doctrinal condemnations of the 16th century, in so far as they relate to the doctrine of justification, appear in a new light."[420] This *new light* is that the "teaching of the Lutheran churches . . . *does not fall under the condemnations from the Council of Trent.* [And], *the condemnations in the Lutheran Confessions do not apply to the teaching of the Roman Catholic Church.*"[421]

Ultimately, no matter how one views the *JDDJ,* it is difficult not to appreciate the efforts and progress made by the LWF and RCC in their

---

415. The Lutheran Church teaches that justification occurs "out of pure grace, because of the sole merit, complete obedience, bitter suffering, death, and resurrection of our Lord Christ alone, whose obedience is reckoned to us for righteousness." See "Righteousness of Faith."

416. According to the official *Catholic Encyclopedia,* justification "comprises not only forgiveness of sin, but also 'sanctification and renovation of the interior man by means of the voluntary acceptation of sanctifying grace and other supernatural gifts." (Pohle, "Justification"). The latter portion is a direct quotation from Trent as the source of the statement's authority, as well as its anchor-point for unpacking the doctrine conceptually.

417. See, for example, Council of Trent, "On Justification," Session 6, Canon 24, which states, "If anyone saith, that the [righteousness] received [in justification] is not . . . increased . . . through good works; but that the said works are merely the fruits and signs of Justification obtained, but not a cause of the increase thereof; let him be anathema."

418. LWF and RCC, *JDDJ,* §38.

419. LWF and RCC, *JDDJ,* §38; italics added.

420. LWF and RCC, *JDDJ,* §41.

421. LWF and RCC, *JDDJ,* §41; italics added

endeavor to repair centuries of fractured relationship. Both bodies invested substantially in this ecumenical exchange. Nevertheless, whether one is Roman Catholic, Lutheran, or otherwise, there remain a number of legitimate questions that require substantive answers.

It is well-known that Luther was the first prominent Protestant Reformer to break from the RCC. In many ways, this makes the LWC (Luther's heirs) the ideal branch of Protestantism to bridge the gap between the RCC and Protestantism. Moreover, the two bodies share a great deal in common. For example, both the RCC and the LWF believe in a type of baptismal regeneration.[422] Both bodies also believe in paedobaptism,[423] and both groups believe that a Christian can lose his or her salvation.[424] These similarities may contribute toward the reconciliation they seek. Furthermore, some of the differences that do exist are merely a matter of *emphasis*, while others were differences of *style*, and still others of *substance*. The question for the architects of the *JDDJ* was, are the differences of substance too deep so as to preclude any official doctrinal unity, or is there sufficient ground to build upon and thus move beyond centuries of hurt and misunderstanding? Avery Dulles notes with some insight that, "Despite the embarrassing nature of the incident leading to *The Annex*, the event itself demonstrates that the *Joint Declaration* was not the product of a false ecumenism."[425] It demonstrated that the Vatican was taking the document seriously—seriously enough to jeopardize the entire process in order to ensure absolute clarity. There is no question that this should have been done sooner, but the fact that the officials risked public embarrassment so that each side would fully understand and be understood is testament to their investment in ecumenical dialogue.

Responses to the *Joint Declaration* have been mixed, with critics and supporters emerging on both sides.[426] Some have been more sour than sym-

---

422. Although there are theological differences between the two groups on this topic, the similarities are striking. Nevertheless, Lutheranism does believe in baptismal regeneration. For example, "Water baptism imparts faith to infants for their salvation" (Barackman, *Practical Christian Theology*, 17). Similarly, the RCC teaches that justification and regeneration occur through the means of the sacrament of baptism. Note Session 5 of the Council of Trent, on the "Decrees Concerning Original Sin."

423. From the Greek *pais*, meaning "infant" or "child."

424. For example, Lutheran pastor and professor Richard Bucher contends that "Scripture clearly teaches that it is possible for [a] believer to fall away from [the] faith—even permanently" (Bucher, "Is a Christian 'Once Saved'"). See also Swan, "Did Luther Believe Salvation."

425. Dulles, "Justification: The Joint Declaration," 108.

426. E.g., Forde, "Critical Response"; Lane, *Justification by Faith*; and Malloy, *Engrafted into Christ*.

pathetic, more critical than caring,[427] while others have been strong allies.[428] However, in a number of instances, the efforts of these detractors have actually (albeit unintentionally) highlighted some of the areas of agreement and progress between the two bodies. Thus the best way forward, regardless of one's position on the matter, is to recognize the genuine achievements of the *JDDJ*, even while recognizing areas of concern and ongoing need.

For now, I simply note two concerns.

1. Perhaps the most obvious concern is what the document does *not* address. The imputation of Christ's righteousness is one of the most obvious examples. This omission appears to be deliberate, allowing each body to teach justification without violating the areas of agreement. One cannot violate what has not been addressed. It is difficult to assess the wisdom of this oversight. If the omission was deliberate, it may suggest a deeper conflict between the groups. If it was unintentional, the lapse seems inexcusable. To be sure, the document does speak of Christ's *imparted* righteousness, using a variety of figures and images,[429] but it was specifically the imputation of Christ's righteousness that was the root of so much controversy during the Reformation and Post-Reformation times.[430] Thus, the absence of any statement on the imputation of Christ's righteousness is both surprising and concerning.

2. Neither body actually retracts their previous anathemas. The *JDDJ* is premised on the idea that the condemnations of the sixteenth century

---

427. For a less than charitable Roman Catholic response to the *JDDJ*, see Sanborn, "Critical Analysis." For an unsympathetic Lutheran response, see McCain, "Betrayal of Gospel."

428. For information and background on a list of supporters, see LWF and RCC, *JDDJ*, 6.

429. For example, justification is spoken of as the "liberation from the dominating power of sin and death" (§11); it "frees human beings from sin's enslaving power" (§22); it encompasses "the renewal of one's way of life" (§26); and "justification and renewal are joined in Christ" (§26). Furthermore, we are told that this teaching "emphasizes the renewal of life" (§27), and that it "truly renews the person" (§28).

430. For Reformation-era treatments on imputation, see Luther, *Lectures on Galatians, 1535*, Ch. 1—4, 122–36, 226–36, 276–91, 313–23, 335–51, 374–92, 430–31, and Luther, "Two Kinds of Righteousness," 31:297–306. Rather than create a list of works endorsing and explicating imputation, we simply note the confessions and catechisms containing statements on the doctrine—statements that were the basis of Trent's condemnation. E.g., the *Heidelberg Catechism* tells us that "*God . . . imputes to me the perfect righteousness, and holiness of Christ*" (*Heidelberg Catechism*, Q. 60–4). Similar statements and summaries can be found in the Anglican *Thirty-Nine Articles*, the Lutheran *Book of Concord*, the London/Philadelphia (Baptist) Confession, etc.

were perfectly valid and, therefore, must be taken seriously. The participants did not "take the condemnations lightly nor [did] they disavow their own past."[431] Obviously, this makes meaningful unity far more difficult to obtain. Additionally, and perhaps more importantly, while the *JDDJ* is viewed as a historic accord by both parties, it is not considered binding by either body—certainly not in the way that Trent is binding on Roman Catholics. This should be borne in mind when reflecting on the document's significance. Both Lutherans and Roman Catholics may find encouragement and comfort in the *JDDJ*, but, at the end of the day, it is the Council of Trent and not the *JDDJ* to which faithful Catholics are required to submit. So, as much as we may appreciate and desire the goals of the *JDDJ*, the document lacks authority; it has no teeth. Hence, the "[d]octrinal condemnations [that] were put forward" by "both in the Lutheran Confessions and by the Roman Catholic Church's Council of Trent" are still considered binding upon Lutherans and Catholics. The important implication of this conclusion is, "These condemnations . . . [continue] to have a church-dividing effect."[432]

Obviously, much more could been said, yet the purpose here is simply to provide an overview of the events that bear directly on the topic of justification. Without doubt, *JDDJ* is a significant work that deserves close attention. It is not, however, a full statement of unity between the two historic bodies, much as we might hope and pray for just such a union.

4.12. CONCLUSION

Reading through a list of summaries and assessments like the above can be a bit disorienting. It is easy to get lost in the minutiae of specific thinkers and movements and lose sight of the bigger picture. In the above, the goal was to place individuals or movements within a larger matrix. In short, how did each person or group impact our understanding of justification? More specifically, how did their specific contribution influence a *pneumatological* understanding of justification? In some instances (Luther and Calvin), they seemed to have presupposed the work of the Spirit but never attempted to flesh out an actual pneumatology of justification. In other cases (Käsemann, and Stendahl), the contribution was preliminary, laying the groundwork that later thinkers would build upon. In still other cases

---

431. LWF and RCC, *JDDJ*, §7.
432. LWF and RCC, *JDDJ*, §1.

(Macchia and Kärkkäinen), the individuals actually attempted to formulate a pneumatologically informed understanding of justification. Finally, in the case of the two major movements we discussed—the New Perspective on Paul and the Joint Declaration on the Doctrine of Justification—they have wielded remarkable influence upon the current conversations on justification. Moreover, it seems fair to say that everyone whom we have analyzed has contributed positively in at least some way to our understanding. Nevertheless, several seem to have created more problems than solutions. Yet each has helped prepared the ground for us as we begin to move forward. As a result, we will now turn from our history of justification to the more constructive portion of this work. In what follows, we will attempt to lay the foundation for a fully trinitarian approach to the Protestant doctrine of justification.

5.0

God's Declaration in Justification and the Role of the Holy Spirit

An Expansion of New Ideas

5.1 GENESIS 1–3 ~ "SPIRIT OF GOD" AND "THE WORD OF THE LORD"

As noted in the preface, the original version of this work had roughly three hundred pages devoted to the exegesis of four NT texts (Rom 3:21–26, Rom 4:1–8, 1 Cor 1:30, and 2 Cor 5:21).[1] Those sections have been removed, but the obvious drawback is that it leaves much of the constructive portion open to the charge of being merely theoretical and without biblical warrant. Nevertheless, the cuts seem necessary. As you will hopefully see, there is still plenty of scriptural support for these ideas, although the detailed legwork is no longer included.

The book of Genesis opens with the declaration that God created the heavens and earth (literally, the "sky" and the "land"). The expression "heavens and the earth" (שָׁמַיִם וְאֵת הָאָרֶץ) is a Hebrew *merism* which expresses the totality of the cosmos.[2] It includes the sun, moon, and stars, and all

---

1. Anderson, "Justification as Speech."
2. *Merisms* are found throughout the Hebrew Bible. A simple example is in Psalm 139:2, where David says, "O Lord, you know my sitting down and my rising up." The

that is in the farthest reaches of space.³ All of this is included in the terse statement, "In the beginning when God created the heavens and the earth" (NRSV). After creating the endless reaches of the cosmos,⁴ God turned his attention to prepare the land for human habitation. Verse 2 gives a very brief description of the earth's landscape (or lack thereof) after God had created the universe. "The land was formless and empty, and darkness was over the surface of the deep" (author's trans). Then, v. 3 tells us that "the Spirit of God was moving over the face of the waters."⁵ This brings us to an important transition in the text.

---

statement that God knows David's "sitting and rising" means that the Lord knows all that there is to know about David. A *merism*, then, is a figure of speech that brings together two antithetical terms in order to indicate the totality of a thing. See Waltke, *Commentary on Micah*, 256.

3. John Sailhamer notes (*Genesis Unbound*, Kindle loc. 604–09):

> In the case of the *merism* 'sky and land,' the terms *shamayim* ('sky') and *eretz* ('land') represent two extremes in the world. By linking these two extremes into a single expression—'sky and land' or 'heavens and earth'— the Hebrew language expresses the totality of all that exists. Unlike English, Hebrew doesn't have a single word to express the concept of 'the universe'; it must do so by means of a *merism*. The expression 'sky and land' thus stands for the 'entirety of the universe.' It includes not only the two extremes, heaven and earth, but also all that they contain—the sun, the moon, and the stars; every seen and unseen part of the universe; the seas, the dry land, and the plants and animals that inhabit them.

4. How long the creative process of v. 1 took is not clear from the Hebrew grammar. The Hebrew word for *beginning* "רֵאשִׁית" (*re'shiyth*) referred to an extended, yet undetermined, duration of time, which preceded an extended series of time periods. Therefore, theoretically, God's creative work "in the beginning" could have taken a few hours, months, or billions of years. The point is that the question of duration is left open. See Sailhamer, *Genesis Unbound*, Kindle loc. 346–74.

5. There is a well known question of how best to translate this text. The ESV, NASB, Young's, and others follow the ASV with the above translation by rendering רוח (*ruach*) as "Spirit of God," that is, as a reference to the Holy Spirit. In contrast, the NRSV translates רוח (*ruach*) here as "a wind from God." The following chart shows the most popular translations:

NASB, NKJV, TEV, NIV, ESV, etc.	"the Spirit of God"
NRSV, JPSOA	"a wind from God"
NJB	"a divine wind"
REB	"the spirit of God"
SEPT	"a breath of God"

While it is possible for *ruach* to denote all the above, the prevailing idea throughout the OT is that of "power," as a parallelism in Micah 3:8 demonstrates: "But as for me, I am filled with power, with the Spirit of the Lord" (ESV). However, when *ruach* is used of God (in roughly a third of the OT occurrences), it does not suggest the idea of "immateriality," "incorporeity," or "non-physicality," although there is little question

Gen 3:1 says, "Then God said, 'Let there be light,' and there was light."[6] Through the rest of the chapter, we see this cycle of God speaking and creation bursting into existence; God declares, and life springs into being. God calls forth vegetation, and the earth produces its vast array of plant life. God commands the waters to be filled with creatures, and the waters teem with life. God calls forth land animals, and the world is filled with creatures that live on the earth's surface. "The spoken word goes forth and brings into being what has been commanded."[7] While humanity may possess its own kind of creativity, we cannot help but see the difference between God's cosmic creative power and whatever creative abilities we may possess. God is the fountainhead of creative work—particularly as it relates to speech; he is the *consummate* communicator—the supreme speaker. And all of God's creative work was done through *the word of the Lord*.

Throughout Genesis and the rest of the OT, the biblical writers frequently use the expression "the word of the Lord" (i.e., *dābār YHWH* or דְבַר־יְהוָה) to describe God's speech.[8] In biblical Hebrew, the speech (דבר or *dābār*) of a person was their spoken word. However, Hebrew frequently conveys far more than when we describe a person's "word" or "speech" in English. It is "that which lies behind."[9] The *dābār* of an individual was regarded as an extension of the personality. Perhaps even more significantly, a person's *dābār* was believed to possess a substantive existence of its own.[10] Within the Pentateuch, "the Word possesses a like power to the God who speaks it and effects his will without hindrance. Hence *the term may refer to*

---

that the general biblical outlook implies as much. Rather, the emphasis is generally on the overwhelming energy, power, and strength of God. "Indeed," says Ferguson (citing Geerhardus Vos), "one might almost speak about the violence of God. 'Divine Spirit' thus denotes 'the energy of life in God,' as in the striking parallelism of Isaiah 31:3: 'The Egyptians are men and not God; their horses are flesh and not spirit.' *The emphasis lies in the contrast between weakness and power*, not in the contrast between material and immaterial. Spirit here contrasts with flesh whose 'characteristic is inertia, lack of power, such as can only be removed by the Spirit of God.'" (Ferguson, *Holy Spirit*, 17; quoting Vos, *Biblical Theology*, 257, and Vos, *Pauline Eschatology*, 300). So, although the NRSV is *possible*, it seems very unlikely. For reasons supporting this rendering, see Whitaker, *Whitaker's Revised*, 50–55, Harris et al., eds., *Theological Wordbook*.

6. NRSV, NASV, ASV, HCSV, NCV, etc.

7. Fretheim, "Word of God," 6:964.

8. The following is only a fraction of the occurrences in the OT, yet it should give the reader an idea of the frequency with which the biblical writers employed this phrase: Gen 15:1, 4; Exod 4:28; Num 15:31; Josh 8:27; 1 Sam 3:1, 7; 15:10; 2 Sam 15:10; 2 Sam 24:11; 1 Kgs 2:27; 6:11; 12:24; 13:1, 2, 20, 21, 32; 15:29; 16:1, 7; 17:2, 8, 16, 24; 18:1, 31; 2 Kgs 1:17; 3:12; 1 Chr 11:3, 17:3; 2 Chr 11:2, 4; 12:7; Ezra 1:1; Ps 18:30; 105:19; Isa 2:3.

9. Birdsall, "Logos," 396.

10. Birdsall, "Logos," 396.

the creative word of God."[11] The word of the Lord is not merely a powerful instrument but is an extension of God himself. It is his creative activity, infused with a kind of determination that will not relent until it has accomplished its mission. "As the rain and the snow come down from heaven, and do not return to it without watering the earth and making it bud and flourish, so that it yields seed for the sower and bread for the eater, so is my word that goes out from my mouth: It will not return to me empty *but will accomplish what I desire and achieve the purpose for which I sent it*" (Is 55:10–11; italics added).

Yet, despite the almost humanizing language used of God's speech, we should be careful to avoid the tendency of disconnecting the word of the Lord from the Lord himself. In other words, the reason the *dābār YHWH* is so powerful and creative is precisely because it is Yahweh's word. The moment someone attempts to separate the word of the Lord from the Lord of the word, is the moment that word ceases to be a powerful force. Earl Kalland writes, "It is God the Creator who does what he will. This will of God is expressed in words of command and they are effective because he makes them so." Interestingly, in its noun form, the Authorized Version translated דָּבָר (*dābār*) eighty-five different ways. This is not poor translation. Rather, it is the result of the word's richness and fecundity, along with the varying senses it conveys in its different contexts. A brief sampling of exactly how the word is translated in the KJV may illustrate just how rich the term actually is. Note the following examples: *W/word, speaking, speech, thing, anything, everything, nothing* (with negatives), *commandment, matter, act, event, history, account, business, cause, reason*, and, in constructions with prepositions, *on account of, because that*, and many more. These few examples give the reader an idea of the word's flexibility. Furthermore, not only does *dābār* describe what a person might say or do, it also describes *a report* of what was said or done.[12] Obviously, there is a difference between those two things, yet the same language is used. Moreover, God's revelatory work is frequently described in the language of "the word of God/the Lord came upon" this or that person (see 1 Chr 17:3; 2 Kgs 3:12). Throughout the book of Psalms, characteristics of God himself are predicated of God's *dābār*. For example, Ps 33:4 teaches us, "The word of the Lord is upright. . ." (NRSV). Ps 119:89 informs us that the *dābār* of Yahweh is settled in heaven: "The Lord exists forever; your word is firmly fixed in heaven" (NRSV). The word of the Lord is described as a lamp that illuminates the path directly in front of us (Ps 119:105). And, perhaps most importantly of all, we are

11. Birdsall, "Logos," 396; italics mine.
12. Kalland, "399," 180.

told that the word of the Lord (*dābār YHWH*) "is true" (Ps 119:160),[13] so we can be utterly confident of it and thus rely on it. As a result, OT scholars conclude that the *dābār YHWH* is an extension of God himself.[14] In fact, the author of Genesis virtually equates the "word of the Lord" with the activity of the Holy Spirit in the early chapters.

As Genesis opens, we are told that darkness covers all, with v. 2 concluding, "And the Spirit of God moved upon the face of the waters" (ASV). This is immediately followed with, "And God said, 'Let there be light: and there was light'" (ASV). These two statements made side by side at the earliest moments of the creation account suggests a relationship. Genesis calls our attention to the Holy Spirit's role in creation just as God declares, "Let there be light." In other words, it appears the Holy Spirit plays an intricate role throughout Genesis and the rest of the biblical narrative, but not in a way that is necessarily obvious. Instead, the role of the Spirit is analogous to the framework found in a modern skyscraper.[15] Without the unseen internal support this framing supplies, the entire structure would collapse. Nevertheless, one rarely sees the internal framing within the walls of a building. The framework is always present, doing its job, but most of the time we do not see it, and so it goes largely unnoticed and unconsidered; yet it is always presupposed. Similarly, the Holy Spirit is the ubiquitous person who perpetually upholds and sustains everything. Although never seen, he is *always* presupposed.

Much has been written on the role of the Son—the Word—in creation.[16] John 1:1 famously tells us, "In the beginning was the Word, and the Word was with God, and the Word was God" (ESV). However, we are given a bit more insight from the Psalmist when he writes, "By the word of the Lord (the Son) the heavens were made, *and* by the *breath (Spirit) of his mouth* all their host" (Ps 33:6 ESV). In other words, the cosmos was created by the triune God. The Son was the spoken word of the Father, and the Spirit was the breath behind that creative Word.[17] This then is a genuinely trinitar-

---

13. "The sum of your word is truth; and every one of your righteous ordinances endures forever."

14. See Fretheim, "Word of God," 964; Brown et al., *Enhanced Brown-Driver-Briggs*, 182ff; Swanson, *Dictionary*; Kalland, "399," 179ff.

15. This illustration is suggested in Horton, *God of Promise*, 12ff. However, in Horton's case, he uses the idea to illustrate the role of covenant within the Bible.

16. E.g., Procksch, "Word of God"; Fretheim, "Word of God"; Thiselton, "Supposed Power of Words."

17. Amos Yong insightfully notes ("Primed for the Spirit," 357):

> While traditional creation theologies have highlighted the creation of the world through the word of God, a pneumatological perspective notices

ian understanding of creation. We see this theme peppered throughout the Bible. For example, we are told that when God sends his "Spirit, they are created, and you renew the face of the earth" (Ps 104:30). Compare that with Acts 17:25, which says God "himself gives all men life and breath and everything else."

We suggest then that when Gen 1:2 says, "And God said . . . and there was . . . ," this is just another way of saying, "And the Holy Spirit did . . . and so there was . . ." Or, perhaps, more fully, "And God said . . . and thus the Holy Spirit did . . . and so there was . . ." That is, the Holy Spirit is the causal agent within the word of the Lord. Or, even more precisely, the Holy Spirit is the *dābār YHWH*. Since the *dābār* of God is understood as an extension of God himself, it seems reasonable to understand the *dābār YHWH* as the Holy Spirit. But how can we arrive at this conclusion? To use the well-known maxim of Euclid, "Things equal to the same thing are equal to each other."[18] The phrases "God said" and "the Holy Spirit created" appear to be synonymous. The Holy Spirit is the breath behind the declared Word, moving it forward to its ordained end. If this is true, then the role of the Holy Spirit in justification may be more overt than previously thought, and justification is necessarily a pneumatologically informed event.

However, before we examine this idea more closely, we first want to demonstrate another set of synonymous statements: "God spoke" and "the Holy Spirit spoke." While grammatically different, these two expressions are conceptually interchangeable within the Bible. To demonstrate this, we will briefly examine how the author of Hebrews easily moves back and forth from "God says" to "the Holy Spirit says."

---

both that the word of God is uttered through the divine breath and that the history of the world is blown or swept along by the presence and activity of the *ruah Elohim*. The partitioning of the waters from land, the emergence of vegetation, the evolution of life itself—each of these can be understood from this pneumatological vantage point as being propelled by the breath of God that transcendentally hovered over the primordial creation.

18. Euclid's "Common Notion 1," from *Elements*, as quoted in Fagin et al., *Reasoning about Knowledge*, 60. This can also be put into more of a mathematical formulation, but it still remains very simple: "If A = C and B = C then A must = B, since things equal to the same thing (A and B are both equal to C) are equal to each other. In geometry it is known as the "transitive property of congruence." See Mercer, "Transitive Property of Congruence."

5.2. THE BOOK OF HEBREWS: "GOD SAYS," "THE HOLY SPIRIT SAYS"

Heb 3:7–11 draws on a quotation from Ps 95. Yet, before he starts the quotation, the author prefaces the citation with the words, "So, *as the Holy Spirit says*" and then follows with the excerpt from Ps 95:7d-11. When we read the original text of Ps 95, we discover something quite instructive.

Ps 95 begins by issuing a call to worship, "O come, let us sing to the Lord; let us make a joyful noise to the rock of our salvation! . . . For the Lord [*YHWH*] is a great God [*ēl*], and a great King above all gods" (Ps 95:1, 3 NRSV). The psalmist continues the same theme down through v. 6 and the first two-thirds of v. 7; but in the latter part of v. 7, there is a definite transition. The writer shifts from a call to worship and a comparison of Israelite dependence upon the Lord (*YHWH*) as sheep to a shepherd, to a solemn warning to the Israelites not to harden their hearts against the Lord as they did when he brought them out of Egypt (Ps 95:6–11 NRSV):

> O come, let us worship and bow down,
> let us kneel before the Lord [*YHWH*], our Maker!
> ⁷For he is our God [*elō he*],
> and we are the people of his pasture,
> and the sheep of his hand.
> O that today you would listen to his voice!
> ⁸Do not harden your hearts, as at Meribah,
> as on the day at Massah in the wilderness,
> ⁹when your ancestors tested me,
> and put me to the proof, though they had seen my work.
> ¹⁰For forty years I loathed that generation
> and said, "They are a people whose hearts go astray,
> and they do not regard my ways."
> ¹¹Therefore in my anger I swore,
> "They shall not enter my rest."[19]

It is this last section of Ps 95 that the author of Hebrews cites in 3:7–11. However, when we look closely at Ps 95, it is clear that the speaker in vv. 8–11 is the Lord God himself, Jehovah, the Lord of Israel—*YHWH*—and he is identified in vv. 1, 3, 6, and 7. This is instructive because the author of Hebrews tells us that it is "the Holy Spirit" who said these things. This is stated without qualification or *proviso*. The point is, for the author of Hebrews, what God says, the Holy Spirit says.

---

19. The author of Hebrews cites the same section of Ps 95 in chap. 4 as well.

The same kind of theological intertextuality emerges again a bit later in Hebrews when the author says (Heb 10:15-17 NRSV; italics added):

> And *the Holy Spirit also testifies* to us, for after saying,
> "This is the covenant that I will make with them
> after those days, says the Lord:
> I will put my laws in their hearts,
> and I will write them on their minds,"
> he also adds,
> "I will remember their sins and their lawless deeds no more."

As before, the author of Hebrews attributes the citation to "the Holy Spirit" without any qualification. However, when we look at the quoted section in Jeremiah, the speaker is the creator himself (Jer 31:31–34 NRSV):

> The days are surely coming, says the Lord [*YHWH*], when I will make a new covenant with the house of Israel and the house of Judah. It will not be like the covenant that I made with their ancestors when I took them by the hand to bring them out of the land of Egypt—a covenant that they broke, though I was their husband, says the Lord. But this is the covenant that I will make with the house of Israel after those days, says the Lord: I will put my law within them, and I will write it on their hearts; and I will be their God, and they shall be my people. No longer shall they teach one another, or say to each other, "Know the Lord," for they shall all know me, from the least of them to the greatest, says the Lord; for I will forgive their iniquity, and remember their sin no more.

Although the biblical writers do sometimes make distinctions between the persons of the Godhead,[20] the doctrine of God does not lend itself to simplistic explanations or easy categorizations. However, when we examine the biblical text closely, when God speaks, it is precisely the same thing as saying the Holy Spirit speaks. Richard Gaffin makes this very point when he writes,

> The diversity of God's speaking is a function of its taking place "through the prophets." With an eye to the preposition "through" (*en*) we may speak advisedly of the prophets as instruments. The way the author of Hebrews views the activity of Old Testament authors is instructive in this regard. In Hebrews 4:7, the quotation from Psalm 95 (Ps 94, LXX) is what God (the implied subject

---

20. E.g., the Son prays to the Father (John 6:11; 11:41–42; 17:1–26); the Father sends the Son (John 3:17; 20:21); when the Son ascends, he sends the Spirit (John 15:25 16:7); the Father sends the Spirit (John 14:26); etc.

from Heb 4:3–5) is saying "through David," while in Hebrews 3:7 the same quoted material is, without qualification, what "the Holy Spirit says." *The Holy Spirit utilizes David such that what David says in the Psalm is primarily and more ultimately what the Holy Spirit says.* Similarly, in Hebrews 9:8 both the actual Day of Atonement ritual and the account of it in Exodus and Leviticus seen together (word focused on deed) are what "the Holy Spirit indicates." In Hebrews 10:15, the promise of the new covenant in Jeremiah 31 is what the Holy Spirit "bears witness to" and "says."[21]

Our conclusion, then, is that "God spoke" and "the Holy Spirit spoke" are synonymous. Put differently, the expressions "God spoke" and "the Holy Spirit created" are interchangeable. Not only did the author of Hebrews readily interchange the Holy Spirit for the God and Lord of the OT, but the author of Genesis, by selecting the word *ruach*, seems to imply as much, for *ruach* denotes "more than simply the energy of God; it describes God extending himself in active engagement with his creation in a personal way."[22] This then bears directly on the subject of justification, and it is to this subject we now turn.

5.3. THE WORD OF THE LORD AND THE SPIRIT OF JUSTIFICATION

We state at the outset that salvation is not a group of disparate redemptive threads but is a single tightly woven fabric. In other words, salvation cannot be limited to justification any more than it can be confined to adoption. Nor can we pick and choose certain elements (e.g., faith and repentance) while leaving out others (e.g., predestination and sanctification). The various elements of our redemption are a package deal. However, that does not mean we cannot distinguish between them. The NT authors did, and so must we. We state this upfront so that no one comes away from the ensuing discussion with the conclusion that we should believe only in justification or that justification is more important than, say, regeneration. All the elements of salvation are essential. Nevertheless, in this section, our focus will be on justification rather than on the other aspects of Christ's redemptive work.

---

21. Accordingly, Hebrews supports something like the classical distinction between God as the primary author of Scripture and the human authors as secondary. See Gaffin, "Redemptive-Historical View," 96; italics added.

22. Ferguson, *Holy Spirit*, 18.

It is a monumental understatement to say that justification has a long history of controversy.[23] However, since the time of the Protestant Reformation, the word has generally come to be understood as a forensic declaration in which God the Father legally declares the believer to be righteous based on the meritorious work of God the Son. A. A. Hodge states the matter in his usual forthright way when he writes: "Justification is a judicial act of God, whereby he declares us to be conformed to the demands of the law as the condition of our life; it is not an act of gracious power, *making* us holy or conformed to the law as a standard of moral character."[24] The magisterial reformers themselves were correct when they insisted that the word δικαιοσύνην could not mean "to make righteous."[25] A simple example will help to illustrate why. Luke 7:29 states: "When they heard this, all the people and the tax collectors *justified* (ἐδικαίωσαν) *God*, having been baptized with the baptism of John."[26] What does it mean that the people "justified God"? Plainly, the people did not "make God righteous." That is, they did not act directly upon his character in some way so as to change him from wicked to holy. Rather, the ESV has captured the basic sense of the Greek text when it translates this passage, "[the people] declared God just." Or, as the NASB puts it, "they acknowledged God's justice.[27] These translations are close to the sense of the Greek. The people saw, recognized and, most importantly, *declared that God was righteous* in sending John the Baptizer. This appears to be the basic idea behind the term δικαιοσύνην as Paul uses it. In fact, one need only try the alternate meaning of "to make righteous" in Luke 7:29 to

---

23. See Gill, *Collection of Sermons*; Broun, "Life of Justifcation Opened"; Buchanan, *Doctrine of Justification*; Baxter, *Imputative Righteousness*; Haslam, *Imputed Righteousness*; Melanchthon, *Loci Communes*, Loci 8; McGrath, *Iustitia Dei*; McGrath, *Intellectual Origins*; Dulles, "Justification in Contemporary Catholic Theology," 256ff; and many, many more.

24. Hodge, *Commentary*. Similarly, Berkhof speaks for many modern Evangelicals when he writes, "Justification is a judicial act of God, in which He declares, on the basis of the righteousness of Jesus Christ, that all the claims of the law are satisfied with respect to the sinner" (Berkhof, *Systematic Theology*, 513).

25. As Augustine and the later Roman Catholic Church maintained. See Calvin, *Canons and Decrees*, 3:116, 113; and Bray, "Late-Medieval Theology," 84.

26. Author's translation. The KJV reads similarly, "And all the people that heard him, and the publicans, justified God, being baptized with the baptism of John" (Luke 7:29).

27. The NRSV translates the passage, "And all the people who heard this, including the tax collectors, acknowledged the justice of God." Still again in the ESV, "When all the people heard this, and the tax collectors too, they declared God just, having been baptized with the baptism of John." The NIV translates the text, "All the people, even the tax collectors, when they heard Jesus' words, *acknowledged that God's way was right*, because they had been baptized by John" (italics added). Although more of a paraphrase, it does capture the basic idea behind the Greek very well.

see the problem it creates: "When they heard this, all the people and the tax collectors *made God righteous*, having been baptized with the baptism of John." The incongruity of such language is striking. As a result, we conclude (along with the Reformed tradition for the past five hundred years and many in the early church before that)[28] that *justification is something God says about someone*, rather than *something he does to* (or *in*) *someone*; it is a decree—a legal decree—he makes regarding them. This is the sense the word frequently conveys through the NT. For example, Rom 5:16 states: "The judgment followed one sin and brought condemnation, but the gift followed many trespasses and brought justification [δικαίωμα]."[29] Similarly, the apostle says that Christ's death, "was to show [God's] righteousness [δικαιοσύνης] at the present time, so that he might be just [δίκαιον] and the justifier [δικαιοῦντα] of the one who has faith in Jesus" (Rom 3:26, ESV).[30] Note again in Gal 2:16, "we know that a person is not justified [δικαιοῦται] by works of the law but through faith in Jesus Christ, so we also have believed in Christ Jesus, in order to be justified [δικαιωθῶμεν] by faith in Christ and not by works of the law, because by works of the law no one will be justified [δικαιωθήσεται]."[31] In each of these instances, the implicit idea is of justification as a forensic reality.

Additionally, when we look closely at Paul's usage of justification language, we discover that he was fond of placing justification in juxtaposition to condemnation—another forensic term. For example, in Rom 5:16, he states: "Again, the gift of God is not like the result of the one man's sin: The judgment followed one sin and brought *condemnation* [κατάκριμα], but the gift followed many trespasses and brought *justification* [δικαίωμα]" (italics

---

28. See Needham, "Justification in the Early Church"; Oden, *Justification Reader*; and Chemnitz, who became known as the "second 'Martin'" of the Reformation and produced, please note, *eight pages* of patristic testimony to the doctrine of justification (Kramer, "Martin Chemnitz," 51ff). Not nearly as optimistic as Chemnitz, but still very much of the opinion that justification by faith alone was taught by segments of the early fathers, was Pelikan, *Riddle of Roman Catholicism*, 50ff.

29. Note the contrast between "condemnation" and "justification." We will look at this contrast on the following page.

30. In this case, the first two instances of the δίκαιο word group do not denote the idea of *to declare righteous*; only the third instance conveys this sense. Instead, the first occurrence (δικαιοσύνης) connotes the simple idea of *righteousness* or *justice*. The second usage (δίκαιον) means *correct* or *righteous*, and, by implication, *innocent*. The third instance (δικαιοῦντα), however, means *to show to be righteous* or *to declare righteous*. Moreover, when we look at the sentence itself, we can see that the first time the δίκαιο root is used, it describes God's character. In the second occurrence, it is used to describe how God exonerates his own righteous character. In the third usage, it describes God as the one who declares sinners to be righteous. See Nestle et al., *Greek New Testament*, 414.

31. Cf. Rom 3:20, 28; 5:1; 8:30, 10:4; Gal 3:24.

added). In v. 18 we see the same contrast, "Therefore just as one man's trespass led to *condemnation* [κατάκριμα] for all, so one man's act of righteousness [δικαιώματος] leads to *justification* [δικαίωσιν] and life for all" (NRSV; italics added). Although a bit different in format, Rom 8:33–34a still expresses the juxtaposition of justification and condemnation: "Who will bring a charge against God's elect? God is the one who justifies [δικαιῶν]; who is the one who condemns [κατακρινῶν]?" (NASB).

What we discover is that condemnation is the legal opposite of justification.[32] Like justification, condemnation is a legal status, but it is a legal pronouncement of guilt. Yet the parallels between the two words are interesting. For instance, it is entirely possible that an individual could be found guilty of a crime in a court of law (condemned) and yet actually be innocent. Nevertheless, within the eyes of the law, the person has been *condemned*— legally condemned. In a reverse of the above situation, a man might commit a crime and thus be actually guilty, yet, when the case comes to trial, be found innocent in the eyes of the law. Such a man will have been *justified*. Although guilty of the actual crime, he has been legally exonerated in the eyes of the state. This analogy illustrates some of the legal realities attending the language of justification and condemnation. Thus, for those who are "in Christ," there is no one who will be able to "bring any charge against God's elect": "Why not? Because it is God who justifies. Consequently, who is it that condemns?" (Rom 8:33–34; author's paraphrase). Wayne Grudem captures the above when he writes,

> To "condemn" someone is to declare that person guilty. The opposite of condemnation is justification, which, in this context, must mean "to declare someone not guilty." This is also evident from the fact that God's act of justifying is given as Paul's answer to the possibility of someone bringing an accusation or "charge" against God's people: such a declaration of guilt cannot stand in the face of God's declaration of righteousness.[33]

In his typical forceful way, John Murray writes, "Justification is a judicial or forensic term and refers to a judgment *conceived, recognized, and declared* with respect to judicial status. It does *not* mean to make righteous or upright or holy in the subjectively factititive and operative sense but to pronounce or declare to be righteous."[34] In other words, justification is something that God *says* about us. He *speaks* or *declares* us to be righteous. This, of course, raises the question, "What does God say in this declaration?"

---

32. Morris, *Epistle to Romans*, 236; Stott, *Message of Romans*, 155.
33. Grudem, *Systematic Theology*, 723.
34. Murray, "Systematic Theology," 204.

Most evangelicals respond that God declares that the believer is forgiven. We can see the close relationship between sin and justification in texts like Rom 3:23–24, "for all have *sinned* and fall short of the glory of God, and are *justified* freely by his grace" (italics added). Our dilemma is that we have not cherished God's glory as the *summum bonum* (the greatest good) and have instead prized other things. The apostle calls this perpetual act of making God inconsequential in our lives *sin*. But note the way the apostle establishes justification as the solution to sin. We have sinned (the problem), so God justifies (the solution). Thus, justification does entail the forgiveness of sins.[35] Forgiveness of sins is an ineffable blessing, but we need to be careful not to conflate forgiveness and justification; they are not synonymous. Justification includes forgiveness, but there is more to justification than forgiveness. When God justifies a believer, he forgives his or her sins, *and* he imputes the righteousness of Christ to him or her. This idea is introduced and developed in the sacrificial system of the Hebrew Bible, so we now turn our attention to this idea in Lev 16—the Day of Atonement.

5.4. IMPUTATION, SUBSTITUTION, AND THE DAY OF ATONEMENT

Every year on *Yom Kippur* (the Day of Atonement), Israel's high priest would take a bull for himself and two goats and "present them before the Lord."[36]

---

35. There seems to be no need to argue that justification involves forgiveness, as it is almost universally conceded.

36. Lev 17:7. The full account is found in Lev 16, part of which is reproduced here (Lev 16:2, 7–10, 15–16, 20–22):"The Lord said to Moses: Tell your brother Aaron not to come just at any time into the sanctuary inside the curtain before the mercy seat that is upon the ark, or he will die; for I appear in the cloud upon the mercy seat. . . . He shall take the two goats and set them before the Lord at the entrance of the tent of meeting; 8and Aaron shall cast lots on the two goats, one lot for the Lord and the other lot for Azazel. Aaron shall present the goat on which the lot fell for the Lord, and offer it as a sin offering; but the goat on which the lot fell for Azazel shall be presented alive before the Lord to make atonement over it, that it may be sent away into the wilderness to Azazel. . . . He shall slaughter the goat of the sin offering that is for the people and bring its blood inside the curtain and do with its blood as he did with the blood of the bull, sprinkling it upon the mercy seat and before the mercy seat. Thus he shall make atonement for the sanctuary, because of the uncleannesses of the people of Israel, and because of their transgressions, all their sins; and so he shall do for the tent of meeting, which remains with them in the midst of their uncleannesses. . . . When he has finished atoning for the holy place and the tent of meeting and the altar, he shall present the live goat. Then Aaron shall lay both his hands on the head of the live goat and confess over it all the iniquities of the people of Israel, and all their transgressions, all their sins, putting them on the head of the goat, and sending it away into the wilderness by means of someone designated for the task. The goat shall bear on itself all their iniquities to a

He would cast lots to determine the respective fates of these two goats. One animal was to be slain as a "sin offering," and its blood sprinkled throughout the holy and most holy places. The future of the other goat, however, was not only different, but it was also more intriguing. A ritual was initiated in the days of Moses that was to be followed by the descendants of Aaron for the generations to come, "a lasting ordinance" (Lev 16:34).

On the Day of Atonement, the high priest was to bathe his entire body in water and then don his priestly garments in preparation for the annual service (vv. 2–3).[37] He would then sacrifice a bull as a sin offering for his own sins. This sacrifice was to be completed before taking any action for the sins of the people.[38] Following his own purification, the high priest would cast lots to decide which goat would be sacrificed for the people and which one was to be the "scapegoat."[39] We should note that as the high priest began the process of casting lots,[40] he was no longer acting as a private person. As he moved from the sacrifice for his own sins to the sacrifice for the sins of the people, he was, likewise, transitioning from acting as a private individual

---

barren region; and the goat shall be set free in the wilderness" (NRSV).

37. See Lev 16:1–10; see also James Smith, *Pentateuch*, Lev 16:1–10; and Harrison, *Leviticus*, 171–2.

38. Seven times in Lev 16 it states that the priest sacrifices the bull "for himself." It was a simple but inviolate assumption that if a priest served as a mediator, his own sins must be dealt with first. However, we note the discontinuity with Jesus Christ as the archetypal high priest. "Unlike the other high priests, he [Jesus] does not need to offer sacrifices day after day, first for his own sins, and then for the sins of the people" (Heb 7:27).

39. The translation of this term (עֲזָאזֵל) has historically been difficult, since its etymology is uncertain, and we have no *clear* word correspondence. Nevertheless, there are essentially three main explanations/translations. First, the term עֲזָאזֵל (ăzā'•zēl) describes an abstract concept of removal. Second, the term is a proper name for the powers of evil with which the sin-bearing goat was associated. And third, some have suggested that it is the name of a wilderness demon (or Satan himself) that needed to be propitiated in some way. Hertz notes: "Any mythological explanation can be dismissed immediately as having no place whatever in the most sacred ordinance of Hebrew cultic worship. The notion that the Israelites ought to make propitiatory or other offerings to such supposed wilderness demons as satyrs was repudiated in the following chapter (Lev 17:7), and thus it cannot be associated with the unique character of the day of atonement. Probably the best explanation is that the word was a rare technical term describing 'complete removal,' i.e., of communal guilt, and that later personifications brought about myths and legends concerning *Azazel* in Jewish writings" (*Pentateuch and Haftorahs*, 481); cf. Smith, *Pentateuch*, Lev 16:1–10ff.

40. In ancient Israel, there were two sacred stones, the *Urim* and the *Thummin*, embedded into the breastplate of the highpPriest (Exod 28:30) that were used for determining the Lord's will in any number of situations. When the high priest cast "lots" (גּוֹרָל) in 16:8 for the goats, it is very likely a reference to these two stones. See also Lev 8:8; Num 27:21; Deut 33:8; 1 Sam 28:6; Ezra 2:63; Neh 7:65, and Harrison, *Leviticus*, 172.

to functioning as a public person in his capacity as high priest. In this position, he was the official representative of Israel. Once the outcome of the cast lots was known, the first animal was sacrificed for the sins of the people. We come now to the pivotal scene. After the sacrifice of the first goat, the high priest would take the second goat, place his hands on its head, and begin to confess the sins of the people—everything they had done in violation of God's law during the previous year. The image is striking: the people's official representative places his hands on the head of a goat, recounting all the corruption, villainy, and debauchery the people had committed. According to the text, the specific actions the high priest carried out were not merely symbolic, they were legal (forensic). The high priest was legally and symbolically placing the sins of the people onto the head of the goat, while simultaneously claiming the innocence of the goat, symbolically and legally, and transferring it to the people. He was overseeing a double transfer.[41] Or, to use a theological term, the high priest was *imputing* the sins of the people to the goat, and, by implication, the innocence of the goat was imputed to the people. Once this rite was completed, the animal was given to someone, led outside the camp, and released into the desert, so that it would carry the sins of the people outside the camp to "a remote area" (ESV).[42] The point of this was to illustrate that the people's sins had been "taken away." If an outsider were to ask, "Where did the sins go?" The answer was, "Away. We don't know where. It's just gone—for good." This was the annual practice for dealing with sin under the Mosaic economy—a practice that was "a shadow" of the salvation that was to come.[43] Just as a person casts a shadow on a sunny day, so we were told that "the good things that are coming," with the inauguration of the new covenant, cast a backwards light onto the Old Testament, creating the shadow of the law. This shadow included the Day of

---

41. I am not suggesting this is the way the passage has always been understood. In his work *Against Marcion*, Tertullian (160–225) interpreted this text allegorically: "Do they not also [i.e., the two goats on 'the great day of atonement'] prefigure the two natures of Christ? They were of like size and very similar in appearance, owing to the Lord's identity of aspect. He is not to come in any other form. He had to be recognized by those by whom he was also wounded and pierced. One of these goats was bound with scarlet and driven by the people out of the camp into the wilderness, amid cursing, and spitting, and pulling and piercing, being thus marked with all the signs of the Lord's own passion. The other, by being offered up for sins and given to the priests of the temple for meat, afforded proofs of his second appearance, when (after all sins have been expiated) the priests of the spiritual temple, that is, the church, are to enjoy the flesh, as it were, of the Lord's own grace. The rest will depart from salvation without tasting it" (*Two Goats*, 3:185).

42. Or "a barren region" (NRSV), an "uninhabited land" (Good News).

43. "The law is only a shadow of the good things that are coming—not the realities themselves" (Heb 10:1).

Atonement. The actual substance "is found in Christ" (Col 2:17). Nevertheless, the events of Lev 16 show us a pattern of the legal exchange in Christ's redemptive work.

Above, we made the claim that justification involves more than just the forgiveness of sins—as wonderful as forgiveness is. We also said that justification includes more than the imputation of our sins to Christ (we saw this through the lens of the Day of Atonement), but also the imputation of Christ's righteousness to us. Here, we suggest that justification not only includes a double imputation but also a double bestowal: the gift of righteousness *and* the gift of the Holy Spirit. One place where we see these elements come into focus is Gal 3:1–14. Therefore, we will now turn our attention to this text and see what it may have to teach us.

5.5. GALATIANS 3 AND THE "BLESSING OF ABRAHAM"

Using a standard literary parallelism, Paul begins Gal 3 by reminding the people[44] that it was, "before your eyes that Jesus Christ was publicly exhibited as crucified!" (Gal 3:1 NRSV).[45] Findlay says it was here that the Galatians began their folly. The first step in their fall backwards was when they ceased to focus on the cross of Christ. "Had their eyes continued to be fixed on Calvary, the Legalists would have argued and cajoled in vain. Let the cross of Christ once lose its spell for us, let its influence fail to hold and rule the soul, and we are at the mercy of every wind of doctrine. . . . If Christ crucified should cease to be its sovereign attraction, from that moment the Church is doomed."[46] Yet, this is what happened with the Galatians believers. Nevertheless, according to the apostle, it is by believing the message of the cross that the gift of the Spirit/the gift of righteousness is given.[47] Just

---

44. "Having begun . . . being perfected" (ESV); "beginning . . . trying to attain your goal."

45. Calvin observes, "Paul hints that their fall [from grace] was more a matter of madness than of mere stupidity. . . . I think that he is referring to the thing itself, which is a spiritual phenomenon. Paul says they were bewitched, not simply because of their disobedience but because they fell away so quickly, in spite of the clear and powerful teaching that they had received. . . . The actual sight of Christ's death could not have affected them more than his preaching had" (*Commentary on the Epistle to the Galatians*, 65–66). Likewise, Prime (also of the Reformation period) notes, "These Galatians were not only fools inwardly but externally bewitched. There is a bodily and there is a spiritual bewitching. . . . The spiritual bewitching is meant here" (*Exposition*, 92, as quoted in Bray, ed., *Galatians, Ephesians*, 89).

46. Findlay, "Epistle to Galatians," 5:854.

47. Luther offers, "It is obvious that the Holy Spirit was granted to the Galatians solely by hearing with faith. . . . The entire book of Acts was written to make this point"

as salvation is through faith, so also the giving of the Spirit and the gift of righteousness is brought about through faith. However, the giving of the Spirit served more than one purpose. For example, it was a *"sign of the true Christian faith."*[48] The gift of the Spirit was the evidence upon which the Jewish believers were persuaded that the Gentiles had been received into the kingdom of God (see Acts 11:15–8). Additionally, the gift of the Spirit was understood as *a guarantee of the age to come*. "[God] set his seal of ownership on us and put his Spirit in our hearts as a deposit [αρραβωνα], guaranteeing what is to come" (2 Cor 1:22). Likewise, in Eph 1:14, Paul tells us that the gift of the Spirit is an "earnest" (αρραβων), that is, a temporary measure until God's redemptive work among his elect people is complete, at which time the full and complete payment of the Spirit will be paid out in full. Moreover, in Acts 1, we see the well known instance of the bestowal of the Spirit upon the early believers with the goal of *empowering them* (Acts 1:8). We could produce other biblical reasons for the conferring of the Spirit; however, the focus here is not why the Spirit was given, but to note that one of those reasons is part-and-parcel with the gift of righteousness. This gift of the Spirit is called the "blessing" (Gal 3:9, 14) or "promise" (Gal 3:16, 18, 29) of Abraham.

Paul reminds the Galatians of their own history in chapter 3. He reminds them of their experience of the Spirit when they were converted. We must not miss that the strength of Paul's argument rests on the Galatians' experience; something dramatic happened. Although we are not told specifically what occurred, it was dramatic enough that Paul could use their experience as a means of establishing his argument. This is significant, because Paul's reasoning is almost exactly the opposite of contemporary evangelicals'.[49] "For Paul the Spirit is the crucial element to all of Christian life; therefore his argument stands or falls on their recalling their own experience of conversion at the beginning in terms of the Spirit."[50] Thus, in v.

(Luther, *Lectures on Galatians, 1535*, Ch. 1—4, 203).

48. Findlay, "Epistle to Galatians," 5:855; italics added. The full context of the above phrase is, "For the 'receiving of the Spirit' was an infallible sign of true Christian faith. This was the very proof which in the first instance had convinced Peter and the Judean Church that it was God's will to save the Gentiles, independently of the Mosaic law (Acts 11:15–8)."

49. In general, modern evangelicals call believers not to rely on their experience and instead trust the Scripture. In calling attention to the above, I am not suggesting that Christians should not trust the Bible. Rather, I am simply pointing out that in Gal 3, Paul sought to establish his teaching through an appeal to the Galatians' experience. As Gordon Fee has observed, "'Paul is speaking like a Pentecostal here and not like an evangelical" (Fee, "Epistle to Galatians," MP3 disk 1).

50. Fee, *Paul*, 87.

3, the apostle points out to the Galatians that they did not receive the Holy Spirit because they obeyed the law of Moses, but because they received the gospel by "hearing with faith" (NASB). We note also that the Galatians were not given the Spirit because they believed "the message of the Spirit," any more than modern evangelicals are given the gift of righteousness because they believe the "gospel of justification."[51] Rather, the Galatians believed the gospel, and, as a result, God gave his Spirit/righteousness to those who believed. The order is important. Finally, we observe also that Paul has no problem equating the gospel with "the message of the cross"—the "one thing" in which he never tires of boasting (Gal 6:14).[52]

It is difficult to appreciate how radically different Paul's message was to much of first-century Judaism. In the Mishnah,[53] Rabbi Phineas ben Jair taught, "Heedfulness leads to cleanliness, and cleanliness leads to purity, and purity leads to separatism, and separatism leads to holiness, and holiness leads to humility, and humility leads to shunning of sin, and shunning of sin leads to saintliness, and saintliness leads to the Holy Spirit."[54] If that was the kind of thing a person was used to hearing, then the indisputable presence of the Spirit given to the Gentiles must have come like an electric shock to Jewish Christians. The Galatians' experience was monumentally different. They were given the Spirit entirely apart from knowing the law and even less by trying to obey its requirements.[55]

After pointing out that the Galatians received the Spirit "through faith" (vv. 2, 5), the apostle puts forward Abraham to illustrate that faith is the means through which righteousness is given. Note here that Paul does not refer to the gift of the Spirit but the gift of righteousness (this is the first instance of righteousness being bestowed). Luther suggests that this statement by the apostle makes faith in God the "supreme act of worship," the

---

51. We note this in contrast to the expression "the gospel of justification" as it is frequently found in evangelical publications. See, for example, Murray, *Redemption*, 117–31; Stumme, *Gospel of Justification*; and Allen, *Justification and the Gospel*.

52. It is interesting to note, however, that although the gospel is never designated "the gospel of justification," it is called by different names at different times. For example, Paul speaks of it as Jesus Christ publicly exhibited as crucified (Gal 3:1); on other occasions, he calls it the message of Jesus, who gave himself for our sins to set us free from the present evil age (Gal 1:4); in some instances, the apostle will boil down the message simply to "him" (Gal 1:16); while on other occasions, he refers to it is as "what was promised" (in the OT Scriptures; Gal 3:22). Perhaps the most succinct metaphors the apostle uses can be seen in Gal 3:25, where he refers to the entire framework of God's redemptive plan simply as the "faith."

53. The codification in the second century AD of Jewish customs and traditions.

54. Phineas ben Jair, as quoted in Hansen, *Galatians*, Gal 3:4.

55. Hansen, *Galatians*, Gal 3:4.

"supreme obedience, and the supreme sacrifice."[56] He says that "faith is omnipotent, and its power is inestimable and infinite; for it attributes glory to God, which is the highest thing that can be attributed to Him. . . . Therefore faith justifies because it renders to God what is due Him; whoever does this is righteous."[57] Luther insists that the reason his opponents are unable to see this is "because they do not understand the true meaning of justification."[58] Paul, however, concludes, "Understand, then, that those who believe are children of Abraham. The Scripture foresaw that God would justify the Gentiles by faith and announced the gospel in advance to Abraham: 'All nations will be blessed through you.' So those who have faith are blessed along with Abraham, the man of faith" (vv. 7–9). Hence, we are told that all who follow Abraham's example of faith will, like him, also receive the gift of righteousness (so, in v. 7, we find a second occurrence of righteousness as the gift of the gospel). This, it seems, is what the Scriptures were literally foreseeing (a remarkable statement, by itself): that God would make righteous those who believe, like Abraham, "the man of faith"[59] (a third instance of righteousness' bestowal). Consequently, according to v. 9, the rest of us who have faith "are blessed along with Abraham." Given the context, it would be difficult to maintain that any other blessing could be in view here other than that we will, likewise, be credited as righteous (a fourth occurrence of righteousness' bestowal). Therefore, we note that within the space of seven verses (vv. 2–9), we have been told *twice* that "the blessing of Abraham" is the gift of the Spirit and *four times* that that it is the "gift of righteousness." In v. 11, we read the famous passage, "Clearly no one is justified before God by the law, because, 'The righteous will live by faith.'"[60] While v. 14 tells us,

---

56. Luther, *Lectures on Galatians, 1535*, 226.

57. Luther, *Lectures on Galatians, 1535*, 226–7, regarding Gal 3:6.

58. Luther, *Lectures on Galatians, 1535*, 233.

59. William Perkins says of faith and its role in the patriarch's life, "Abraham's faith was a faith against hope. For he believed the promise of a seed when his body was half dead and Sarah was barren. In like sort we, keeping true religion and good conscience, must in all our temptations, crosses, miseries, infirmities, against reason, sense and feeling, believe the promise of remission of sins and life everlasting" (Perkins, *Commentary on Galatians*, 58).

60. Quoting Hab 2:4. Of this verse Calvin says,

> Faith is not mere belief . . . but involves a relation to the Word of God that enables people to rest and trust in God. . . . Righteousness is not something we have in ourselves but that we obtain by imputation, in that God accounts our faith as righteousness. We are therefore said to be justified by faith, not because faith infuses into us some habit or quality but because we are accepted by God. Faith is only the instrumental cause of our justification. Properly speaking, our righteousness is nothing but God's free acceptance of us, on which our salvation is founded . . . . Righteousness

"[Christ] redeemed us in order that the blessing given to Abraham might come to the Gentiles through Christ Jesus, so that by faith we might receive the promise of the Spirit." These final two verses again tell us that those who receive the blessing of Abraham are justified before God, and that this is brought about by faith. Paul says that justification is inextricably connected to righteousness and that those who receive the "blessing of Abraham" (v. 14) receive "the promise of the Spirit." As a result, in this short paragraph we have been told *three times* that the blessing or promise of Abraham is "the gift of the Spirit" (vv. 2, 5, and 14), and *five times* we have been told that the blessing or promise of Abraham is the "gift of righteousness" (vv. 6–9, 11). In every case, it is given *through* or *by means of* faith.

What then? Was the promise to Abraham a promise of righteousness (i.e., justification), or was it a promise of the Holy Spirit (i.e., baptism of/in/with the Holy Spirit, an outpouring of the Spirit, etc.)?[61] What are we to make of these seemingly different assertions? It is inescapable that both assertions are firmly embedded in the letter. Moreover, both the "gift of the Spirit" and the "gift of righteousness" are thoroughly interwoven together in Paul's thought. Which direction, then, should we go? Of course, to phrase the question this way is to set up a false dilemma. It is a bit like asking if cricket is played with a bat *or* if it is played with a ball. For it seems the apostle wants us to understand that the blessing of Abraham is the gift of righteousness *and* the gift of the Spirit. This appears to be Luther's conclusion as well, for he notes as much with great adamancy:

> Now is not the fact that faith is reckoned as righteousness a receiving of the Spirit? So, either [Paul] proves nothing or the reception of the Spirit and the fact that faith is reckoned as righteousness will be the same thing. And it is true; it is introduced in order that the divine imputation may not be regarded as amounting to nothing outside of God, as some think that the Apostle's word 'grace' means a favorable disposition rather

---

is not a quality inherent in human beings but the pure gift of God, and it is possessed by faith only. It is not even a reward for our faith, because faith is only the means by which we receive what God freely gives. We are justified by the grace of God, Christ is our righteousness, the mercy of God is the cause of our righteousness, righteousness has been obtained for us by the death and resurrection of Christ, righteousness is bestowed on us through the gospel, we obtain righteousness by faith" ("Gal 3:6–9" in *Commentary on Galatians and Ephesians*).

61. According to Luther, "Now the blessing is nothing else than the promise of the Gospel. And that all the nations are blessed means that all the nations hear the blessing, or that the divine blessing, which is the promise, is preached and spread among all nations through the Gospel" (Luther, *Lectures on Galatians, 1535, Ch. 1—4*, 245).

than a gift. For when God is favorable and when he imputes, the Spirit is really received, both the gift and the grace.[62]

This conclusion opens certain avenues that might otherwise be closed off to us. By understanding "the blessing of Abraham" as a two-sided coin—one side being the bestowal of the Spirit, and the other the gift of the righteousness—it will allow us to hold together what might otherwise be put asunder. This is not to suggest that we should no longer make distinctions between justification, sanctification, glorification, etc. We can and should continue to distinguish between the different stages of redemption. Yet it seems equally clear that when the apostle wrote on the topic, both ideas were thoroughly intertwined. So while we may be able, for the sake of systematic theology (and it should be borne in mind that this project is an exercise in systematics), to distinguish between the two concepts in Gal 3:2–15, it is equally evident that the two ideas were of one fabric in the apostle's mind. G. Walter Hansen appears to find agreement with Luther when he writes, "But by quoting the entire text of Genesis 15:6, Paul also sets up a parallel between the bestowal of the Spirit upon the Galatians and the crediting of righteousness to Abraham. This parallel points to the close connection between the bestowal of the Spirit and the crediting of righteousness."[63]

The point of the above excursus is to demonstrate that, although the blessing of Abraham may mean more than merely a declaration of righteousness (*contra* classical evangelicalism), it does not—indeed, cannot—mean less. When God made his promise to Abraham, the implications of his oath were incalculable. It appears that the severing of righteousness from the gift of the Spirit is what is behind the angst of authors like Macchia et al. To their credit, they note with palpable frustration as authors attempt not to distinguish the two sides of God's promise, but to actually separate them one from the other, as if such a separation were possible. Thus, they rightly wince at these attempts, because they recognize that any such separation is dangerous. Yet it is no answer to deny the "gift of righteousness," or to so thoroughly downplay and harp against this side of the coin so as to functionally negate it (as Macchia does). It seems as though more and more authors are attempting to take the route of offering a very brief disclaimer at the beginning of their respective works, in which they begrudgingly affirm a forensic aspect to justification, but then write protracted refutations of the very thing they insist they uphold. Regardless of what critics or supporters might say, it seems clear that, for Paul, the promise to Abraham was a promise to be received by faith. This promise was about the gospel,

---

62. Luther, *Lectures on Galatians, 1519*, 252.
63. Hansen, *Galatians*, Gal 3:6.

a gospel that could be summarized as simply "the message of the cross" (1 Cor 1:18) or "what was promised" (Gal 3:22, Heb 6:15, 17). To believe the gospel was to receive the promise made to Abraham, and this promise was two-sided: one side being the gift of the Spirit, the other side being the gift of righteousness—or, put still differently, justification. Both the gift of the Spirit and gift of righteousness are received "by faith," but it is not faith in the gifts themselves, but faith in the gospel. Even more accurately, it is not faith itself that saves, as faith is only the means *through* which God saves us. Rather, it is Christ who saves *through* faith, and all of this is gratuitous. Thus we are saved by grace through faith in "the message of the cross." P. T. Forsyth was right when he wrote, "Christ is to us just what his cross is. All that Christ was in heaven or on earth was put into what he did there. . . . Christ, I repeat, is to us just what his cross is. You do not understand Christ till you understand his cross."[64] It is through this message of the cross that God freely gives us of his Spirit and the righteousness of Christ, and here we return to the idea of imputation.

5.6. THE SPEECH OF THE SPIRIT AS JUSTIFICATION

The verb *to impute* (ἐλογίσθη) means *to attribute to*, *to credit*, or *to reckon*. Consequently, *to impute* means "to attribute anything to a person or persons, upon adequate grounds."[65] It is here, I think, that we can see the role of the Holy Spirit in justification. To use the language of speech-act theory, the Holy Spirit is the speech-act of the Father. That is, where Jesus provided the basis for the illocutionary statement of justification, the Holy Spirit is the perlocutionary agent of justification. Just as the Spirit was the *dābār YHWH* in the creation of the cosmos—not merely a spiritual presence resident in and with the Father and Son, but the actual speech and energizing force of the Father's creativity—so also the Spirit is the speech of the Father in the declaration of the sinner's righteousness. In more traditional language, in justification, the Holy Spirit *is* the declaration of the Father—the declaration of our legal righteousness. This righteousness is based entirely on the work of the Son, a righteousness earned by and imputed from the Son and spoken by the Father. The Spirit is the legal utterance spoken, the agency through which this righteousness is given to us—in short, a pneumatologically robust understanding of justification.

The advantage of this approach is that it preserves what the Reformers regained, *and* it offers a genuinely trinitarian understanding of justification.

64. Forsyth, *Cruciality of the Cross*, 44–45.
65. Hodge, *Systematic Theology*, 2:194.

We do not need to choose between the historic Protestant view of forensic justification and a pneumatologically rich view of justification. There is no need to eschew forensic justification in order to have a pneumatologically robust view of justification. This approach allows us to heed Luther's caution, "[Justification is] the chief article of Christian doctrine.... For if we know this article, we are in the clearest light; if we do not know it, we dwell in the densest darkness. Therefore, if you see this article impugned or imperiled, do not hesitate to resist Peter or an angel from heaven; for it cannot be sufficiently extolled."[66]

Moreover, such a proposal keeps together what the apostle delivered together—the gift of the Spirit *and* the gift of righteousness (Gal 3). Paul wove both ideas into a single fabric, and we will do well to keep them tightly bound together. There is no need to isolate one from the other; nor does there appear to be any need to place additional emphasis on one spiritual gift over-against another. In the apostle's mind, the greatest need the Galatians had—the greatest need we have today—is to believe the message of the gospel. Again, not to believe the gift of the Spirit, nor to believe in justification, but to believe the gospel. The Christian life is a life of delving ever deeper into this "good news." The gospel is the whole of our message. "The gospel is not only the most important message in all of history; it is the **only** essential message in all of history."[67] It is not simply "the first 'step' in a 'stairway' of truths, rather, it is more like the 'hub' in a 'wheel' of truth.... The gospel is not just the minimum required doctrine necessary to enter the kingdom, but the way we make all progress in the kingdom."[68] Thus, we never move *beyond* the gospel; we never move *past* it to some "deeper truths"—whether they be sanctification, holiness, the tabernacle, etc. Rather, we go ever deeper into the message and meaning of the gospel. All the topics just mentioned should be taught and displayed in their relation to the gospel. This is what Luther meant when he said there is not "a word in the Bible ... which can be understood without reference to the cross."[69] Paul's great heartbreak over the Galatians was their defection from the centrality of the gospel to a "different gospel" (Gal 1:6). His opponents "claimed not

---

66. Luther, *What Luther Says*, 2:705. When Luther spoke of *justification*, he self-consciously used the term in a forensic sense.

67. Bridges, *Discipline of Grace*, 46.

68. Keller, "Centrality of Gospel."

69. Luther, *Table Talk*, as quoted in Grace of Calvary Lutheran, "Martin Luther." We note the similar theme to Thomas Jones's statement, "Therefore no doctrine of Scripture may faithfully be set before men unless it is displayed in its relationship to the cross" (as quoted in Chappell, *Christ-Centered Preaching*, 271).

to be opposing Paul but to be supplementing his message."[70] But the moment we add something to the gospel—to supplement it—it ceases to be the gospel. The message Paul preached had ceased to hold the Galatians under its spell, and as a result, it had ceased to transform them. The good news, however, is that such a situation can be undone: if we fix our eyes on the message of the cross and marvel at its meaning, then we will bear the fruit of its power in our lives—the gift of the Spirit and the gift of righteousness. Like the psalmist, we want to see God's holiness and righteousness and declare that it is "beautiful" (Ps 29:2, 96:9 ASV). And as we continue to center our lives on the message and meaning of the εὐαγγέλιον, it will transform us, not just once but continually. The gospel alone has the power to destroy the guilt of sin, and then, through that same gospel, the power of sin can be conquered. Once the guilt of sin has been severed, its days of power in the life of the believer are truly numbered. The Christian is in a truly unique and wonderful position, because he has been justified before the judge of all the earth, and there is no condemnation for those in Christ Jesus (Rom 8:1).

---

70. Longenecker, *Galatians*, 106.

6.0

Speech-Act Theory

God's Words of Power

6.1. INTRODUCTION

Up to this point in this work we have looked at a few snippets of justification's history, the role of the *dābār* YHWH in creation, how the author of Hebrews saw the speech of the Spirit in the OT, and how the blessing of Abraham refers to both the bestowal of the Spirit and the gift of righteousness. In this section, however, we will raise some first-order questions of methodology. This means our objective will be a bit different than in the previous segments. Within this section, we intend to look at the development of a branch of linguistic philosophy known as speech-act theory. To this end, we will look at two modern scholars who, knowingly or unknowingly, have utilized a number of the tools developed by linguistic philosophers. Specifically, we will sample the work of Pentecostal theologian Kenneth Archer[1] and the English NT scholar James Barr, and we

---

1. We readily acknowledge that both Barr and Archer move considerably beyond the realms of linguist philosophy in their respective works. However, we include two moderately popular representatives like Barr and Archer because too often the debt that modern scholarship owes to linguistic philosophy goes unrecognized altogether. It is not that linguistic philosophy is the bedrock of modern biblical studies and related fields, but it has assisted these critical fields repeatedly over the past few decades.

will note the way in which Tradition (with a capital "T") was used in the ancient church and how it might be utilized today. Following our look at Barr and Archer, we will look more closely at speech-act theory, what it is, with whom it originated (J. L. Austin), and who has subsequently exercised the greatest influence on its development (John Searle). From this, we will examine a question which, on the surface, appears to be simple enough, but upon closer reflection proves to be far more troublesome: the question of meaning. What is the meaning of meaning? How do we move from marks on a page to real, understandable meaning—meaning so real it can move a person to tears, or to take action, or to cause someone to commit his or her entire life to a cause? We will not only survey the subject of meaning in general, but we will also consider what Searle and Austin had to say on the question of meaning, authorial intent, and authorial responsibility. These subjects concerned both Austin and Searle, so we will assess both authors on these questions and on how the role of the author might affect the meaning of a text. More specifically, does the author play a meaningful role in the creation of meaning? Does the author contribute anything at all? Although authorial intent used to be the first and most basic assumption upon which Enlightenment interpretive methods were built, a number of contemporary approaches (i.e., postmodern) have rejected a determinative role for the author in the creative and interpretive process. This subject will bring us to two very significant authors, Hans-Georg Gadamer and Paul Ricœur. Both Gadamer and Ricœur believed in the primacy of the "horizon" of the text, which, by an interesting turn of fate, brought the author back into the picture—not in the same way as the Enlightenment methodologies of classical evangelicalism, but within the interpretive process nonetheless. Our survey of Gadamer and Ricœur's work will raise the subject of tradition and the appropriate role it might play as we interpret. Finally, we will arrive at what is, perhaps, the most significant material of this segment. Here, we will examine a few of the specifics found in Gadamer, Ricœur, and Austin's work, and from these we will explore some of the practical implications to which they give rise. These three philosophers have contributed to the world of hermeneutical theory in ways that very few can be said to have done. The practical takeaways from both Gadamer and Austin will wrap up this section and bring us to the conclusion of this work.

6.1.A. Kenneth Archer and an Alternative Approach to Interpretation

Pentecostal theologian Kenneth Archer has taken great exception to many of the modernistic assumptions in contemporary evangelicalism.[2] The primary concern for Archer is the thorny issue of how we move from what the text *meant* (to its original audience) to what the text *means* (to us today).[3] Archer states: "An exegetical approach that focuses only upon what the original inspired author *meant* and/or intended his first readers to understand will not completely satisfy the requirements of [this] hermeneutical strategy."[4] What is needed, he insists, is an approach that not only explicates the original meaning of the biblical text (the supposed function of the historical-critical methodologies), but also one that answers the question of what the text *means* for us today. In other words, says Archer, "the . . . hermeneut will want to comprehend the biblical passage in such a way that the illusive dichotomy of what a text *meant* and what a text *means* is overcome."[5]

Put simply, Archer's proposal is a "narrative approach that embraces a tridactic negotiation" to ascertain meaning between the Bible, the Holy Spirit, and the community. But to accomplish this end, we cannot utilize the classic Reformed approach of, say, Louis Berkhof, who believed that "*Scripture has but a single sense.*"[6] Berkhof was not unique in this conviction. Popular theologian R. C. Sproul stated repeatedly that, "A particular [biblical] statement may have numerous possible personal applications, but *it can only have one correct meaning.*"[7] For his part, Archer responds in what we might consider an *a*typical Pentecostal way. This is not to suggest that he is altogether out of step with his Pentecostal brethren, but that Archer has sought to cut his own path through the underbrush of hermeneutical foliage, while striving to explore the vexing problem of meaning and where it resides. Moreover, Archer wants to understand how meaning is actually accessed, once it is located. He wants to know if meaning is retrieved via

---

2. Kenneth Archer is associate professor of theology at the Church of God Theological Seminary in Cleveland, TN, and is an ordained bishop within the Church of God. He completed his PhD at the University of St. Andrews, Scotland, and his doctoral dissertation, "Forging a New Path: A Contemporary Pentecostal Hermeneutical Strategy for the Twenty-First Century," was eventually published as *A Pentecostal Hermeneutic*.

3. This is obviously not a new question. However, for two recent yet helpful introductions to the subject, see Marshall, *Beyond the Bible*, and Meadors, *Four Views*.

4. Archer, *Pentecostal Hermeneutic*, 142; italics in original.

5. Archer, *Pentecostal Hermeneutic*, 142; italics in original.

6. Berkhof, *Principles of Biblical Interpretation*, 57; italics added.

7. Sproul, *Knowing Scripture*, 39; italics added.

the reading process, through the agency of the Holy Spirit, by participation within the dynamic of church-life, or through another means or some combination of all of these. Consequently, Archer would undoubtedly echo Richard Bauckham's comment to Berkhof, Sproul, et al. when he says, "The Bible's meaning for today cannot result automatically from the correct use of a set of hermeneutical principles."[8] It appears that Archer has embraced the ideas driving Rickie Moore's project when Moore said, "Pentecostals . . . want to approach interpretation as a matter of *the text, the community*, and also *the ongoing voice of the Holy Spirit*."[9] Within Archer's own program, this last citation is significant, for it captures and summarizes well the outline of his interpretive program.

From the outset, Archer wants to conduct the interpretive task as a self-conscious Pentecostal. As such, he maintains that, "*Meaning . . . is arrived at through a dialectical process based upon an interdependent dialogical relationship between Scripture, Spirit* and *community*."[10] In other words, rather than the Reformation cry of *sola scriptura*, Archer utilizes a polyvalent approach where "*meaning is created* in the process of dialogue with a text."[11] Put simply, Archer advocates a kind of reader-response approach to meaning and understanding. It is not that meaning is *retrieved* from a given text and then brought to bear in the present world in new and creative ways. Much less is this Fee and Douglas' version of exegesis and then hermeneutics (i.e., analysis and interpretation of the text and then application).[12] Rather, according to Archer, it is actually the "creation of meaning" that occurs between the interplay of text and reader.

Archer is careful, however, in articulating his thesis, lest someone come away with the misconception that he is suggesting that an individual could go to the Bible, read it, and come away with whatever meaning he or she might desire and then simply give the Holy Spirit credit for it. In fact, Archer repeatedly states that there are only so many things the text can potentially say to anyone in any given situation. Each text is circumscribed

---

8. Bauckham, *Bible in Politics*, 19. I state above that Archer would "undoubtedly respond . . . by citing Richard Bauckham" precisely because it is Bauckham and Moore whom he *does* cites in his essay. See Archer, "Spirit and Theological Interpretation."

9. Moore, "Canon and Charisma," 75; italics added. The idea of a triatic approach to biblical interpretation (Word, Spirit, and Community) is a common theme in recent Pentecostal scholarship. In addition to the above, see Yong, *Spirit-Word-Community*; Purdy, *Distinct Twenty-First Century Pentecostal Hermeneutic*; and Peterson and Moore, *Voice, Word, and Spirit*.

10. Archer, *Pentecostal Hermeneutic*, 157; italics added. This statement captures in its most succinct form the essence of Archer's hermeneutical program.

11. Archer, *Pentecostal Hermeneutic*, 149; italics added.

12. See Fee and Douglas, *How to Read the Bible*, 17–88.

in such a way as to avoid a limitless number of readings. Thus, Archer insists he is not advocating an approach that would open up the proverbial floodgates of meaning (contra Fee and Douglas),[13] enabling the reader to simply impose upon the text any sense he or she may desire. Rather, it is only as the individual is in full participation within his or her local community, facing the new problems and situations that arise, seeking the direction of the Holy Spirit, that this new meaning is created. "Hence, it is the reading of the Scripture from a new *praxis* and in community that opens up valid yet multiple meanings of biblical texts."[14] Archer argues that it is the nature of eschatological community for God to speak in new and fresh ways in each generation. "The Pentecostal community's theological conviction that the word of God speaks to the present eschatological community collapses the distance between the past and present allowing for creative freedom in the community's acts of interpretation."[15] Interestingly, the primary constraint that Archer's interpretive method has built in is not from the text of Scripture (as is the case within evangelicalism) but from his own Pentecostal tradition.[16] Again, we should be careful to observe what Archer is *not* saying. He is not advocating a kind of isolated individualism that would allow the reader to mentally run with a text wherever he likes. Rather, this model wants to "keep the making of meaning in creative interdependent dialectic tension between the text and the community, which is always moving into new and different contexts. In this manner, the making of meaning is a constructive ongoing cooperation between the text and community of faith."[17]

Archer does appear to have a valid concern regarding the evangelical methodology. A particular group, be it evangelical, Pentecostal, or otherwise, shapes its interpretive methods. These methods, in turn, reshape the community. Methods are never neutral. They are rooted in specific worldviews and are anchored in the epistemological background of the community. Intentionally or not, methods reflect what a community deems to be true or valid. And it is just here that evangelicalism is, perhaps, most vulnerable.

---

13. Fee states that "the only proper control for hermeneutics is to be found in the original intent of the biblical text. . . . *Otherwise biblical texts can be made to mean whatever they mean to any given reader. But such hermeneutics becomes total subjectivity, and who then is to say that one person's interpretation is right, and another's is wrong? Anything goes*" (*How to Read the Bible*, 29–30). Archer, however, insists: "This does not imply that the biblical passage can mean whatever a community wants or desires it to mean" (*Pentecostal Hermeneutic*, 157).

14. Archer, "Spirit and Theological Interpretation."

15. Archer, "Spirit and Theological Interpretation."

16. Archer, "Spirit and Theological Interpretation."

17. Archer, "Spirit and Theological Interpretation."

Evangelicalism has long maintained, often implicitly, an assumption of *a*historicity in its methodological approach. That is, evangelicals have typically understood that the job of the interpreter is to seek a neutral stance before the text in order to obtain the objective meaning of the text. Once subjectivity is eliminated, the reader can access the objective propositional content within the text, and clear, unbiased meaning results (or is, at least, very likely). Such an approach was the bread-and-butter of evangelical authors like Carl F. H. Henry,[18] Gordon Clark,[19] and, to a far lesser degree, J. I. Packer.[20] But such a neutral stance simply does not exist; there is no such thing as a view from nowhere. We all have our biases, and the methodology of even the most ardent evangelical is value-laden. We must take seriously John Goldingay's prophetic warning that those who "pretend to be objective and critical and then find their own (Enlightenment or existential or feminist) concerns in the texts they study need to take a dose of self-suspicion."[21] Perhaps the most dangerous person is the one who claims to have no bias. "We all have traditions and that man who thinks he has none is the man who is the most enslaved to them."[22]

The fact is, we simply do not, indeed we *cannot*, come to a text *tabula rasa*, waiting for it to write its message upon us. There is no "virgin approach" to the Bible or any other text. Rather, it is normal for us to develop our understanding of God and our methodology simultaneously. "Experience and interpretation are mutually informing and correcting elements in any community."[23] There is an interdependent relationship between theology and hermeneutics. "God must be our first thought, Scripture our second thought, and hermeneutics our third and last thought."[24] Yet these concepts do not merely build upon one another like the foundation of a building, with the first floor being laid, then the second floor, then the third. Rather, they interact with each other dynamically, developing synergistically. In looking at Archer's proposal, one might be justified in wondering if such a radical solution is necessary or even desirable. Is the sickness so serious that

---

18. Henry, *God, Revelation and Authority*, 3:481. Although Henry devotes only the first volume of this work to explaining and defending the propositional nature of revelation, it is apparent that his entire six-volume magnum opus is devoted to fleshing out this notion.

19. Clark, *God's Hammer*; *Language and Theology*; *Today's Evangelism*; *In Defense of Theology*.

20. Packer, *God Has Spoken*.

21. Goldingay, *Models for Interpretation*, 45.

22. Hunt and White, *Debating Calvinism*, 173.

23. Yong, *Discerning the Spirit(s)*, 181.

24. Vanhoozer, *First Theology*, 9.

the surgery suggested must be so severe? Is the patient truly so terminal? The answer, of course, depends upon whom you ask. If we were to consult someone like D. A. Carson, no doubt he would see and diagnose many of the same problems (something he has done in print on numerous occasions).[25] Yet it is doubtful that he would counsel the same drastic measures. However, if we were to turn to someone like the English NT scholar James Barr, it is possible that he would concur with many of Archer's diagnoses[26] and possibly even some of his drastic measures. It is to Barr, therefore, that we will now turn our attention.

6.2.B. The Critical View of James Barr: Holy Scripture: Canon, Authority, Criticism

Like Archer, James Barr, in his volume *Holy Scripture: Canon, Authority, Criticism*, upbraids the modern evangelical church for their "thoroughly modern" views, and more particularly, for their view of canon and inspiration. He insists that modern Christians have inverted the proper order of things, and he therefore states: "Now the strange thing was that, in ... taking its stand upon the canon as a complete entity, the church—and especially the Protestant branch of it—was actually taking its stand, to a considerable extent, outside the Bible rather than within it."[27] The solution, says Barr, is to enter into the experience of the man or woman of the ancient world,[28] who had no Bible—at least not in the same way that modern believers today possess. Since early Christians did not possess the Bible *per se*, they could not appeal to it and formulate doctrines in the same way that modern believers do. Thus, for example, when 2 Tim asserts, "All Scripture is inspired by God and is useful for teaching, for reproof, for correction, and for training in righteousness ..." (3:16 NRSV), Barr contends that the passage could not be referring to the New Testament material, because the only canon available in the first century was the Old Testament (i.e., the Hebrew Bible).[29] The upshot is that Barr sees a fundamental flaw in the anachronistic tendency

---

25. See specifically Carson, *Gagging of God*; Carson, ed., *Biblical Interpretation and the Church*; Carson and Woodbridge, eds., *Hermeneutics, Authority, and Canon*; Carson, ed., *Church in the Bible*; Carson and Williamson, eds., *It is Written*; Carson and Porter, eds., *Discourse Analysis*; Carson, *Collected Writings on Scripture*; and Carson, "Redaction Criticism," 115-42.

26. Although it is also likely that he would find many of Archer's methods wanting and see in Archer much of the fundamentalism he so thoroughly loathes.

27. Barr, *Holy Scripture*, 3.

28. Barr, *Holy Scripture*, 7-8.

29. Barr, *Holy Scripture*, 8-22.

of moderns to impose their view of canon and inspiration onto the people of the early church—how much greater the travesty when this is done to those that lived within the time of the canon itself.[30] Such an approach, he argues, is deductive, rather than the inductive method which he advocates.[31] Moreover, "it becomes impossibly artificial to attribute divine inspiration particularly to the writing of the texts in their final form. If there is inspiration at all [which Barr does not concede], then it must extend over the entire process of production that has led to the final text."[32] Yet he asserts that Scripture was a *product* of the believing community.[33] This, of course, is true as far as it goes; but Barr appears to understand this as the imposition of the concept by external post-biblical councils.[34] He insists that the modern notion of canon is as foreign to the Bible as the modern computer. He states, for example: "[The previous] considerations are, I suggest, fatal to the notion that the idea of the canon is of first-rate importance for biblical Christianity. Scripture is essential, but canon is not. Canon is a derivative, a secondary or tertiary, concept, of great interest perhaps but not of the highest theological importance."[35] He goes further and claims that the actual process of canonization, as it has been historically understood, is also "foreign" to the Bible. James Sanders, however, has helpfully pointed out that this claim of Barr's is not supported by even a little credible evidence, and it is difficult to maintain in the face of the many different forms of literary and historical criticism that have provided the necessary tools to describe, in at least some measure, the canonization process and to "ferret out the hermeneutics by which the formative process took place."[36]

30. Barr, Holy Scripture, 28

31. Barr insists that the deductive approach, advocated by many, presupposes a great many things, including an "accessible and articulate authority." If such an authority exists, "is it not necessary that it should be divinely given and constructed, in such a way that human tampering cannot have affected it? If it is so divinely given, does it not necessarily follow that it is free from any kind of error?" Such are the assumptions of a deductive methodology. However, the inductive approach advocated by Barr "will begin from a quite different set of observations: is it not the case that the Bible itself contains only rather limited assertions about the existence and function of scripture within Christianity? Did not the men of the New Testament live by personal contact and oral tradition rather than by submission to a written document? Does not the Bible itself contain very various estimates of the place, role, and authority of different parts of itself? Does it not contain pseudonymous documents and the like? The importance of the difference between these two approaches [is] continuously before us" (*Holy Scripture*, 22).

32. Barr, Holy Scripture, 27.

33. Barr, Holy Scripture, 26, 41, 42, 48.

34. See Sanders, Review of Holy Scripture.

35. Barr, Holy Scripture, 63.

36. Sanders, Review of Holy Scripture, 502.

The practical upshot of Barr's assessment appears to be both positive and negative. Positively, it is a step forward any time that someone can provoke thoughtless conservatives (and there are many of us) with a dose of realism over the nature and structure of the canon and the canonization process. That being said, although it may be easy to commend Barr's rigid adherence to the available facts (whether they be literary, historical, or otherwise), it is difficult to miss the unblushing antipathy he holds towards conservatives (*fundamentalism* being his preferred designation),[37] and it appears that this antagonism has influenced his critique in several significant, yet occasionally subtle, ways. For example, Barr overstates his case concerning 2 Tim 3:16 when he pontificates that the text could *only* apply to the OT, because the church did not yet possess the NT canon at the time of 2 Timothy's composition.[38] Such a contention simply does not fit with the testimony of the text itself (the very litmus test Barr insists upon again and again, and the criterion he claims conservatives repeatedly fail live up to). Here is why: 1 Tim 5:17–8 states: "Let the elders who rule well be considered worthy of double honour, especially those who labour in preaching and teaching; for the scripture says, 'You shall not muzzle an ox while it is treading out the grain,' and, 'The labourer deserves to be paid'" (NRSV). We take special note of the two texts cited in the passage. The first is a citation from Deut 25:4[39] while the second is drawn from Luke 10:7.[40] The choice of texts is significant because the author drew from *both* the OT and the book of Luke. But according to Barr, this could not have happened! Barr insists the NT canon had not yet been formed, thus the author could not have used the Lukan text; and yet this is exactly what 2 Tim does. As a result, the claim that 2 Tim 3:16 could not have referred to the New Testament or had it in view in any way is fallacious. Although Barr's canonical scheme may not allow for it, it the author of 2 Timothy did, in fact, refer to Luke's Gospel as "Scripture."[41] We

---

37. Barr has authored several works on the subject, indicating that he is less than objective in his overall approach. See *Escaping from Fundamentalism*; *Beyond Fundamentalism*; and *Fundamentalism*.

38. I am not assuming Pauline authorship at this point. Since Barr rejects Pauline authorship, I accept his assumption for the moment, as it does not affect the point being made.

39. "You shall not muzzle an ox while it is treading out the grain" (Deut. 25:4 NRSV).

40. "Remain in the same house, eating and drinking whatever they provide, for the laborer deserves to be paid. Do not move about from house to house" (Luke 10:7 NRSV).

41. 2 Pet 3:15–7 could also be adduced as evidence that the authenticated Pauline writings were considered as Scripture even in the early days of the church. Peter writes, "So also our beloved brother Paul wrote to you according to the wisdom given to him, speaking of this as he does in all his letters. There are some things in them hard to

highlight this even while recognizing the very real challenges present within Barr's thesis. Before we move on, however, there is one additional matter that we should look at before we move on to the full subject of speech act theory: the possibility of Tradition as a teacher and light into the biblical text.

6.2.C. Tradition, the Church, and Interpretation

Although it is quite true that modern ideas of inspiration are just that—modern—and that the early Christians did not have access to the Scripture in the same way that believers do today, it is entirely misleading to suggest (in the way that Barr and others do)[42] that the early church could not formulate doctrine because "they did not have the NT canon." For the NT itself speaks of a body of normative teaching that existed objectively within the early church. This is not to suggest that the early church formed doctrine in quite the same way we do today, but they did formulate doctrine, and they articulated and defended these beliefs against perceived threats.[43]

For example, in Rom 6, the apostle speaks of the "the form of teaching to which you were entrusted" (v. 17 NRSV), while in the book of Acts this teaching is called "the whole counsel of God" (Acts 20:27 ESV), and in the letters to Timothy it is referred to as "the standard of sound teaching" (1 Tim 1:13 NRSV) and "the good deposit that was entrusted to you" (1 Tim 6:20, 2 Tim 1:14 ESV). This "body of truth," we are told, is the very means by which we have the Father and the Son, because, "Whoever abides in [this] teaching has both the Father and the Son. [And] Everyone who goes on ahead and does not abide in the teaching of Christ, does not have God" (2 John 9–10 ESV). From the beginning, the gospel consisted of an account of events that took place in actual history; from that historical account, real, specific meaning was identified and written down to be preserved and transmitted to future generations. Aberrations were also recognized and rejected. J. Gresham Machen captured the all-important connection between real

---

understand, which the ignorant and unstable twist to their own destruction, as they do *the other scriptures*. You therefore, beloved, since you are forewarned, beware that you are not carried away with the error of the lawless and lose your own stability" (RSV; italics added). Peter puts the writings of Paul on the same level as the "other Scriptures."

42. See also Dunn, "Authority of Scripture" in *Living Word*, 89–135. Many of Barr's arguments are restated in Dunn's essay. In a number of instances, Dunn has articulated them more succinctly and clearly than Barr, and certainly with less venom, although he seems equally immovable as Barr.

43. E.g., Jude 3, "Beloved, although I was very eager to write to you about our common salvation, I found it necessary to write appealing to you to contend for the faith that was once for all delivered to the saints" (ESV).

history and doctrine when he wrote: "'Christ died'—*that* is history; 'Christ died for our sins'—*that* is doctrine. Without these two elements joined in an absolutely indissoluble union, there is no Christianity."[44] There is no minimizing of what took place in redemptive history without minimizing redemption itself. This brings us back to the all-important epistemological question: How is a person to decide between rival interpretations? Or should we allow multiple, potentially conflicting readings?

The late Peter Toon, a respected Anglican priest and theologian helpfully wrote:

> Since the Reformation of the sixteenth century, the Anglican approach to doctrine, worship, discipline, and polity has been deeply influenced by the commitment to norms found in the patristic period of the early church. This commitment has been put simply in terms of 1, 2, 3, 4, and 5. The Anglican Way rests upon *one* canon of Scripture with *two* testaments, *three* creeds (Apostles,' Nicene, and Athanasian, summarizing the essentials of the catholic faith as found in Holy Scripture), *four* ecumenical councils (from Nicaea in AD 325 to Chalcedon in 451, setting forth dogma, doctrine, and canon law), and *five* centuries of historical development (of polity, canon law, liturgy, etc.). Thus, any exposition of Anglican polity or church government is always an exercise in the use of *Scripture* and *Tradition*. The full authority of Scripture is not in question or doubt, but the way in which it is received and interpreted is significant.[45]

This approach of utilizing Scripture and Tradition accords well with what we know of other major episcopal bodies (i.e., the Roman Catholic and Orthodox Churches). Tradition not only provided the necessary matrix for the content of the early church (that is, the gospel: what had been held in common by all believers from the beginning),[46] it also provided an essential unity for the church—a unity built around apostolic teaching and an ongoing continuity. All of these features were contained within the context of the interpretive community that we call the church.[47] Consequently, it was understood that *only within the framework of authentic church-life could believers develop the appropriate set of virtues necessary to form the proper sympathies*

---

44. Machen, *Christianity and Liberalism*, 27.

45. Toon, "Episcopalianism," in Engle and Cowan, eds., *Who Runs the Church*, 23. For more information on Toon, see "Peter Toon."

46. Or, as Thomas Oden has put it, "the cohesive central tradition of general lay consent to apostolic teaching, not through its centrifugal variations but in its centripetal centering" (*Systematic Theology*, 3:vii).

47. See Florovsky, *Bible, Church, Tradition*, chap. 5.

required to correctly interpret the biblical text. Hence, a life lived in close community (within the larger church community) was thought to be a necessary requirement if one aspired to be an interpreter of the biblical text.[48] "Oh, how the mighty have fallen!"[49] Consider the climate of today's theological environment, and ask if a life lived within the closeness of authentic church-life is thought to be utterly essential to properly understanding the Bible. Although we might say yes, by our actions we generally live no.

We will return to the subject of tradition further down, but for now we simply note that, for the early church, it was not the Bible as such that held ultimate authority, nor was it even the perception of God's will that held the place of greatest power, but it was the "the interaction of both past revelation (i.e., the Word) and present revelation (i.e., the Spirit)."[50] Hence, what may be most important is not the intended meaning of the author, nor the original sense of the text itself (assuming for the moment that authorial and textual meaning could even mean something different); rather, it is the meaning of the text as interpreted in light of the advent and event of Jesus Christ. According to Dunn, the way of "bridging the gap"[51] between the text of the past (i.e., what the text *meant*) and the present situation (what the text *means*), is through "the continuity of *living tradition*."[52] And it is precisely at this point that both Gadamer and the Orthodox Church may have something to contribute to those of us in the western church.

For the Orthodox, Tradition is monumentally important. The living tradition has always been a part of the ongoing life of Orthodoxy. This can also be said of the Roman Catholic Church as well, but it may be safe to say that an emphasis on the *living* tradition does not always come through as clearly in the Roman Catholic Church as it does in the Orthodox Church. "For the Orthodox . . . Tradition means not primarily the acceptance of formulae or customs from past generations, but rather the ever-new, personal and direct experience of the Holy Spirit in the present, here and now."[53] Yet

---

48. Vanhoozer, *Is There a Meaning*, 379.
49. 2 Sam 1:19.
50. Dunn, *Living Word*, 119.
51. See Lambert and Moser-Mercer, eds., *Bridging the Gap*.
52. Dunn, *Living Word*, 154. Italics in original.
53. Ware, *Orthodox Way*, 60–62. Ware writes, "Each is called to verify for himself what he has been taught, each is required to re-live *the Tradition* he has received. 'The Creed,' said Metropolitan Philaret of Moscow, 'does not belong to you unless you have lived it'" (*Orthodox Way*, 55–56). Later, he adds, "The Bible . . . is the book of the Church, containing God's word. And so, we do not read the Bible as isolated individuals, interpreting it solely by the light of our private understanding, or in terms of current theories about source, form or redaction criticism. We read it as members of the Church, in communion with all the other members throughout the ages. The final

before we conclude that Tradition is the ultimate solution to our interpretive challenges, there is another thread we need to introduce into the interpretive tapestry we have been weaving. Although already alluded to, we come now to the topic of speech-act theory as a potential window through which to view God's glorious work of justification.

6.2.D. An Introduction to Speech-Act Theory

Speech-act theory originated in the seminal work of J. L. Austin, in his 1955 William James lectures at Harvard University and in his posthumously published work of 1962. Austin was a philosopher of language who made some "common sense observations" about the world around him that were critical in breaking the "stranglehold" of the "distinctively modern" view of the world.[54] That is to say, prior to Austin, *the major view of language was that it was thought to function primarily as a vehicle through which to communicate facts and states of affairs*, and to these two areas it was essentially limited. Austin was the man that jarred us free from the captivity that Wittgenstein described as "a picture [that] held us captive.... We could not get outside it."[55]

However, explaining speech-act theory can be difficult, as the discipline itself has become extraordinarily complex. Yet there are aspects which are simple enough. For example, when we speak, write, argue, laugh, cry, stew, etc., we are doing different things with our words. Sometimes we simply recount the events of the day: "I went to the store this afternoon," or "I taught a Bible study this morning," and so on. But other times we do not describe events (i.e., states of affairs) but actually *do* something with our words.[56] For example, as an ordained minister, I am sometimes called upon to perform wedding ceremonies. At a specific point in the ceremony, I say, "By the power invested in me, as a minister in the State of Washington, *I now pronounce you* husband and wife. You may kiss the bride." When I reach the point where I say, "I now pronounce you husband and wife," I am no longer describing a simple state of affairs; I am actually *doing* something

---

criterion for our interpretation of Scripture is the mind of the Church. And this means keeping constantly in view how the meaning of Scripture is explained and applied in Holy Tradition: that is to say, how the Bible is understood by the Fathers and the saints, and how it is used in liturgical worship" (*Orthodox Way*, 1991–6).

54. Briggs, "Speech Act Theory," in Vanhoozer et al., eds., *Dictionary for Theological Interpretation*, 763.

55. Wittgenstein, *Philosophical Investigations*, 115.

56. Richard has pointed out that it is also in these kinds of examples that Austin found his most frequent examples. See Briggs, "Speech Act Theory," in Vanhoozer et al., eds., *Dictionary for Theological Interpretation*, 764.

with my words. In short, I am wedding the couple. I am effecting an action through my words.[57] The words I use in such a situation have been endowed with a particular kind of authority, so that when they are spoken by the right person, under the right circumstances, at the right time, they possess the power to *do* something—something they would not normally be able to do. Although simplified, this illustrates speech-act theory.[58]

For his part, J. L. Austin identified three distinct types of speech-acts that people regularly perform (often unknowingly): locutionary acts, illocutionary acts, and perlocutionary acts.

1. A *locutionary act* is the performance of an utterance. It is the actual utterance, as well as its ostensible meaning. It is comprised of phonetic, phatic, and rhetic acts, which correspond to the verbal, syntactic, and semantic parts of any meaningful utterance.[59]

2. An *illocutionary act* is the semantic force (the illocutionary force) of the utterance. That is, it is the real and intended meaning of the locutionary act.[60]

3. A *perlocutionary act* is the actual effect of the utterance upon an individual, such as the actual persuading of someone, or convincing of an individual; this may involve scaring, enlightening, inspiring, or otherwise getting someone to do or realize something, whether this is intended or not.[61]

---

57. Similarly, the bride and groom who say, "I do," at the appropriate place during the wedding ceremony cannot a few moments later follow it up with, "Actually, I've decided that I don't." Why not? Because "the conventions that make the first utterance a promise of marriage are not in place to make the second utterance an undoing of that promise" (Briggs, "Speech Act Theory," in Vanhoozer et al., eds., *Dictionary for Theological Interpretation*, 763).

58. Austin focused on institutionalized uses of speech-acts, such as when a queen names a ship, a wedding ceremony, etc. But, as Briggs notes, while such examples have "memorable pedagogical values," they "obscure the more fundamental point that most speech acts operate outside of institutionalized settings, and thus invite consideration of just how it is (and by whom) that words are taken in a certain way" (Briggs, "Speech Act Theory," in Vanhoozer et al., eds., *Dictionary for Theological Interpretation*, 764).

59. Austin helped describe the function of an illocutionary act when he said it was the "performance of an act *in* saying something as opposed to performance *of* an act of saying something" (*How to Do Things*, 99–100).

60. In another place, Austin said, "The act of 'saying something' in this full normal sense I call, i.e., dub, the performance of a locutionary act, and the study of utterances" (*How to Do Things*, 94).

61. Austin adds (*How to Do Things*, 101):
There is yet a further sense (C) in which to perform a locutionary act, and therein an illocutionary act, may also be to perform an act of another kind. Saying something

An illocutionary act is performed whenever we say something. More accurately, it is performed *in* saying something. For example, "I promise I'll be on time," or "I believe in God, the Father Almighty, the Maker of heaven and earth." The speech-act in this example is not so much about the specific words as it is the particular action performed in uttering the words by virtue of what they mean in their context. To use another wedding example, the statement "I do" carries tremendous significance within the context of the wedding ceremony. However, if someone were to address a small group of people after the ceremony (say, during the reception) and say, "My car battery is dead. Does anyone here have a pair of jumper cables?" If I responded by saying, "I do," obviously the statement, although meaningful (and an illocutionary statement in its own right), would not convey anywhere near the same significance, even though it is verbally identical to the one spoken during the ceremony. Nevertheless, the insights that have come as a result of the illocutionary speech-act alone are overwhelming. As Richard has noted, it is likely that the illocution is the most significant analytical tool to be produced and found in the speech-act tool kit.[62]

Although Austin is noted for first uncovering and distinguishing the above three types of speech-acts (as the "father" of speech-act theory), it was his student, John Searle, who has become known for formalizing Austin's largely oral system into a full-fledged discipline, framed within a logical structure of five fundamental speech-acts. Searle summarized speech-acts in the following five basic categories:

1. *Assertives*: speech-acts that commit a speaker to the truth of the expressed proposition, e.g., reciting a creed.

2. *Directives*: speech acts that are to cause the hearer to take a particular action, e.g., requests, commands, and advice.

3. *Commissives*: speech-acts that commit a speaker to some future action, e.g., promises and oaths.

---

will often, or even normally, produce certain consequential effects upon the feelings, thoughts, or actions of the audience, or of the speaker, or of other persons: and it may be done with the design, intention, or purpose of producing them; and we may then say, thinking of this, that the speaking has performed an act in the nomenclature of which reference is made either (C. *a*), only obliquely, or even (C. *b*), not at all, to the performance or of the locutionary or illocutionary act. We shall call the performance of an act of this kind the performance of a "perlocutionary" act, and the act performed, where suitable—essentially in cases falling under (C. *a*)—a "perlocution."

62. Briggs, "Speech Act Theory," in Vanhoozer et al., eds., *Dictionary for Theological Interpretation*, 763.

4. *Expressives*: speech-acts that express the speaker's attitudes and emotions towards the proposition, e.g., congratulations, excuses, and thanks.

5. *Declarations*: speech-acts that change the reality in accordance with the proposition of the declaration, e.g., baptisms, pronouncing someone guilty, or pronouncing someone husband and wife.[63]

Although Searle has exercised significant influence upon the emerging discipline, we will continue to use Austin's nomenclature and categories of speech-acts (i.e., the locutionary, the illocutionary, and the perlocutionary) throughout this work. An important observation of most (but not all) locutions is their frequent multilayered character.[64] *Locutions* regularly hold room for multiple *illocutions*, depending upon the angle (or agenda) from which they are approached, albeit these *illocutions* are frequently unintentional.[65] We might attempt to express this phenomenon in the form of a question by asking, Which illocution(s) does the text support? Austin himself argued that the meaning of any given text was best understood as the "illocutionary act potential."[66] As to the *perlocutionary*, it relates to the

---

63. Searle, "Taxonomy of Illocutionary Acts," 345; cf. Searle, *Expression and Meaning*, 1–29.

64. This insight is frequently overlooked as well. Whether this oversight is intentional or unintentional is not a question we are prepared to answer, just an observation we are making.

65. It is this characteristic that has made room for Ricœur's metaphorical concept of the "surplus of meaning." See below. Furthermore, one can see in the roots of historical-criticism the mingling of many of the same questions as the speech-act theorist.

66. Austin, *How to Do Things*. However loose it may be, there appears to be an analogy between what Austin (and later Ricœur) is suggesting here on a linguistic level and what we find in the field of physics. Since the days of Gottfried Leibniz (1646–1716), scientists typically categorize different kinds of energy into two main classes: *kinetic* and *potential*. Kinetic energy is the form of energy we see when a given body is in motion; it is energy in action. However, potential energy (the energy with which we are concerned) is the energy latent within a given object. This energy *holds the potential* to do work. It is not the actual work itself. It is, rather, the image of a yew bow in the relaxed position, waiting to be bent in order to send the arrow to its target; it is the arm of the warrior at rest, waiting to pick up the sword and strike down his adversary. Potential energy is energy or strength at rest, yet fully present and waiting to go to work. This appears to be a similar notion to what Austin is suggesting linguistically. Thus, when Austin speaks of the "illocutionary act potential," he appears to have in mind the idea of a statement where real semantic force resides on at least a secondary or tertiary level. Consequently, this "semantic force"—the illocutionary force—may or may not be accessed in the reading/dialogue process. It is *potentially* there (just as the energy is potentially present within the yew bow while it is at rest); whether it is accessed or not is another question. We should clarify that the expression *potential energy* was not coined until later in the nineteenth century by the Scottish engineer/physicist William Rankine (even while the term, by Rankine's own admission, still maintained strong

actual effect a speech-act has (or hopes to have) on the reader, above and beyond the regular meaning we would expect from a sentence (i.e., beyond the semantic and syntactical—the *locutionary* meaning). In other words, there is what we might consider the regular or traditional meaning of a sentence. Beyond this normal meaning that we would find in or draw from a sentence, an author is usually attempting to do something in his or her writing. In a middle-school science textbook, for example, it might be to explain a particular hypothesis. In a work of poetry, it could be to move the heart of the reader. In the sermons of Jonathan Edwards, the perlocutionary goal was usually to persuade or convince, to plead or to encourage the listener or reader. Even more to the point, the main perlocutionary goal of this project is to persuade you, the reader, that the classic Protestant understanding of forensic justification is properly pneumatological—that is, even though the Protestant Reformers did not explicitly state it as such, the presence and activity of the Holy Spirit is latently present. Moreover, it is important for the reader to recognize that the perlocutionary intent of this work is not haphazardly related to its illocutionary meaning. In actual fact, they are tied together in the closest of ways. We might illustrate this using the *filioque* clause[67]—the clause that divided the Eastern and Western churches in 1054.[68] The language of "procession" that was used in the early trinitarian formulation in the west seems apropos; for as the Spirit proceeds from the Father and the Son, so too the "literary act proceeds from the author, and so too does the perlocution (persuading, convincing) proceed from the illocution (claiming, asserting)."[69] If taken seriously, this impacts a host of related issues, not the least of which is our understanding of Scripture itself. For example, Kevin Vanhoozer says, "To view the Bible as 'Scripture' best accords *not* with the *illocutionary* but rather with the *perlocutionary* aspect of communicative action. That is, Scripture intends, by and through its communicative action, to function in a way that leads to Christ and to the righteousness of God. To call the Bible *Scripture* does not make its warnings or its promises something other than warnings and promises, but rather reorients them to the larger purpose of 'making wise unto salvation.'"[70] We

---

ties to the philosopher Aristotle and his concept of *potentiality*). On this subject, see Rankine, "On the General Law."

67. "And from the Son."

68. I recognize not everyone embraces the *filioque* clause in the creed, and, like Vanhoozer, I have no wish to stake my entire hermeneutical approach on it. The point here is simply to illustrate how a text can have an illocutionary meaning *and* a perlocutionary intent. See Vanhoozer, *Is There a Meaning*, 410.

69. Vanhoozer, *Is There a Meaning*, 410.

70. Vanhoozer, *Is There a Meaning*, 380.

will return to this idea further down. For now we simply note the importance of the perlocutionary in the interpretive task and observe its potential to reorient the vantage point from which we view linguistic reality.

6.2.E. Textual Meaning Versus Authorial Meaning: Gadamer and Barth

Thus far, all we have shown is how, using speech-act theory, an utterance might be able to do more than one thing at a time. That is, it can convey its illocutionary meaning while also communicating its perlocutionary aims; yet there are additional questions and difficulties. What takes place in the act of communication? What do we mean by the word *understanding* or *meaning*? Communication is generally experienced rather than assessed; it is something to be practiced rather than probed. Huston Smith was surely right when he said, "We always know more than we know how we know it, from which it follows that to channel our knowing through methods we are explicitly aware of restricts our field of vision."[71] For example, as I write these words, I assume that eventually someone will read them, and the reader will be able to understand them. But how is this meaning conveyed? Where is the meaning located? It is easy to assert that meaning is within the words themselves. But if so, why is misinterpretation so prevalent? If meaning is not anchored in the actual words, is it possible, then, that the locus of meaning is to be found somewhere else? In the author, perhaps? Authorial intent has come under serious scrutiny during the past few decades. "[I]n the current hermeneutical climate it is open season on the concept of the author. And virtually no one thinks the author's order can stave off the conflict of interpretations."[72] So where does this leave us? Ultimately, to grapple

---

71. Smith, "Methodology, Comparisons, and Truth," 174.

72. Vanhoozer, "Discourse on Matter," 4. As an example of *the rejection of authorial intent*, Kenneth Archer, building on the work of Umberto Eco, argues that "in order to avoid over interpretation (an improper interpretation of the text) . . . the reader must be sensitive to the intention of the text" (*Pentecostal Hermeneutic*, 160). Eco himself does not collapse the intention of the text back into the intention of the author (*intention auctoris*). Rather, he claims that the intention of the author is "very difficult to find out and *frequently irrelevant for the interpretation of a text*" (Eco, *Interpretation and Overinterpretation*, 25; italics added). But Vanhoozer is surely correct when he notes, "It is doubtful, however, whether much sense can be made out of textual intent because texts, lacking consciousness, cannot have intentions." He continues, "It is not the narrative but the properly canonical shape that renders the authoritative subject matter of Scripture" (Vanhoozer, "Intention/Intentional Fallacy," 328). And, finally, "Texts have neither meanings nor intentions apart from being considered someone's. In short: discourse is always someone's performance" (Vanhoozer, "Discourse on Matter," 20).

with the question of meaning and understanding, we need to grapple with Gadamer, whose magnum opus, *Truth and Method*,[73] is still "the most comprehensive and influential description of the event of understanding."[74]

Kevin Vanhoozer offers an analysis of Gadamer's methodology[75] and the approach adopted by Karl Barth—no small task. Vanhoozer's insightful essay breaks down the various possibilities of who is active and who is passive in the event of understanding. He writes, "In describing the event of understanding, my major concern will be to gain clarity as to *who is doing what to whom*. Is understanding a type of active mastery or a passive happening? Is it something the interpreting subject does or is understanding done to the interpreter by the subject matter?"[76] Unlike historic evangelicalism, Gadamer (and Ricœur) believed the active agent in the event of understanding was the *Sache* (the "matter of the text"), rather than the author. For Gadamer, language was not the object of thought, but the medium. He employed an analogy from the incarnation to demonstrate the relationship between human speech and thought, an analogy aptly captured and summarized in Philippe Eberhard's work, *The Middle Voice in Gadamer's Hermeneutic*. Eberhard writes, "The spoken word reveals thinking to us because speaking and thinking are *homoousios*."[77] The "miracle"[78] of understanding is precisely the miracle of an "inner word" becoming an "external word," all the while remaining itself.[79]

Despite Gadamer's appeal to the incarnation, however, the notion of the *Sache* swallowing up words "conjures up a rather unorthodox picture in which the 'inner word' overwhelms the historical particularities of discourse. The actual text assumed by the *Sache* is not the *locus* of the miracle, as was Christ's flesh. Rather, the miracle concerns the self-presentation of the *Sache* through the veil of textual flesh to those caught up in the contemporary

---

73. Gadamer, *Truth and Method*.

74. Vanhoozer, "Discourse on Matter," 4.

75. I place "method" in quotation marks as Gadamer's approach is *almost* self-consciously anti-methodological.

76. Vanhoozer, "Discourse on Matter," 4.

77. Eberhard, *Middle Voice*, 182. Cf. Gadamer: "The mystery of the Trinity is mirrored in this miracle of language.... This is more than a mere metaphor, for the human relationship between thought and speech corresponds, despite its imperfections, to the divine relationship of the Trinity. The inner mental word is just as consubstantial with thought as is God the Son with God the Father" (Gadamer, *Truth and Method*, 421).

78. Gadamer's preferred term.

79. There are some superficial similarities between this analogy and Andreas Osiander's image of the "inner" and "outer" word.

conversation about it."[80] Although Gadamer speaks of effective historical consciousness, a Christian may rightly desire, instead, to explore the idea of an effective *pneumatic* consciousness.

As Vanhoozer turns to Karl Barth's methodology, one is struck at the dissimilarity in approaches. Barth came to Scripture "not so much to discover God but to be discovered by God."[81] Vanhoozer proceeds to place his finger on a notorious blind spot within evangelicalism: "To read (the Bible) for [only] the human author's intention fails to do justice to the freedom of God's Word speaking in Scripture."[82] The mistake theologians so often make is to attempt to find the *Sache* in the human author's intentions rather than the divine author's. The Bible's *Sache* is not an object, a thing we can master, nor is it something at our immediate disposal—a point that should not be minimized. Exegetes are not simply spectators of the Word, but by the grace of God, they are participants who may be "caught up into the subject matter (viz. the fellowship-creating triune economy)."[83] It is this living subject matter (*Sache*), therefore, and not some method that is to be normative for biblical interpretation, according to Barth. In conventional terms, according to Barth, both inspiration and illumination are necessary ingredients not only for divine revelation but also for the process (or, better, "the event") of understanding Scripture. In short, God "gives himself as the subject matter of this thinking."[84] To put it differently, according to Barth, what takes place in the event of understanding is not the result of simple natural or semantic connections between sense and referent. Instead, understanding is an act of divine disclosure, it is a gift from God. The specific subject matter or *Sache* of the Bible is not a subjective religious experience (*contra* theological liberalism),[85] nor is it the objective history of the historian and literary critic (*contra* conservative evangelicalism). It is, rather, the redemptive self-presentation of the triune God in the person and history of Jesus Christ.[86] Likewise, revelation

---

80. Vanhoozer, "Discourse on Matter," 23.

81. Vanhoozer, "Discourse on Matter," 8.

82. Vanhoozer, "Discourse on Matter," 9. This "blind spot" is not universal; there are exceptions. But, in general, they are just that: exceptions. However, this is an area where evangelicals can learn a great deal from their Pentecostal brethren, for Pentecostals are trained to read the Bible as God's word addressed *to them*. See Archer, *Pentecostal Hermeneutic*, 69ff, and Fee, *Listening to the Spirit*. For two additional exceptions, see Bock, "Single Meaning, Multiple Contexts," and Vos, "Theology of the New Testament" in *Redemptive History*, 503–9.

83. Vanhoozer, "Discourse on Matter," 9.

84. Barth, *Word of God*, 33.

85. Cf. Schleiermacher, *Christian Faith*.

86. Vanhoozer, "Person of the Book," 46. See also Barth's "Preface to the Second

is not simply the transmission of information about God, but it is God's own self unveiling. Barth's own preferred way of defining revelation was, "God is who He is in the act of His revelation."[87] Additionally, Barth claims that revelation happens when, and only when, God in his freedom chooses to make it happen. Thus, "revelation," in Barth's thought is always an "event."[88] Richard Burnett captured this aspect of Barth when he wrote, "Because God is free . . . any attempt to bind or contain Him or any attempt to force Him to conform to any method or hermeneutic came down not simply to a matter of inadequacy, but to a matter of reduction and distortion."[89] In other words, all attempts to reduce the interpretive process to methods, whatever they may be, would ultimately result in misunderstanding. The fundamental question for Barth then was not human understanding but the being of God himself.[90] Gianni Vattimo appears to have drawn the same conclusion when he wrote, "We are led to the hypothesis that hermeneutics itself, as a philosophy with certain ontological commitments, is the fruit of secularization as the renewal, pursuit, 'application' and interpretation of the substance of the Christian revelation, and preeminently the dogma of the incarnation of God."[91] What is clear is that, as it relates to the biblical text, the question of meaning cannot be accounted for simply on the basis of anthropological or sociological analysis. All critical methods, be they biblical, textual, higher, source, redaction, rhetorical, reader-response, form, genre, and every other kind of historical critical method of which we can think, apart from God's own self-disclosure, are ultimately dead end streets. "The gap between what is written (the sense) and what is written about (the reference) is closed, from above, by the Holy Spirit."[92]

This brings us to an all-important point, a point that is simple enough to acknowledge yet precariously easy to neglect: the essential role of the Holy Spirit. The apostle to the Gentiles tells us that, "The man without

Edition" in *Epistle to the Romans*, 2–15.

87. Barth, *Church Dogmatics*, 2/1, 257.

88. While not unique, this idea was instilled into me by Earl Palmer, former member of the Board of Governors for Princeton Theological Seminary, Regent College, New College Berkeley, and Whitworth University. However, Palmer is probably best known for his extraordinary expository preaching—a task he carried out for sixty-two years. Throughout his ministry he was frequently invited to lecture as a subject matter expert on Karl Barth, Deitrich Bonhoeffer, J. R. R. Tolkien, and C. S. Lewis. For more information, see the Earl Palmer Collection at Princeton Theological Seminary Library. The collection contains over thirty-five hundred audio and video recordings of Palmer.

89. Burnett, *Karl Barth's Theological Exegesis*, 49.

90. Burnett, *Karl Barth's Theological Exegesis*, 49.

91. Vattimo, *Beyond Interpretation*, 52.

92. Vanhoozer, "Discourse on Matter," 10.

the Spirit does not accept the things that come from the Spirit of God, for they are foolishness to him, and he cannot understand them, because they are spiritually discerned" (1 Cor 2:14). There is a most basic interpretive function which the Holy Spirit fills, without which no amount of training, skill, or other preparation will bring about what we might call "accurate understanding." The fundamental hurdle is not intellectual but moral. We are told that "the man without the Spirit" (Ψυχικὸς ἄνθρωπος, "the natural man") is incapable of receiving the things that come from the Spirit, because they strike him as ridiculous. This is an astonishing claim. It shows us that the unbelieving interpreter's problem is not an ignorance of methods, languages, or critical tools. An unbeliever may possess all of these in an abundance, and yet precisely because he does not believe, he is "programmed" to go astray in understanding the biblical text. Amos Yong captured this idea when he wrote, "Words in and of themselves are misunderstood, ineffectual, and ultimately, unintelligible. Meaning is finally borne in and by the Spirit through the medium of the Word."[93] Likewise, Karl Barth wrote with the sense of majesty he so frequently conveyed on the subject, "When God's Word is heard and proclaimed, something takes place that for all our hermeneutical skill cannot be brought about by hermeneutical skill."[94]

The conclusion of this for Vanhoozer is simple, yet also, perhaps, a bit surprising. His basic thesis is that for authentic Christian interpretation to take place, we cannot use the same categories in the same way as philosophical hermeneutics (please note: it is not that we *should not*, nor even that we *must not*, but that we *cannot* use the same categories). "My proposal, as radical as it is unapologetic, is that we employ specifically Christian categories not only notionally but operationally for the sake of a description of the miracle of understanding and of the being whose being consists in understanding."[95] Vanhoozer recalls how Augustine employed Christological concepts operationally in his *De Magistro* to claim that "understanding dawns not from an 'inner word' but from an 'inner teacher,' namely, Jesus

---

93. Yong, *Spirit-Word-Community*, 40. As an example of the need for the Spirit in the rational process, Yong notes 1 Cor 2:14, "The man without the Spirit does not accept the things that come from the Spirit of God, for they are foolishness to him, and *he cannot understand them*, [precisely] because they are spiritually discerned."

94. Barth, *Church Dogmatics*, 1/1, 148. At one point in 1932, Barth was questioned as to why the Holy Spirit did not appear more explicitly in the section on the "revealed Word" in the *Church Dogmatics*. Barth responded: "I wanted to place a strong emphasis on the objective side of revelation: Jesus Christ. If I had made much of the Holy Spirit, I am afraid I would have led back to subjectivism, which I wanted to overcome" (as quoted in Fackre, "Revelation," 4).

95. Vanhoozer, "Discourse on Matter," 25.

Christ."⁹⁶ This was Augustine's solution to the paradox of which came first: "a knowledge of the sign or a knowledge of the reality to which the sign refers."⁹⁷ According to Augustine, the reality to which a sign refers is known through consulting this inner teacher, Jesus Christ, through whom all things were made. Moreover, it is important for us to *feel* the truth that the Christian faith not only seeks understanding; it mediates it. As a result, we note with approval Eberhard's comment that, "Faith as an object of our knowledge and faith as a gift from God are exclusive alternatives only as long as one keeps thinking in terms of subject and object instead of subject and verb."⁹⁸ Faith is not something one merely does or even has, but it is the *Sache*, the subject that gets involved but never controls. Interpreting faith is something we understand while we are doing it, even while it happens to us. Consequently, the miracle of understanding *cannot* take place apart from the direct intervention of the Holy Spirit; it is this element of the interpretive process that we dare not downplay. Therefore, to elaborate on these ideas, we will continue to focus our attention on a few specifics of Gadamer and Ricœur.

6.2.F. Specifics of Interpretive Theory in Gadamer and Ricœur

It is quite possible that Ludwig Wittgenstein, Hans-Georg Gadamer, and Paul Ricœur exercised greater influence upon the interpretive enterprise over the last century than any other three men.⁹⁹ Here, however, we will not focus on the work of Wittgenstein and his language games, but will instead keep our attention on Gadamer and Ricœur. Historically, the discipline of hermeneutics (i.e., the reflection and practice of the appropriate principles that guide accurate interpretation of texts) was thought to be the subject matter for specialists such as exegetes and philologists. In more recent times, however, hermeneutics has become the domain of linguistic philosophers who want to know not simply what a particular text *means*, but *what understanding itself means*.¹⁰⁰ The dilemma that vexed interpreters for years

---

96. Vanhoozer, "Discourse on Matter," 26.
97. Vanhoozer, "Discourse on Matter," 26.
98. Eberhard, *Middle Voice*, 209.

99. Probably more than any other ten people. Vanhoozer states, "Perhaps no twentieth-century philosophers have done more on behalf of hermeneutics than Hans-Georg Gadamer and Paul Ricœur" (*Is There a Meaning*, 106). On Wittgenstein's influence, see Richter, "Ludwig Wittgenstein."

100. The specific philosophers we have in mind here would include Martin Heidegger, Hans-Georg Gadamer, and Paul Ricœur. See Vanhoozer, *Is There a Meaning*, 19.

came from a simple question: Does a text shape the interpretation, or does the interpretation shape the text? Both Gadamer and Ricœur rejected this either-or, take-it-or-leave-it approach in favor of something more akin to a both-and. Gadamer in particular viewed meaning as the outcome of an encounter between reader and text. *Knowing* an object and *understanding* a text are not the same thing, says to Gadamer, and understanding is not as simple as traditionally thought. Gadamer writes:

> In the process of understanding, a real fusing of horizons occurs—which means that as the historical horizon is projected, it is simultaneously superseded. To bring about this fusion in a regulated way is the task of what we called historically effected consciousness. Although this task was obscured by aesthetic-historical positivism following on the heels of romantic hermeneutics, it is, in fact, the central problem of hermeneutics. It is the problem of application, which is to be found in all understanding.[101]

While the typical Cartesian method pursued mental neutrality before a given text and sought to mirror that object within his mind, Gadamer, in contrast, observed that the reader was not a neutral, detached observer of the text, and meaning was not something that we could simply "explain." Instead, understanding is something that "happens" to us. It is an event that occurs when an interpreter "participates" in and with a text. He states in one place that, "interpretation is not an occasional, *post facto* supplement to understanding; rather, *understanding is always interpretation*, and hence *interpretation is the explicit form of understanding*. In accordance with this insight, interpretive language and concepts were recognized as belonging to the inner structure of understanding."[102]

The well-known "hermeneutical circle"[103] highlights the subject's ever-present involvement in the interpretive enterprise.[104] The result is that the reader, far from being a disinterested observer, stands in a crucial position (what Gadamer refers to as a "situation").[105] He defines this situation by say-

---

101. Gadamer, *Truth and Method*, Kindle loc. 4696–9.

102. Gadamer, *Truth and Method*, Kindle loc. 4703–4; italics added.

103. Conceptually improved by Osborn's hermeneutical "spiral." See Osborne, *Hermeneutical Spiral*.

104. See Vanhoozer, *Is There a Meaning*, 106. For a few treatments of Gadamer's interpretive theory, see Palmer, *Hermeneutics*; Hoy, *Critical Circle*; Thiselton, *Two Horizons*, chap. 11; Warnke, *Gadamer's Hermeneutics*.

105. Gadamer, *Truth and Method*, Kindle loc. 4680, 4690.

ing it "represents a standpoint that limits the possibility of vision."[106] *This situatedness, then, both conditions and limits what may be known about a text.* This should not be thought of as a limitation outside of history, but as an arrangement within history itself—a limitation that is "the result of previous interpretations."[107] This crucial "location" that the reader occupies, Gadamer calls a "horizon." But what is this horizon? According to Gadamer, a horizon is "the range of vision that includes everything that can be seen from a particular vantage point."[108] When applied to the field of philosophy, the word *horizon* characterizes "the way in which thought is tied to its finite determinacy, and the way one's range of vision is gradually expanded."[109] Thus, to "have a horizon," entails not merely being confined to what is only nearby, but also being able see what is farther away. The individual who is self-conscious of his or her horizon instinctively recognizes the relative significance of all things within that horizon, whether those things be great or small, near or far, etc. Likewise, as one works through his or her hermeneutical situatedness, this will entail obtaining the proper horizon of investigation appropriate to each encounter, unique to each tradition.[110] The implication of this view is that, in order to genuinely understand, we must place ourselves in the situation of the other.[111] That is to say, until we at least provisionally take on the viewpoint of the text/author and adopt his or her horizon of ideas, thoughts, feelings, and dreams, we will be incapable of genuine understanding. That is not to say that we must agree with him or her, but it does mean that we must attempt to think like them in order to understand them.[112]

106. Gadamer, *Truth and Method*, Kindle loc. 4631.
107. Vanhoozer, *Is There a Meaning*, 106.
108. Gadamer, *Truth and Method*, Kindle loc. 4631.
109. Gadamer, *Truth and* Method, Kindle loc. 4634. This is true at least since the time of Friedrich Nietzsche and Edmund Husserl. See, for example, Kuhn, "Phenomenological Concept of 'Horizon.'"
110. Gadamer, *Truth and Method*, Kindle loc. 4634-9.
111. Gadamer, *Truth and Method*, Kindle loc. 4640-1. This is very similar to the standard evangelical call to the interpret the Bible existentially. See Sproul, *Knowing Scripture*, 46ff.
112. Gadamer, *Truth and Method*, Kindle loc. 4645-6. In a brief but somewhat cryptic section, Gadamer cautions that if we attempt the interpretive task utilizing *only* the tools of the critical scholars, we will delude ourselves, if we think that such labors will lead to authentic *understanding*. For, he says, if we attempt to "see the past" from *strictly* a historical viewpoint (i.e., we attempt to place ourselves into the historical situation and attempt to reconstruct the "historical horizon"), we will have effectively given up every claim to finding anything meaningful for ourselves from the past, any truth that might have been considered valid, or any hope of locating anything intelligible for us or for those around us (*Truth and Method*, Kindle loc. 4650-1). The reason for this

Thus, according to Gadamer, when we approach the subject of historical understanding, we must always speak of horizons, especially when referring to the claims of historical consciousness to see the past on its own terms—not in terms of our contemporary criteria and prejudices, but within its own historical setting. The task of historical understanding involves acquiring an appropriate historical horizon, so that what we understand can be seen in the fullness of its dimensions.[113] Again, the horizon of our present state is always in the process of being reformed, precisely because we continually test and retest our assumptions and prejudices. A significant part of this process occurs when we recognize our past and become genuinely self-aware of our own tradition. The upshot of this is that the horizon of the present cannot be formed and reformed apart from the past. We can no more isolate our present (current) horizon than we can make a self-contained historical horizon. Both tasks are simply not possible. Instead, our objective is to bring these two horizons together and thus acquire understanding. According to Gadamer, "In a tradition this process of fusion is continually going on, for there old and new are always combining into something of living value, without either being explicitly foregrounded from the other."[114]

In contrast to the traditional approach of Schleiermacher, Dilthey, and large segments of modern evangelicalism, the interpretive process envisaged by Gadamer is far more dynamic than static. That is, a given horizon is something that is continuously in flux. It invites the individual reader (in the memorable words of C. S. Lewis) to come "further up, and further in!"[115] To move, to grow, to change, and develop.[116] Consequently, the horizon which

---

rather paradoxical assertion, he says, is because "[a]cknowledging the otherness of the other in this way, making him the object of objective knowledge, involves the fundamental suspension of his claim to truth" (*Truth and Method*, Kindle loc. 4649–52).

113. Gadamer, *Truth and Method*, Kindle loc. 4634–9.

114. Gadamer, *Truth and Method*, Kindle loc. 4687–90.

115. Lewis, *Last Battle*, chap.15. Gadamer states, "In the sphere of historical understanding, too, we speak of horizons, especially when referring to the claim of historical consciousness to see the past in its own terms, not in terms of our contemporary criteria and prejudices but within its own historical horizon. The task of historical understanding also involves acquiring an appropriate historical horizon, so that what we are trying to understand can be seen in its true dimensions" (*Truth and Method*, Kindle loc. 4634–9).

116. Gadamer observes, "The historical movement of human life consists in the fact that it is never absolutely bound to any one standpoint . . . the horizon is, rather, something into which we move and that moves with us. Horizons change for a person who is moving. Thus, the horizon of the past, out of which all human life lives, and which exists in the form of tradition, is always in motion" (Gadamer, *Truth and Method*, Kindle loc. 4657–60). Finally, Gadamer builds further on the concept of horizon when

created the matrix into which we have moved with its flow of experience is likewise parallel to an "equally comprehensive horizon intentionality on the objective side. For everything that is given as existent is given in terms of a world and hence brings the world horizon with it."[117] The horizon we bring to the text is a cultural-historical perspective. This horizon delimits the boundaries that we can (and cannot) see, because it is circumscribed, in part, by our own prejudices, practices, and experiences. Each of us looks at the world in ways unique to ourselves. One of the practical upshots of this is that we all come to the text with our own preunderstanding.[118] Yet, even

---

he explains what he means by "transposing ourselves." He states (*Truth and Method*, Kindle loc. 4666-72):

> What do we mean by "transposing ourselves"? Certainly not just disregarding ourselves. This is necessary, of course, insofar as we must imagine the other situation. But into this other situation we must bring, precisely, ourselves. Only this is the full meaning of "transposing ourselves." If we put ourselves in someone else's shoes, for example, then we will understand him—i.e., become aware of the otherness, the indissoluble individuality of the other person—by putting ourselves in his position. Transposing ourselves consists neither in the empathy of one individual for another nor in subordinating another person to our own standards; rather, it always involves rising to a higher universality that overcomes not only our own particularity but also that of the other. The concept of "horizon" suggests itself because it expresses the superior breadth of vision that the person who is trying to understand must have. To acquire a horizon means that one learns to look beyond what is close at hand—not in order to look away from it but to see it better, within a larger whole and in truer proportion.

117. Gadamer, *Truth and Method*, Kindle loc. 3745-7. Gadamer notes Dilthey's *Leben Schleiermachers*.

118. Preunderstanding can be far more powerful than many people realize. In 1971, Dooling and Lachman conducted an experiment (using the paragraph below) that demonstrates the incredible influence that preunderstanding can have. Half of their subjects in their experiment read the paragraph without being given a title and had very poor recall. In fact, only four out of one hundred eighty (about two percent) were able to understand the passage the first time through without the aid of a title. But the other half were given the simple title, "Columbus Discovers America," and for them everything made perfect sense. See Dooling and Lachman, "Effects of Comprehension," 217.

> With hocked gems financing him, our hero bravely defied all scornful laughter that tried to prevent his scheme. "Your eyes deceive," he had said. "An egg, not a table, correctly typifies this unexplored planet." Now three sturdy sisters sought proof. Forging along, sometimes through calm vastness, yet more often very turbulent peaks and valleys, days became weeks as many doubters spread fearful rumors about the edge. At last, from nowhere, welcome winged creatures appeared, signifying momentous success.

This simple experiment demonstrates that understanding depends upon more than just decoding skills. For, presumably, the participants were able to decode the words.

while the reader comes to the text with his or her own presuppositions (i.e., horizon), the text also has a horizon of its own, for it also carries within it the prejudices of its own time and historical setting. Thus, the task of interpretation is not so much a one-way street where the interpreter draws out something that lies dormant within inert text (meaning), but is more of a dynamic interchange between reader and text, where the reader lays him or herself open to the specific text, while simultaneously the text is laid bare to the interests and concerns of the reader. Understanding is what emerges in this encounter. It is what occurs when the horizons of reader and text are "fused" together.[119] *That*, according to Gadamer, is at the very essence of understanding.

If Gadamer is correct in his concept of the "fusion of horizons," then it follows that interpretation is more complex than initially thought. It is a process that cannot be reduced to "one correct interpretation."[120] Why is this? Because as each reader approaches the text, he or she comes to it with a distinctive background, assumptions, experiences. Thus, when the reader's horizon is fused with that of the text, it is virtually impossible that anyone else would come to the same text with the same background, knowledge, experiences. It is a truly unique encounter. Consequently, it is impossible that the understandings of two persons will be absolutely identical. This, of course, is just another way of saying there are multiple readings of any given text (since there are multiple horizons). It is precisely here that confusion sometimes occurs. When Gadamer speaks of meaning as an event, there is a sense in which meaning is *created*; yet we must be careful to circumscribe this idea. We must not think of this as creation *ex nihilo*. We do not create meaning by divine *fiat*; we do not create in the same way God creates. It is, rather, more appropriately described as *a miracle*, as when referred to as "the miracle of understanding."[121] For through the process of reading, the author gives the reader something through the text. Even though the author is no longer present with the reader, the text guides the reader into this "new" understanding.[122] Moreover, this suggests that there cannot be one single

---

Yet almost none of them could actually make sense of them. See Ornstein, *Evolution of Consciousness*.

119. Gadamer, *Truth and Method*, Kindle loc. 4695.

120. Sproul, *Knowing Scripture*, 39; Berkhof, *Systematic Theology*, 57; Fee and Douglas, *How to Read*, 34, 77.

121. Gadamer favored this expression, as was evident by its repetition in his work. See Gadamer, *Truth and Method*, Kindle loc. 4498, 4750, 5174, and 2633. For references in the original German edition, see Gadamer, *Wahrheit und Methode*, 169, 297, 316, and 347.

122. Not all authors are equally circumspect on this point. For his part, Gadamer

hermeneutical formula for the fusing of the horizons. Just as each person is a distinct individual, and each text is a unique work, so the encounter between the two will likewise be distinct. Yet, for as long as we continue to meet the text, we may appropriately apply it, as each new setting opens up new horizons of opportunities.[123] Gadamer himself states, "To understand a text always means to apply it to ourselves and to know that, even if it must be understood in different ways, it is still the same text presenting itself to us in different ways."[124] Meaning, then, is not limited to being in the text; instead, meaning is the event that takes place in the very act of our reading. It is the outcome of our "interpretive fusion."[125] As Vanhoozer succinctly states, "Gadamer's description of the miracle of understanding ultimately suggests a process of—why not say it?—grace."[126] However, this would seem to raise the question of the meaning of meaning.

6.2.G. The Meaning of Meaning

It has been suggested that instead of thinking of meaning as something that words or sentences "have" (that is, conceiving of meaning as a noun), we should reconceive of meaning primarily as an act, as something someone does (i.e., meaning as a verb).[127] Put differently, a text possesses meaning (in the sense of a noun) only when a person means something by it (a verb). We do not blame or praise books in the strictest sense; rather, we blame or praise the authors who wrote the books, because the texts themselves do not have the power of agency.[128] Only persons possess such powers; only people have

---

is marvelously nuanced when he speaks of *meaning, creation,* and the *miraculous event of understanding*; but other authors are not nearly as careful, bluntly speaking of the Christian community "creating meaning" (or similar statements) often without qualification. For example, Archer says, "The making of meaning and the validation of that meaning will take place primarily within the community, thus *meaning rests in the pragmatic decision of the community.*" A bit later he cites with approval Stanley Fish (*Is There a Text*) and then goes on to say, "Fish is correct in his argument that *interpretive communities do have the final decision in proclaiming what a text means* and establish the hermeneutical ground rules for interpreting texts" (Archer, *Pentecostal Hermeneutic*, 99n32; italics added).

123. The idea of ongoing change with the horizons is not an inference from the above but arises from Gadamer himself. See Gadamer, *Truth and Method*, Kindle loc. 4659–60.

124. Gadamer, *Truth and Method*, Kindle loc. 6031–2.
125. Vanhoozer, *Is There a Meaning*, 106.
126. Vanhoozer, "Discourse on Matter," 24.
127. This is one of the basic contentions of Vanhoozer, *Is There a Meaning*.
128. Vanhoozer, *Is There a Meaning*, 215.

the ability to say something about something to someone.[129] But from this we can see that *meaning*, like the word *act*, not only refers to what is done, but also to the actual act of doing it. Thus, what has been said of guns might also be said of meaning: "Words don't kill (or state, or convince, or promise, or whatever else); people do." Meaning then is not an indeterminate thing (even less, an intermediate state of being, as in a "sleeping text" that we must awaken to life); instead, it is a determinate action.[130]

Such a shift in the way we approach texts and meaning may be helpful for several reasons and has been argued at length elsewhere,[131] so we will not take the time to do so here. However, even if there are exceptions to such an approach, as a general rule, such a shift in our thinking is helpful, as it anchors the focus of our attention in the source of the action, rather than the vehicle by which it is carried. Even though we cannot get at the potentially "hidden states" or disclosed reasons of the author's minds, there are advantages to keeping the author within the interpretive process. Yet, before we ever come to the interpretive process, there is a more fundamental question, a question of the text's ontology. If the matter of the text—the *Sache*—is something outside of our direct control (Gadamer), and if God himself gives himself as a gracious gift in the interpretive process so that what we experience is a divine revelation, not so much as a process but as an event (Barth), thus making understanding a miracle of God's grace (Vanhoozer), then we might wonder about the very nature of the texts we examine, particularly biblical revelation. What exactly are they? Yes, there is a miracle that takes place when we understand what we read, but what specifically happens when understanding occurs? To say that God's Spirit enables us, or that God's grace helps us, may answer the question; but it is also quite possible that it might not. Sometimes people "explain" something or a situation by describing it as a *miracle* or *God's grace* (or something similar), when all they have done is to place a familiar word on the event and move it one step further away. In such cases, we have not actually explained anything. It is only the appearance of an explanation; it may sound like an explanation, but, in reality, it is only a pseudo-explanation, a kind of verbal sophistry.[132] Real answers are often hard to come by, and sometimes what

---

129. Vanhoozer, *Is There a Meaning*, 216.

130. Vanhoozer, *Is There a Meaning*, 202–3.

131. Vanhoozer, *Is There a Meaning*, 200–231.

132. Years ago, I heard a debate between a philosopher and a scientist. At one point, the scientist ridiculed the philosopher because "philosophy was so imprecise and theoretical." The philosopher appealed to the scientist, suggesting that he could surely relate to the difficulty. The scientist responded with a contemptuous negative. So, the philosopher asked him to define "energy." "That's easy," said the scientist, "energy is the

initially appears to be an answer turns out to be little more than the linguistic equivalent of cotton candy.

It may be true that, when we think of language, we first think of linguistic signs, but it is not true that meaning is nothing more than linguistic signs. Just as a body is more than the sum of its physical parts, and a man or woman is more than the sum of his or her bodily movements, so also a sentence is more than the sum of its linguistic parts (or signs). We might say of meaning what was said of God in some of the discussions of the 1960s—that it/he is both transcendent and immanent. So also meaning is more than vocabulary and syntax, hence its transcendence. Yet without vocabulary and syntax, it would be incomprehensible—in fact, there would be nothing—hence its immanence. Rightfully, therefore, did Jerry Gill note, "Linguistic deeds and events are vital features of reality, as substantial and significant as chairs, jumps, persons, and ideas."[133] Put differently, incorporeal reality exists, and it includes things like meaning; yet we usually come to know such intangible reality—this reality we call *meaning*—through the corporeal world (which includes things like linguistic signs, sounds, and marks), even though we can never reduce one to the other, nor can we equate one with the other. "Meaning is neither read off, nor read into, language, but is rather encountered in it."[134] The upshot is that, when we look at language, a text becomes the medium for the author's intentions. The author then may no longer hold the pride of place in the interpretive process, and this raises the question, Where does that leave us? For some, it is a great relief to be free from the author. For others, it is a calamity of the highest order. For our own project, such a conclusion (if shown to be true) would be of genuine concern, particularly when one considers that our overall thesis is built, in part, upon the book of Genesis, which could ostensibly argue for dual authorship (divine and human). If we remove the author from the interpretive equation, where then does this leave the biblical interpreter? If the author really is cut off from the text, then "we are to be pitied more than all men" (1 Cor 15:19).[135]

---

ability to do work." "I don't want to know what it can *do*," said the philosopher, "I want to know what energy *is*." The scientist responded, "Oh, I see what you mean. Still, it's not *that* hard. Energy is e=mc2." "No," said the philosopher, "I don't what a mathematical equivalent. I want to know what energy *is—ontologically*." It was only then that the scientist began to grasp the complexity of the problem. He had been using familiar phrases to describe energy, but, in the end, he could not actually define energy. This is the type of dilemma I am describing above.

133. Gill, *Mediated Transcendence*, 120.

134. Gill, *Mediated Transcendence*, 126.

135. A comment from the apostle in an entirely different context.

6.2.H. Gadamer and Ricœur on Author and Text

Although Gadamer and Ricœur had their differences, both authors privileged the idea of the "horizon" or "intention" of the text, over the actual author.[136] Additionally, both Ricœur and Gadamer viewed texts as possessing a kind of potential meaning from which individual readers could derive distinct understandings. Put differently, "the text has a sense potential, but actual meaning is the result of an encounter with the reader."[137] Ricœur defines a text as a "discourse [that is] fixed by writing."[138] Like audible speech, the intent of a text is to say something to someone about something. Each work (text) possesses its own unique sense (what it says), and its own unique reference (subject matter). Ricœur says, "The dialogical situation has been exploded. The relation writing-reading is no longer a particular case of the relation speaking-hearing."[139] For Ricœur, the disconnection of a text from its author is not a loss; it is, rather, a great gain. Why? Because it is in the autonomy of the text that the appropriate conditions are met for what Ricœur refers to as the text's "surplus of meaning."[140] That is, when the text has been severed from its author and made autonomous, it is enabled to transcend its original setting, thus placing it in a position to speak to readers in other ages. Ricœur writes, "What the text signifies no longer coincides with what the author meant; *henceforth, textual meaning and psychological meaning have different destinies.*"[141] More specifically, once the text is cut off from its author, it possesses a three-fold semantic independence: 1. autonomy from its author, 2. autonomy from its original audience, and 3. autonomy from its original referent.[142] The result is that, through the medium of writing, "the text's career escapes the finite horizon lived by its author."[143]

We may understandably wonder where Ricœur is taking us with such conclusions. For both Gadamer and Ricœur, their answers are as intriguing as they are at times unnerving. Ricœur maintains that as interpreters we do not meet a mind behind the text when we read. Instead, we discover an entirely new way of seeing things, a world of the possible, and this world lies

---

136. Cf. Vanhoozer, *Is There a Meaning*, 104, 107.
137. Vanhoozer, *Is There a Meaning*, 106.
138. Ricœur, *Interpretation Theory*, 26.
139. Ricœur, *Interpretation Theory*, 29.
140. Ricœur, *Hermeneutics and the Human Sciences*, 139.
141. Ricœur, *Hermeneutics and the Human Sciences*, 139; italics added.
142. Ricœur, *Interpretation Theory*, 30.
143. Ricœur, *Interpretation Theory*, 30.

in front of the text.[144] For Ricœur, a text is not part of the world to which it makes reference *per se*. That is, it is not part and parcel of an empirical verification model that describes an actual states of affairs. Instead, texts exhibit different potential ways of seeing or experiencing the world.[145] This "fusion of horizons" consists in unlocking the sense of the text in order to unpack its referent.[146] One of the obvious questions critics have raised (appropriately, I think) is, What is to keep readers from seeing their own meaning in the texts? How do we keep the reader from hijacking a written work? What is to obstruct a reader from taking "every text captive" to his or her own egotistical imagination? Isn't there a real danger that readers will simply use the text as a mirror into which they project themselves? According to Stephen Moore, there is a considerable danger precisely at this point: "Reader theory in literary studies is a Pandora's box into which we, infant literary critics of the Bible, have barely begun to peer."[147] According to other authorities, this is not a danger to be avoided but an opportunity to be embraced, an occasion to be celebrated. Yet, when it comes to the biblical text, participation within the community of the saints is a fundamental criterion for a proper understanding. Nevertheless, this does not answer the question: Is Ricœur correct about the autonomy of the text from its author? And, if the text does enjoy such semantic independence from its originator, is such a separation something we should celebrate? In brief, we believe the answer to both questions is *no*.

6.2.I. Tradition and the Necessity of the Author

According to some,[148] the Bible can never be properly understood until it is interpreted and lived out within the living tradition, passed down from apostolic times to the present. Although "tradition" was understood differently in the ancient church than it is often viewed in the modern west, it is language itself that is specifically the focus of our attention here. The intent of language, or its *design plan*,[149] is to function as a kind of intermediary of

---

144. This seems strikingly similar to some of the ideas in the field of possible world semantics. See Soames, *Philosophy of Language*.

145. See Vanhoozer, *Biblical Narrative*, for a full examination of the way in which Ricœur applies this understanding of texts to Scripture.

146. Vanhoozer, *Is There a Meaning*, 108.

147. Moore, *Literary Criticism*, 107.

148. Particularly those in the ancient church, as well as the Orthodox, Roman Catholic, and Anglican communities.

149. Vanhoozer's preferred expression. See *Is There a Meaning*, 204–7, 223–4, 267, 288.

covenantal relations between God and others in the world. It is the medium through which God fulfills his covenantal relationships.[150] We cannot help but notice that language is the instrument through which we relate and communicate to others. As such, each speaker is responsible for his or he own linguistic actions (i.e., what he or she says). "Language is not a code that bespeaks the subject, but a covenant that bestows dignity and responsibility on the agent of language."[151] As such, language is the organ through which we relate to the outside world and seek to understand it. This returns us to the subject of speech-act theory. For where locution pertains to the specifics of a given system of signs (or *langue*),[152] illocution and perlocution pertain to language that is in action (or *parole*).[153] It was the idea of the illocutionary act that allowed Austin to make the important distinction between the what of what we say (i.e., the content, including the sense and references of our sentences) and the impact of what we say (i.e., the force of what we say, what we are trying to *do* with our words). Austin's concept of the illocution calls us to keep the author or speaker ever present, perhaps not always at the forefront, but always, at least, in the background. We can never finally dismiss the author/speaker from the dialogue/conversation. It is this point that Vanhoozer highlights in his work, constantly emphasizing the importance of the author (albeit not always centrally). Put simply, *illocutionary speech acts require the ongoing presence of the author*. Although such a statement is astonishingly simple, it is incomparably important. "The speaker is a doer. It is precisely this aspect of illocution—what is done in saying or writing something—that Undoers overlook. For the Undoer, a text is a code to be unraveled rather than a force to reckon with."[154] Since Austin, however, it is no longer as easy to separate the speaker from her speech. This, it seems, is one of the great debts we owe Austin: he reunited what was previously thought to be inseparable, and, once separated, was thought to be incommensurate. Austin himself accentuated the connection which exists in popular expressions like, "Our word is our bond."[155] William

---

150. See Plantinga, *Warrant and Proper Function*, 11–17, 21–31. "A thing's design plan is the way the thing in question is 'supposed' to work" (21).

151. Vanhoozer, *Is There a Meaning*, 206.

152. French for *language*.

153. French for *speech*.

154. Vanhoozer, *Is There a Meaning*, 209.

155. Austin, *How to Do Things*, 10. We see a similar idea with the English word *integrity*. Originating from Latin, the word meant "soundness" or "wholeness." It was the idea that every part of an individual was fully informed by every other part. There was nothing that was out of sync. The practical upshot was that such a person could not lie for such an aberration would be a violation of the very "wholeness" or "perfect

Alston underscores the significance of Austin's work when he states, "The concept of an illocutionary act is the most fundamental concept in semantics and, hence, in the philosophy of language."[156] Once again, the role of the illocutionary takes on a role of monumental importance. In this case, it is not because it is fulfilling its primary objective (of persuading, convincing, arguing, etc.), but because it is accomplishing an unanticipated secondary objective: it is demonstrating *the ongoing connection with the author*, that *the author is the one who is persuading, convincing, arguing*, etc. To sever that connection is to sever the connection to meaning, to understanding. Consequently, we cannot let go of the author and maintain a grip on meaning.

6.3. PRACTICAL IMPLICATIONS OF SPEECH-ACT THEORY

The purpose of the above has been to introduce the various threads of linguistic philosophy, speech-act theory, pneumatology, and historic Reformed theology into a single fabric from which we can create a pneumatologically informed understanding of justification. All of the above topics have been addressed in a merely cursory fashion, but it is hoped that such an introduction might plant the seeds for future discussion. So where does this leave us? What does speech-act theory have to do with our present concerns? A great deal, it turns out. The utilization of speech-act theory in the service of systematic theology is not new,[157] but its introduction into the specific combination of pneumatology and theology may provide some insight into the ways in which God produced both creation and redemption. To use the idea of a text as an example, we could say that each text has its own unique mission—a mission of meaning. We might tentatively define this mission of meaning in relation to its illocutionary outcome. In other words, the objective of any literary act is to achieve its desired goal, to accomplish the purpose for which it was sent (see Isa 55:11). In the Bible, the *dābār* YHWH also has a mission. This mission, in turn, circumscribes the mission of the Spirit.[158] But it is precisely here that things frequently become muddled, because if the history of interpretation has taught us anything, it is that the interpretive enterprise is invariably a disputed affair. Interestingly,

---

condition" in which they lived. See "Integrity," *Dictionary*

156. Alston, *Philosophy of Language*, 39.

157. E.g., Vanhoozer writes, "I propose rethinking the relation of Word and Spirit with the aid of speech act theory." Vanhoozer, *Is There a Meaning*, 410. Cf. Horton, *Covenant and Eschatology*, 127ff.

158. Vanhoozer, *Is There a Meaning*, 410.

however, evangelical theologian Donald Bloesch has pointed out that both the church fathers and the Protestant Reformers understood the Word of the Lord (i.e., the *dābār YHWH*) as something that was more than merely a text; it is the Word of God.[159] As Hebrews insists, the word is "living and active" (4:12). Bloesch argues that the Spirit breathes life into the inert letters of the page. This, he insists, is far more than God merely repeating himself. The question is, How are we to understand this life-breathing activity? According to Bloesch, it is nothing less than a divine speech-act. What then is the take-away?

Undoubtedly, too much has been made over the years about the difference between "what the text meant" versus "what the text means." Kevin Vanhoozer is probably correct when he says, "Exegetes and theologians alike should take care . . . not to exaggerate the dichotomy between 'what it meant' and 'what it means'; one must beware of pitting Word *against* Spirit."[160] It is this danger we wish to avoid. The Holy Spirit does not add to or improve upon his word, so what is the work that the Spirit of God performs? Based on his reading of Acts 2, James McClendon suggests that Scripture is addressed not so much to the "original audience" as it is to "today's readers."[161] For example, Peter states clearly to the people "this is that" which the prophet Joel had promised. Peter was speaking of the event of Pentecost to his listeners. Yet, according to McClendon, what is taking place in Acts 2 was more than a kind of literary license (where Peter simply projected upon his audience some kind of historical-presence), but was instead the result of the Spirit's direct leading. If McClendon is correct, we must ask if such an endowment can also be attributed to participation within the life of the church, which enabled Peter to see that "this" was in fact "that." In other words, can we also draw upon biblical texts and, like Peter, say "this is that"?

Richard Hays follows a similar line of thinking similar when he notes that it was the Holy Spirit *alone* that enabled the apostle Paul to understand diverse OT promises to be fulfilled ultimately in the Church. Hays states that the apostle "read Scripture in light of his experience of the Spirit rather than vice versa."[162] To read Scripture in this way is, in effect, to proclaim that "this is that." That is, "this" promise (or prophecy, assurance, guarantee, contract, agreement, etc.) that was once made about the nation and people of Israel is "that" (prophecy, assurance, guarantee, contract, agreement, etc.), and

---

159. Bloesch, *Holy Scripture*, 21–22.

160. Vanhoozer, *Is There a Meaning*, 410.

161. McClendon, *Ethics*, 1:31–33.

162. Hays, *Echoes of Scripture*, 108. Note the similarity to the claims of Fee under the section "Galatians 3 and the 'Blessing of Abraham.'"

it was ultimately made about the church. This is uncomfortable business, because no amount of critical analysis will tell us when and where this can and should be done. "Only a prayerful reading that invokes the Spirit can perceive the true meaning in what is otherwise a dead letter."[163] As Curtis Freeman has perceptively written, this kind of Spirit-led reading "restores the interpretive activity of the spiritual community as the connecting link between text and reader."[164] In addition, we might also cite the agreement of Stanley Hauerwas who maintains that *Scripture can be read and interpreted correctly only from within a believing and practicing community*—the church."[165] But, and here is the rub, what is necessary for such interpretive practice is not the tools of the scholarly guild but training in godliness. The very endeavor to understand the biblical books "on their own terms" can end up being little more than "vain nonsense." How so? Because in the end, "it is little more than an attempt to know Jesus 'after the flesh.'"[166] Hauerwas himself makes the rather astonishing suggestion that there is no such thing as a/the "real meaning" in Paul's letters to the Corinthians. He claims that once we truly grasp that they are not *Paul's* letters at all, but the *church's* Scripture, only then will we see his point.

There are, however, at least a couple of concerns. It is easy to claim that Scripture can only accurately be interpreted from within the believing community—and I believe this. But we need to reflect carefully on the relationship between the believing interpreter and the believing community. I am thinking here specifically of Jer 8:8: "How can you say, 'We are wise, and the law of the Lord is with us'? But behold, the lying pen of the scribes has made it into a lie." The point is that a communal reading of Scripture is not a guarantee of accuracy. Perhaps even more concerning, though, is that the most outspoken champions of a community reading do not appear to submit and verify their work to a community of thought in a way all that dissimilar to others. "Does, say, a Joel Green or a Stanley Grenz, who emphasize the importance of community in the interpretive process, actually reflect a community or submit his findings to a community in a way in which, say, Millard Erickson or I. Howard Marshall does not?"[167] All interpretation is shaped to some degree by individual interpreters, who, in turn, are influenced by the communities from which they come. Nevertheless, as D. A. Carson notes, "to suspend all the weight of meaning from this

---

163. Vanhoozer, *Is There a Meaning*, 411.
164. Freeman, "Toward a *Sensus Fidelium*," 170ff.
165. Hauerwas, *Unleashing the Scripture*, chap. 2; italics added.
166. Vanhoozer, *Is There a Meaning*, 411.
167. Carson, "The Many Facets," 594.

solitary insight would mean it is impossible for different individuals and communities to study common texts with a view, so far as it is possible, to come to a meeting of minds as to what those texts say."[168] As already stated, I believe that we must read within the framework of church-life, but, as with all tools, no single instrument works perfectly in every situation. There is no single solution for all interpreting woes.

Looking back over this section, we might ask, What was the main point? Although we could suggest several answers, surely one legitimate answer is that *saying is a form of doing*. Many of the things we say—our utterances—are also, in fact, performatives, and if we are able to grasp this point in particular, the doctrine of justification may take on a new significance. When God speaks, he *performs* his utterance through his Spirit. That is, he is *doing* something with and through his words. All along, Protestants have argued that, in justification, God *says* something about us. He *declares* us to be a certain way—that is, righteous. Moreover, Protestant Christians have historically argued that what God says about them in this proclamation is first and foremost a *legal statement*. Yet in arguing for this legal statement, Protestants have never contended that salvation is only forensic. It is not. Those who depict evangelicals as concerned with only the forensic side of salvation (justification) are misrepresenting them—one-sided, misleading works. Whether one reads the Protestant Reformers, the early or late Puritans, the Princeton theologians, or some of the modern-day representatives, conservative evangelicals have simply not presented the gospel in the kind of one-sided way that critics so frequently portray. There are always exceptions, of course, but exceptions do not make the rule.[169] Protestant history is replete with examples of even the most ardent proponents of forensic justification unambiguously insisting on the need for repentance and good works. For example, Luther himself spoke of the impossibility of separating genuine faith and good deeds when he wrote, "It is impossible, indeed, to separate works from faith, just as it is impossible to separate heat and light from fire."[170] In a similar vein, Calvin wrote, "Thus it appears how true it is that we are justified not without, and yet not by works."[171] "We must understand, then, that faith and works can never in themselves (or together, for that matter) save anyone. *It is sovereign grace alone that forms the basis for*

---

168. Carson, "The Many Facets," 596.

169. I think here of the way John MacArthur has depicted Pentecostals and Charismatics by finding wild and weird examples and then presenting those examples as if they are normative for P/Cs. Such portrayals are misleading and unfair. Even so, it is disheartening to see P/C authors do the same type of things to their evangelical siblings.

170. As quoted in Dillenberger, ed., *Martin Luther*, 24.

171. Calvin, *Institutes* (Beveridge), 2:99 or 3.16.1.

eternal salvation. Good works 'complete' the testimony of faith by witnessing to the fact of that faith's existence; they serve to justify us before *men*, who cannot *see* the grace or the faith that has already justified us before God."[172] Yet, despite this disclaimer, justification is, and always has been, a distinctive of Protestantism. And in speech-act theory we can see how the Holy Spirit, as God's declaration, performs the task of executing our justification.

6.4. HARDNESS OF HEART AND OUR NEED OF THE GOSPEL

Not every question or critique is equally valid. While this may be obvious, it still must be said plainly sometimes. For example, when Mark C. Taylor characterizes the work of interpretation as "a hostile act in which [an] interpreter victimizes [a] text,"[173] we view such a cynical definition to be out of touch with linguistic reality. Or Geoffrey Hartman's hyper-skepticism, where he concludes, "What constitutes a text is a slippery thing to define."[174] There are times when cynicism and unbelief become so overwhelming that you either give yourself over to them or you resist and run the risk of being considered naïve or close-minded. But this puts us in a difficult place.

Often, unbelief does not appear to be all that bad. It seems to suggest a kind of intellectual credibility. Most academics do not want to be thought of as naïve or simplistic. Most of us would rather be thought skeptical than gullible, critical than susceptible. However, we should remember that the sin Jesus rebuked so frequently in his opponents was not the sin of credulity but of unbelief. Unbelief is subtle because it looks sophisticated, even academic. It can adopt the very appearance of professionalism, allowing the doubter to be respected as he or she works within the halls of academia. But professionalism has nothing to do with Christian ministry—even when it is an academic ministry. There is no such thing as professional "tenderheartedness" (Eph 4:32). It is hard to "pant after God" (Ps 42:1) in a dignified way. If we accede to Jesus's call to hunger and thirst after righteousness, to be filled with the Spirit, then we must run the risk of being thought credulous, and consciously resist skepticism and academic respect, placing our faith afresh in the gospel. For justification is always by faith (Acts 13:39). We say with

---

172. Martin, *Essential Christianity*, 73; italics added.

173. Taylor, "Text as Victim," 65. Such statements strike me as self-stultifying. The only way for Taylor to make such an assertion is to have interpreted the various approaches to interpretation. Thus, his own approach would "a hostile act in which [he] victimizes [the] text." So it seems impossible to take such a claim seriously.

174. Hartman, *Fate of Reading*, 13.

Luther, "Let skeptics and academics keep well away from us Christians. . . . Permit us to be assertors, to be devoted to assertions and delight in them . . . for *the Holy Spirit is no skeptic*, and it is not doubts or mere opinions that he has written on our hearts, but assertions more sure and certain than life itself and all experience."[175] One of the implications of this is that we must think deeply about the gospel. While it is certainly true that part of the academic task is to digest all types of theological works, we also need to include a steady diet of gospel-centered works—works that continually bring us back to the centrality to Jesus Christ and his redemptive work. We need to pray with the David, "Search me, O God, and know my heart; test me and know my anxious thoughts. See if there is any offensive way in me and lead me in the way everlasting" (Ps 139:23-24). A steady diet of critical or cynical works will eventually distort our thinking and thus our affections.

Two of the most troubling pericopes in the NT are found in Mark 6 and 8. In Mark 6, we read Mark's account of Jesus walking on the water. As we know, Jesus' stroll on the water "terrified" the disciples because they thought he was a ghost. In vv. 50b-52, we are told, "Immediately he spoke to them and said, 'Take courage! It is I. Don't be afraid.' Then he climbed into the boat with them, and the wind died down. They were completely amazed, for they had not understood about the loaves; their hearts were hardened." It is the last line that is so disconcerting. Ultimately, the disciples were incapable of understanding the events because "their hearts were hardened." Their inability to understand was not because of inadequate information or an insufficient education. They could not understand because their hearts were hard. Commenting on this text, Jonathan Edwards says,

> Now, by a "hard heart" is plainly meant an *unaffected* heart, or a heart not easy to be moved with virtuous affections, like a stone, insensible, stupid, unmoved, and *hard to be impressed*. Hence the hard heart is called a *stony heart*, and is opposed to a *heart of flesh*, that has feeling, and is sensibly touched and moved . . . what is a tender heart, but a heart which is easily impressed with what ought to affect it?[176]

We find a similar situation in Mark 8 following the feeding of the four thousand. Again, Jesus and his disciples are in a boat, but in this instance, Jesus cautioned the disciples against "the yeast of the Pharisees and that of Herod." The disciples misunderstood the comment and thought it to be a rebuke for neglecting to bring bread along for the journey. But with some

---

175. Luther, *Bondage of the Will* (Lehmann), 22, 24; italics added.
176. Edwards, *Religious Affections*, in *Works*, 1:29388-9; italics added, except for "stony heart" (italicized in original).

apparent frustration, Jesus asks them, "Why are you talking about having no bread? Do you still not see or understand? Are your hearts hardened?" (8:17). As before, Jesus draws a connection between the disciples' inability to understand the events happening to them and the hardness of their hearts. "The very notion of hardness of heart implies moral inability."[177]

This should give us pause. Reading, interpreting, and understanding are all part of the academic task. But these tasks are not morally neutral, and thus they are affected by the condition of our hearts. Like the disciples, if our hearts our hard, we will not be able to understand things correctly. We will misinterpret texts and events. If this book addressed all the major subject heads of interpretive theory yet did not mention something about the dangers of a hard heart, it would be a monumental oversight. It would be a bit like trying to explain the game of baseball to someone who has never heard of or seen the game and neglecting to mention that a bat is used. They would have many right ideas about the game, but they also would be left utterly confused. As Calvin observed, "The assent we give to God . . . is more a matter of the heart than the head, of the affection than the intellect."[178] This means engagement with God himself. Walter Martin used to say, "It is always a mistake to talk about God as if he is not in the room."[179] If we are to avoid such a mistake, then we must genuinely engage with God. "Engagement with God means being sufficiently grasped, disturbed, or troubled by the gospel *and its dispute with us*."[180] Thus, we must be prepared for God to "search and know [our] hearts" and respond appropriately. This includes coming to the interpretive task hungering and thirsting for righteousness (Matt 5:6). We desperately need the help of the Holy Spirit as we read the Bible and seek to understand it. Apart from such aid, we will eventually find ourselves entangled in a kind of philosophical straitjacket that keeps a text from meaning what it means.

---

177. Edwards, *Religious Affections*, in *Works*, 1:8823.

178. Calvin, *Institutes* (Beveridge), 3.2.8.

179. I heard Martin say this years ago on an audio lecture. Unfortunately, I was unable to locate the source.

180. Webster, *Culture of Theology*, 133.

7.0

Conclusion

At the beginning of this project, we suggested that, although the Protestant Reformers did not explicitly teach a view of justification informed by pneumatology, one can argue that such a pneumatology is, nevertheless, latently present within their work. Therefore, the many recent attempts at creating pneumatological views of justification are, in the best instances, helpful reminders of how Father, Son, and Holy Spirit act harmoniously to bring about redemption. Conversely, the worst examples appear to be little more than misguided efforts that abandon the Reformation heritage, redefining the very language through which the doctrine has come.

In arguing for a pneumatology of justification, it is easy to get lost along the way. In the process of researching the many related issues, one can easily lose sight of the forest for the trees. A distinct problem arises when we recognize the concerns that different individuals have raised throughout the years, whether they be the original concerns of the Roman Catholic Church, or the more intermural concerns of Andreas Osiander, or even as we move forward in time, until we arrive at the present and examine the misgivings of many. The potential problem is that, by considering each of these issues, one after the other, one slowly gets the impression that they are equally valid; that is most emphatically not the case. Not all critiques are equal. Although this is perfectly obvious, sometimes in the day-to-day encounter of book after book after book, reading one review after another, one periodical following the next, the arguments begin to bleed into each other, and they begin to weigh upon the reader, eventually producing the feeling that all views have equal weight. They do not, of course, but, over time, even the most radical ideas begin to have the appearance of reasonableness. We have seen repeated examples where relatively peripheral issues take on central importance. Nowhere is this more true than in the doctrine of justification. We have, for example, already observed where evangelicals refer to "the gospel of justification by faith."[1] In such instances, these authors are taking a biblical doctrine and, knowingly or not, making it synonymous with the gospel itself, thereby giving it greater weight than the authors of the biblical texts did. By using the expression "the gospel of justification," they have made justification tantamount to the gospel itself.

To be sure, justification is a crucial element of the gospel, but it is only one aspect. At best, justification might be a synecdoche for the gospel, in which a single part represents the whole. Thus, the doctrine is very important, but we must also be careful not to emphasize it beyond measure. While justification addresses the legal aspect of our redemption, other facets address the other areas of our sinful condition. For example, the NT teaching of Christ as our ransom is designed to address, at least in part, our enslavement to sin and what we suffer as a result of it. Other aspects of the gospel address the problems of shame, fear, etc., each focused on specific aspects of our sinful condition. The point here is that justification, rather than being a central organizing principle for the apostles' theology, seems instead to be one of several theological concepts that constitute the gospel. It should not be equated with the gospel, but is itself a part of the gospel message.

The upshot of this is that when we survey large amounts of intellectual material it is easy to unintentionally assign equal significance to all the elements. Conversely, in guarding against such a danger, an alternate risk would be to unconsciously attribute too much importance to certain ideas and/or not enough to others.[2] There is a *tertium quid* (i.e., a third option),

---

1. For example, Martin Luther, in his commentary on Galatian, argues for "the gospel of justification by faith" (Luther, *St. Paul's Epistle*, 206). Likewise, some of the best-known evangelicals throughout history were known for using this kind of nomenclature, e.g., Buchannan, *Doctrine of Justification*, 221, 226, 227, 330, 331, 345; the published sermons of Spurgeon, *Justification by Faith*; and, more recently, Bornkamm, *Jesus of Nazareth*, 128; Sproul, *Focus on the Bible*, 173; and Longman and Garland, eds., Rom 4:31 in *Romans—Galatians*.

2. Carson expressed a similar concern when he wrote, "I fear that the cross, without ever being disowned, is constantly in danger of being dismissed from the central place it must enjoy, by relatively peripheral insights that take on far too much weight. Whenever the periphery is in danger of displacing the center, we are not far removed from idolatry" (*Cross and Christian Ministry*, 26).

however. This third choice is to proceed with the survey of the intellectual material, while deliberately and self-consciously identifying those things of greatest importance and those that are less significant. This is the path we have attempted.

Sections 5 and 6 represent, perhaps, our most constructive contribution in this project. Up to that point, most of what is addressed can be found in other works. However, in sections 5 and 6, we began examining the creation account. Yet our focus was not so much on the typical questions found related to Gen 1–3 (e.g., alternate creation myths, literal vs. figurative days, authorship of Gen., etc.), but was instead on the recurring expression, "God said . . . and there was . . ." This was set in tension with the assertion that it was "the Spirit of God" which was "over the face of the deep." Our conclusion is that the expression "God said" is equivalent to "the Holy Spirit said" and/or "the Holy Spirit did . . ." Nor should we confine this relationship to Genesis, since the author of Hebrews repeatedly quotes statements from Yahweh in the Hebrew Bible, only to preface these citations with the words, "As *the Holy Spirit* says . . . " The conclusion is that what "Yahweh says," the "Holy Spirit says." Moreover, we noted the Hebrew expression for "the word of the Lord" (דְּבַר־יְהוָה, *dābār YHWH*), is vastly more flexible than our English translations suggest. When we compare the usage of this phrase in the LXX we again discover that "what God says" means "the Holy Spirit does."

Further, as we looked at the way the NT authors used the expression δικαιοσύνη (*righteousness* or *justice*), a number of seemingly disparate pieces coalesced nicely. We noted, for example, that when the NT writers use this term (δικαιόω), it means *to declare righteous*.[3] What Protestants have observed for the past five hundred years is still true: justification is first and foremost something God *says* about a person—he declares them to be a certain way. Thus, in saying something about them, the Holy Spirit is also doing something for them and in them. What that something is, must

---

3. Contra Macchia, who writes, "*declared* or *imputed* righteousness tends to be inadequate to capture the full depth and breadth of justification" (Macchia, *Justified in the Spirit*, 50). At one level, Macchia is certainly correct. No individual word or term can capture the "full depth and breadth of justification." However, at another level, he is mistaken. The biblical authors themselves seemed to think the δικ- word group was an adequate medium to express their ideas. For example, as stated previously, in Luke 7:29, ἐδικαίωσαν (third person, plural, aorist, active, indicative) clearly means *to declare*. "And all the people that heard *him*, and the publicans, *justified God* (ἐδικαίωσαν), being baptized with the baptism of John" (ASV; italics added). Macchia's aversion to such forensic language is palpable in several places. For example, he writes that he wants to "deliver" the doctrine of justification from "a Spiritless declared righteousness" (Macchia, *Justified in the Spirit*, 73).

be explained exclusively in terms of justification itself (for that is how Paul himself circumscribes the use of the idea). However, if we acknowledge the imputation of Christ's righteousness as an aspect of justification (we recognize that not everyone will), we can at least say that, in justification, the Holy Spirit is the active agent in the legal application of Christ's righteousness to the believer. As for the specific means through which this takes place, it is accomplished through faith. Such an approach preserves the Protestant Reformers' rediscovery of the biblical doctrine of justification by faith alone, with its distinction between our judicial standing and acceptance before God and our actual and progressive growth in holiness. On the other hand, it addresses the concerns raised by Frank Macchia[4] and others that justification must be pneumatologically informed.

By way of reminder, since the days of the Cappadocian fathers, the church has universally maintained that "the external works of the Trinity are undivided" (*opera trinitatis ad extra sunt indivisa*). This is to say, that in every act God performs, all three persons of the Godhead are involved. With this in mind, the question was asked, Where is the Holy Spirit in the Protestant formulation of justification?[5] Since the Protestant Reformation, justification has been understood as a legal declaration which the Father makes regarding the believer, based upon the work of the Son. As Macchia et al. have noted, the problem with the classic Protestant formulation is the absence of the Holy Spirit. However, rather than jettisoning the Protestant understanding of justification as suggested by Macchia et al., this proposal addresses that concern. We are saying, in effect, that the Holy Spirit is intricately involved in the Protestant understanding of justification, as he is the very agent of its implementation—its execution. As Daniel Gilbert notes, "The Holy Spirit is . . . the Person who executes the whole work of God the Father and God the Son. Without God the Spirit, the work of [justification] cannot be accomplished."[6] Thus, there is no need to throw-out the Reformation understanding of justification and redefine it from the ground up as a number of contemporary theologians have attempted (e.g., Macchia,[7]

4. Macchia, "Justification through New Creation," 207–17.

5. Macchia, "Justification through New Creation," 216.

6. Gilbert, "Pneumatic *Charismata*," 17.

7. Justification is understood fundamentally as the "divine embrace." See Macchia, *Justified in the Spirit*, 24. Macchia cites with approval Eberhard Jüngel, when Jüngel wrote, "To put it briefly: We are talking about the raising of Jesus Christ from the dead and about our participation in his life and resurrection" (as quoted in Macchia, *Justified in the Spirit*, 71). Macchia states his understanding more specifically when he writes, "In my view, the notion of covenant faithfulness as a description of justifying righteousness needs to be expanded by such concepts as righteousness as a redemptive reality, justification as vindication of the messianic ruler, and, ultimately, the gift of

Wright,[8] et al.). Rather, we can build *on* the work of the Reformers, extending it and elaborating it in the places where they were silent.

The ideas under the section on speech-act theory may be the most original and, simultaneously, may hold the most potential for future study. However, I want to be clear about my personal objectives—my perlocutionary aims. Unlike some of my colleagues, I do not view novelty to be an appropriate goal in theological exploration. If there are genuinely novel ideas within this work, novelty itself has not been the goal. Rather, in keeping with the early church, my primary objective has been to "receive and reappropriate the faith" within my own context. This, of course, may involve a kind of innovation all its own. Nevertheless, my goal has been more pastoral in nature: it is to faithfully receive the biblical message and contextualize it within my own environment. In this case, that has meant receiving the message of justification and addressing the lacuna of pneumatology. Thus I do not view originality with hostility *per se*, but only with a kind of caution, recognizing that it, like a number of other things (such as money, power, etc.) can easily be misused and become an end in itself. The kind of underlying concern I have had throughout the process of writing this work was articulated by Thomas Oden, when he stated that his goal was to develop a theology built primarily from the leaders of the first five centuries of the church:

> I do not quote these theologians in order to make intellectual heroes of them or to treat them as geniuses or creative innovators. Oddly enough, most of them, insofar as they were orthodox, were self-consciously *un*original in desiring not to add anything to an already sufficient apostolic faith *but only to receive and reappropriate that faith creatively in their particular historical setting and language.* They were not seeking to invent new ideas but simply and plainly to understand God's goodness and purpose. There was indeed creative genius at work in the communities of orthodoxy, but the individual teachers who best served those communities did not think of themselves as creative geniuses; they knew that it was the community itself that was brilliant and made brilliant by the power of the Spirit. The

---

righteousness through 'God with us' or the outpouring of the Spirit" (Macchia, *Justified in the* Spirit, 105).

8. "'Justification' in the first century was not about how someone might establish a relationship with God. It was about God's eschatological definition, both future and present, of who was, in fact, a member of his people. In Sanders's terms, it was not so much about 'getting in,' or indeed about 'staying in,' as about 'how you could tell who was in.' In standard Christian theological language, it wasn't so much about soteriology as about ecclesiology; not so much about salvation as about the church" (Wright, *What Saint Paul Really Said*, 119).

most powerful writers . . . were those who most ably and simply gave expression to the faith that was already well understood generally by the community.[9]

Thus I feel the freedom to utilize innovation within the theological discipline, in so far as it is in the service of the much greater end of God's glory. Jonathan Edwards summarized the point I am trying to make: "The great end of God's works, which is so variously expressed in Scripture, is indeed but *one*; and this one end is most properly and comprehensively called, *The Glory of God*."[10] We are to do all things—*all things*, including research, reading, writing—to God's glory. John Piper captured the pathos of this conviction well:

> We were made to know and treasure the glory of God above all things; and when we trade that treasure for images, everything is disordered. The sun of God's glory was made to shine at the center of the solar system of our soul. And when it does, all the planets of our life are held in their proper orbit. But when the sun is displaced, everything flies apart. The healing of the soul begins by restoring the glory of God to its flaming, all-attracting place at the center. We are all starved for the glory of God, not self. No one goes to the Grand Canyon to increase self-esteem. Why do we go? Because there is a greater healing for the soul in beholding splendor than there is in beholding self.[11]

Nor is this some mere ephemeral idea. It is, rather, *the* idea pervading virtually all the biblical material, from beginning to end. The cross of Christ, which the apostle so emphatically sought to "glory" in, is itself intended as

---

9. Oden, *Systematic Theology*, 1:xi; italics added, except for "*un*original" (italicized in original). For example, at the beginning of Oden's final volume, he reiterates what he refers to as his "Modest Reaffirmations"—convictions that guided his three-volume work. He writes, "At the end of this journey I reaffirm solemn commitments made at its beginning:
- To make no new contribution to theology.
- To resist the temptation to quote modern writers less schooled in the whole counsel of God than the best ancient classic exegetes.
- To seek quite simply to express the one mind of the believing church that has been ever attentive to that apostolic teaching to which consent has been given by Christian believers everywhere, always, and by all.

Oden goes on to say, "I am dedicated to unoriginality . . . I am pledged to irrelevance if relevance means indebtedness to corrupt modernity. What is deemed relevant in theology is likely to be moldy in a few days" (*Systematic Theology*, 2:vii). See also Oden, *Systematic Theology*, 1:322–5, 341–51.

10. Edwards, *Dissertation* in *Works of Jonathan Edwards*, 1:119.

11. Piper, *Seeing and Savoring*, 21.

a means of bringing glory to God. It seems clear from the Bible that "God loves His glory! He is committed with all His infinite and eternal might to display that glory and to preserve the honor of His name."[12] Moreover, when we are overwhelmed by the ubiquitous biblical truth of God's preeminence in his own mind, then his supremacy in our minds is utterly irresistible.[13] There is another reason to feel the sense of overwhelmedness at God's preeminence in his own mind. "Many people are willing to be God-centered as long as they feel that God is man-centered. It is a subtle danger. We may think we are centering our lives on God, when we are really making Him a means to self-esteem."[14]

The catechism teaches that humanity's "chief end" (or "primary purpose") is to "glorify God and enjoy him forever."[15] So, too, God's primary purpose is to glorify God and enjoy himself forever.[16] God declares, with a kind of sledgehammer force, "*For my name's sake* I defer my anger, *for the sake of my praise* I restrain it for you, that I may not cut you off.... *For my own sake, for my own sake*, I do it, for how should my name be profaned? My glory I will not give to another" (Isa 48:9, 11 ESV; italics added). Through this kind of repetition, the God of glory makes plain *his* central concern: "For *my* name's sake ... for the sake of *my* praise ... for *my* own sake! For *my* own sake ... *my* glory I will not give to another!" This passage bellows forth the centrality of God's glory in his own mind and affections. Thus that which drives God's actions is not, in the first instance, paternal love (although it is certainly true that God loves us paternally). While there is no question that God's redemptive purpose is motivated by his love, such goals are penultimate, not ultimate, because man is penultimate, not ultimate. This idea may seem odd, because we are "more accustomed to think about our duty than God's design. And when we do ask about God's design, we are too prone to describe it with ourselves at the center of God's affections."[17] But the impetus behind God's actions—his primary purpose—is that "all the earth will be filled with the glory of the Lord" (Num 14:21).[18] God's

---

12. Piper, *Brothers*, 8.
13. See Piper, "Supremacy of God in the Life of the Mind."
14. Piper, *Brothers*, 6–7.
15. The first question/answer of the *Westminster Shorter Catechism* reads: "Q. What is the chief end of man? A. Man's chief end is to glorify God, and to enjoy him forever." Similarly, a modernized version (one I used with my own children) asks, "Q. What is humanity's primary purpose? A. Our primary purpose is to glorify God and enjoy him forever!" See Meade, *Training Hearts*, 3.
16. See Piper, *Desiring God*, 40.
17. Piper, *Desiring God*, 31.
18. Cf. Ps 72:19; Isa 6:3; Hab 2:14.

highest commitment is to himself. Even God's redemptive work is driven by the allegiance he has to the honor of his name. "I, I am He who blots out your transgressions *for my own sake*, and I will not remember your sins" (Isa 43:25 NRSV; italics added). Christ's saving work—including justification—is driven by a desire within the Godhead to purchase men for God from "every tribe and language and people and nation" that he might be glorified (Rev 5:9). We receive the forgiveness of our sins, the imputation of Christ's righteousness, and everything else we need "for life and godliness" (2 Pet 1:3), and God is glorified. We are helped, he is honored; we are exonerated, he is exalted. It is without doubt the greatest arrangement the world has ever known.

Bibliography

Adam, A. K. M., ed. *Postmodern Interpretations of the Bible: A Reader*. Atlanta: Chalice, 2001.
Akin, James. "Setting the Record Straight." http://www.catholicculture.org/culture/library/view.cfm?recnum=1369.
Aland, Kurt. *Four Reformers: Luther, Melanchthon, Calvin, Zwingli*. Minneapolis: Augsburg, 1979.
Albertus Magnus. *Opera Omnia*. Edited by S. C. A. Borgnet. 38 vols. Paris: Vives, 1809.
Albrecht, Daniel. *Rites of the Spirit: A Ritual Approach to Pentecostal/Charismatic Spirituality*. Sheffield, UK: Sheffield Academic, 1999.
Albright, William Foxwell. *From the Stone Age to Christianity*. Baltimore: Johns Hopkins University Press, 1946.
Alexander of Hales (attributed). *Summa theologica*. 4 vols. Quaracchi, It.: Typographia Collegii S. Bonaventurae, 1924–48.
Alexander, Archibald. *The Doctrine of Justification*. Charlotte, NC: Strait Gate, 1992.
Alexander, Donald L. *Christian Spirituality: Five Views on Sanctification*. Downers Grove, IL: InterVarsity, 1988.
Alexander, Eric J. "The Basis of Christian Salvation: Urbana 1984 Exposition of Ephesians 1:1–14." https://urbana.org/transcript/basis-christian-salvation.
Alexander, T. Desmond. *Abraham in the Negev: A Source-Critical Investigation of Genesis 20:1–22:19*. Carlisle, UK: Paternoster, 1997.
―――. "Authorship of the Pentateuch." In *Dictionary of the Old Testament: Pentateuch*, edited by T. Desmond Alexander and David W. Baker, 61–73. IVP Bible Dictionary Series 1. Downers Grove, IL: InterVarsity, 2003.
―――. *From Paradise to the Promised Land: An Introduction to the Pentateuch*. Grand Rapids: Baker Academic, 2002.
Allen, R. Michael. *Justification and the Gospel: Understanding the Contexts and Controversies*. Grand Rapids: Baker Academic, 2013.
Alonzo Church. "A Formulation of the Simple Theory of Types." *Journal of Symbolic Logic* 5, no. 2 (June 1940) 56–68.
Alston, William P. *Philosophy of Language*. Englewood Cliffs, NJ: Prentice-Hall, 1964.

Alter, Robert. *Ancient Israel: The Former Prophets: Joshua, Judges, Samuel, and Kings: A Translation with Commentary*. New York: W. W. Norton, 2013.

———. *The Art of Biblical Narrative*. New York: Basic, 1981.

———. *The Five Books of Moses: A Translation with Commentary*. New York: W.W. Norton, 2004.

———. *The Invention of Hebrew Prose: Modern Fiction and the Language Revolution*. Seattle: University of Washington Press, 1988.

Althaus, Paul. *The Theology of Martin Luther*. Minneapolis: Fortress, 1966.

Ames, William. "Justification." https://www.apuritansmind.com/puritan-favorites/william-ames/justification/.

———. *Marrow of Theology*. Edited and translated by John D. Eusden. Durham, NC: Labyrinth, 1968.

Anderson, Jeffrey K. "The Holy Spirit and Justification: A Pneumatological and Trinitarian Approach to Forensic Justification." *Evangelical Review of Theology* 32, no. 4 (Oct. 2008) 292–305.

———. "Justification as the Speech of the Spirit." PhD diss., Regent University, 2015.

Anselm of Canterbury. *Basic Writings*. Translated by S. N. Deane. La Salle, IL: Open Court, 1962.

———. *Cur Deus Homo*. In *Saint Anselm: Basic Writings*, translated by S. N. Deane, 198–251. La Salle, IL: Open Court, 1968.

———. *Proslogion*. Edited and translated by M. J. Charlesworth. Notre Dame, IN: University of Notre Dame Press, 1979.

Aquinas, St. Thomas. *Summa Theologica*. Translated by the Fathers of the English Dominican Province. 5 vols. New York: Christian Classics, 1948.

Archer, Kenneth. *A Pentecostal Hermeneutic for the Twenty-First Century: Spirit, Scripture, and Community*. New York: T. & T. Clark International, 2004.

———. "The Spirit and Theological Interpretation: A Pentecostal Strategy." *Cyberjournal for Pentecostal-Charismatic Research* 16 (Jan. 2007). http://www.pctii.org/cyberj/cyberj16/archer.html.

Archimandrite George of Mount Athos. *Theosis: The True Purpose of Human Life*. Mount Athos, Greece: Holy Monastery of St. Gregorios, 2006.

Athanasius. *Letter 60, to Adelphus: 4*. In *Nicene and Post-Nicene Fathers*, edited by Philip Schaff, 4:1334–40. Peabody, MA: Hendrickson, 2004.

———. *The Letters of Saint Athanasius Concerning the Holy Spirit*. Edited and translated by C. R. B. Shapland. Reprint, Eugene, OR: Wipf & Stock, 2006.

Augustine. *St. Augustin: Anti-Pelagian Writings*. Vol. 5 of *Nicene and Post-Nicene Fathers*, 1st ser., edited by Philip Schaff. Albany, OR: AGES, 1997.

———. *Sermon 52*. In *The Works of Saint Augustine: A Translation for the Twenty-First Century*, edited by John E. Rotelle, translated by Edmund Hill, 3:22–51. New York: New City, 1994.

Aulén, Gustaf. *Christus Victor: An Historical Study of the Three Main Types of the Idea of the Atonement*. Eugene, OR: Wipf & Stock, 2003.

Aune, David E. *Rereading Paul Together: Protestant and Catholic Perspectives on Justification*. Grand Rapids: Baker Academic, 2006.

Austin, J. L. *Collected Papers*. Edited by J. O. Urmson and G. J. Warnock. Oxford: Oxford University Press, 1979.

———. *How to Do Things with Words*. Cambridge, MA: Harvard University Press, 1975.

———. "Three Ways of Spilling Ink." Edited by L. W. Ferguson. *Philosophical Review* 75, no. 4 (Oct. 1966) 427–40. http://www.jstor.org/stable/2183222.
Bailey, Daniel P. "Jesus as the Mercy Seat: The Semantics and Theology of Paul's use of *Hilasterion* in Romans 3:25." PhD diss., Cambridge University, 1999.
Baillie, D. M. *God Was in Christ: An Essay on Incarnation and Atonement*. New York: Charles Scribner's Sons, 1948.
Bainton, Roland H. *Erasmus of Christendom*. New York: Charles Scribner's Sons, 1969.
———. *Here I Stand: A Life of Martin Luther*. N.p.: Read Books, 2014. Kindle.
Baird, William. *History of New Testament Research: From Deism to Tübingen*. Minneapolis: Fortress, 1992.
———. *The Quest of the Christ of Faith: Reflections on the Bultmannian Era*. Waco, TX: Word, 1977.
Barackman, Floyd H. *Practical Christian Theology: Examining the Great Doctrines of the Faith*. 3rd ed. Grand Rapids: Kregel, 2001.
Barr, James. *Beyond Fundamentalism: Biblical Foundations for Evangelical Christianity*. Louisville: Westminster, 1984.
———. *Escaping from Fundamentalism*. London: SCM, 2012.
———. *Fundamentalism*. Louisville: Westminster, 1978.
———. *Holy Scripture: Canon, Authority, Criticism*. Philadelphia: Westminster, 1983.
Barrett, Matthew, ed. *The Doctrine on Which the Church Stands or Fall: Justification in Biblical, Theological, Historical, and Pastoral Perspective*. Wheaton:, IL: Crossway, 2019.
Barth, Karl. *Church Dogmatics*, 1/1. Edited by G. W. Bromiley and T. F. Torrance, translated by G. W. Bromiley. Edinburgh: T. & T. Clark, 1975.
———. *Church Dogmatics*, 2/1. Edited by G. W. Bromiley and T. F. Torrance, translated by G. W. Bromiley. Edinburgh: T. & T. Clark, 1975.
———. *The Epistle to the Romans*. Translated by Edwyn C. Hoskyns. Oxford: Oxford University Press, 1933.
———. *The Word of God and the Word of Man*. Translated by Douglas Horton. Grand Rapids: Zondervan, 1935.
Bartholomew, Craig G. "Postmodernity and Biblical Interpretation." In *Dictionary for Theological Interpretation of the Bible*, edited by Kevin J. Vanhoozer et al., 600–7. Grand Rapids: Baker Academic, 2005.
Bartsch, Hans-Werner. "Bultmann and Jaspers." In *Kerygma and Myth: A Theological Debate*, edited by Hans-Werner Bartsch, translated by Reginald H. Fuller, 199–221. London: SPCK, 1962.
Basil the Great. *On the Holy Spirit*. New York: St. Vladimir's Seminary Press, 1980.
Bartos, Emil. *Deification in Eastern Orthodox Theology: An Evaluation and Critique of the Theology of Dumitru Stăniloae*. Carlisle, U.K.: Paternoster, 1999.
Bauckham, Richard. *The Bible in Politics: How to Read the Bible Politically*. Louisville: Westminster/John Knox, 1989.
Baxter, Richard. *Imputative Righteousness: Truly Stated, According to the Tenour of the Gospel*. London: J. D., 1679.
Bayer, Oswald. *Martin Luthers Theologie: Eine Vergegenwärtigung Taschenbuch*. Tübingen, Germ.: Mohr Siebeck, 2007.
Berkhof, Louis *Principles of Biblical Interpretation*. Grand Rapids: Baker, 1977.
———. *Systematic Theology*. Grand Rapids: Eerdmans, 1938.

Beza, Theodore. *The Life of John Calvin*. Translated by Henry Beveridge. London: Forgotten Books, 2013.
Birdsall, J. N. "Logos." In *The New Bible Dictionary*, edited by D. R. W. Wood, 395–6. Wheaton, IL: Tyndale, 1962.
Blatt, Lauren. "Luther and the Holy Spirit in the Catechisms." *Thinking Theologian*, Jan. 1, 2014. http://thinkingtheologian1.blogspot.com/2014/01.
Bloesch, Donald G. *A New Handbook of Christian Theology*. Nashville: Abingdon, 1992.
———. *Holy Scripture: Revelation, Inspiration and Interpretation*. Christian Foundations 2. Downers Grove, IL: InterVarsity, 1994.
Bock, Darrell L. "Single Meaning, Multiple Contexts and Referents: The New Testament's Legitimate, Accurate, and Multifaceted Use of the Old." In *Three Views on the New Testament Use of the Old Testament*, edited by Kenneth Berding, 105–51. Grand Rapids: Zondervan, 2009.
Bornkamm, Gunther. *Jesus of Nazareth*. New York: Harper & Brothers, 1960.
Bouman, Herbert. "The Doctrine of Justification in the Lutheran Confessions." *Concordia Theological Monthly* 26, no. 11 (Nov. 1955) 801–19.
Bouwsma, William J. *John Calvin: A Sixteenth-Century Portrait*. New York: Oxford University Press, 1988.
Bray, Gerald L. "Late-Medieval Theology." In *Reformation Theology: A Systematic Summary*, edited by Matthew Barrett, 67–110. Wheaton, IL: Crossway, 2017.
———, ed. *Galatians, Ephesians*. Reformation Commentary on Scripture: New Testament 10. Downers Grove, IL: InterVarsity, 2011.
Bridges, Jerry. *The Discipline of Grace: God's Role and Our Role in the Pursuit of Holiness*. Colorado Springs: NavPress, 1994.
Broun, John. "The Life of Justification Opened: A Treatise Grounded upon Gal. 2." https://quod.lib.umich.edu/e/eebo/A29752.0001.001?view=toc.
Brown, Francis, Samuel Rolles Driver, and Charles Augustus Briggs. *The Enhanced Brown-Driver-Briggs Hebrew and English Lexicon*. Oak Harbor, WA: Logos, 2000. Logos.
Buchannan, James. *The Doctrine of Justification*. Grand Rapids: Solid Ground Christian Books, 2006.
Bucher, Richard P. "Is a Christian 'Once Saved Always Saved'?" http://lutherantheologystudygroup.blogspot.com/2013/08/is-christian-once-saved-always-saved-dr.html.
Burnett, Richard E. *Karl Barth's Theological Exegesis*. Tübingen, Germ.: Mohr Siebeck, 2001.
Calvin, John. *Autobiographical Sketch from the Dedication of the Commentary on the Psalms*. In *Calvin: Commentaries*, edited by Joseph Haroutunian, 53. Library of Christian Classics. Philadelphia: Westminster John Knox, 1979.
———. *Calvin's Commentaries*. 22 vols. Translated by William Pringle. Grand Rapids: Baker, 1996.
———. *Canons and Decrees*. In *Selected Works of John Calvin: Tracts and Letters*, edited and translated by Henry Beveridge, edited by Jules Bonnet, 3:17–188. 7 vols. Reprint, Grand Rapids: Baker, 1983.
———. *Commentary on Galatians and Ephesians*. Christian Classics Ethereal Library. https://ccel.org/ccel/calvin/calcom41.html.
———. *Commentary on the Epistle of Paul the Apostle to the Romans*. Translated by Henry Beveridge. Vol. 38 of *Calvin's Commentaries*. Grand Rapids: Baker, 1979.
———. *Commentary on the Epistle to the Ephesians*. Reprint, Albany, OR: AGES, 1998.

———. *Commentary on the Epistle to the Galatians*. Translated by Theodore Graebner. Albany, OR: AGES, 1998.

———. *Commentary on the Epistle to Titus*. Reprint, Albany, OR: AGES, 1998.

———. *Grace and Its Fruits: Selections from John Calvin on the Pastoral Epistles*, edited by Joseph Hill. Darlington, UK: Evangelical, 2000.

———. *Institutes of the Christian Religion*. Edited by John T. McNeill, translated by Ford Lewis Battles. Louisville: Westminster John Knox, 2011.

———. *Institutes of the Christian Religion*. Translated by Ford Lewis Battles. Grand Rapids: Eerdmans, 1995.

———. *Institutes of the Christian Religion*. Translated by Henry Beveridge. Bellingham, WA: Logos Bible Software, 1997. Logos.

———. *Tracts Relating to the Reformation*. 3 vols. Translated by Henry Beveridge. Eugene, OR: Wipf & Stock, 2002.

Calvin, John, and Theodore Beza. *Tracts Relating to the Reformation*. 7 vols. Carlisle, PA: Banner of Truth, 2009.

Campbell, Douglas A. *The Deliverance of God: An Apocalyptic Rereading of Justification in Paul*. Grand Rapids: Eerdmans, 2013.

———. *The Quest for Paul's Gospel: A Suggested Strategy*. London: Continuum, 2005.

Carson, D.A. *Basics for Believers: An Exposition of Philippians*. Grand Rapids: Baker, 1996.

———. *Collected Writings on Scripture*. Wheaton, IL: Crossway, 2010.

———. *The Cross and Christian Ministry: An Exposition of Passages from 1 Corinthians*. Grand Rapids: Baker, 1993.

———. *The Gagging of God*. Grand Rapids: Zondervan, 2002.

———. "Redaction Criticism: On the Legitimacy and Illegitimacy of a Literary Tool." In *Scripture and Truth*, edited by D. A. Carson and John D. Woodbridge, 115–42. Grand Rapids: Zondervan, 1983.

———. "The Many Facets of the Current Discussion." In *The Enduring Authority of the Christian Scriptures*, edited by D. A. Carson, loc. 373–1248. Grand Rapids: Eerdmans, 2016. Kindle.

———. "Three More Books on the Bible: A Critical Review." In *Collected Writings on Scripture*, loc. 5532–6964. Wheaton, IL: Crossway, 2010. Kindle.

Carson, D. A., ed. *Biblical Interpretation and the Church: Text and Context*. Reprint, Exeter, UK: Paternoster, 1984.

———. *The Church in the Bible and the World: An International Study*. Grand Rapids: Baker, 1987.

———. "Introduction." In *The Complexities of Second Temple Judaism*, edited by D.A. Carson et al. Vol. 1 of *Justification and Variegated Nomism*. Grand Rapids: Baker, 2001.

Carson, D. A., et al., eds. *The Paradoxes of Paul*. Vol. 2 of *Justification and Variegated Nomism*. Grand Rapids: Baker Academic, 2004.

Carson, D. A., and Stanley E. Porter, eds. *Discourse Analysis and Other Topics in Biblical Greek*. Sheffield, UK: JSOT, 1995.

Carson, D. A., and H. G. M. Williamson, eds. *It is Written: Scripture Citing Scripture—Essays in Honour of Barnabas Lindars, SSF*. Cambridge, UK: Cambridge University Press, 1988.

Carson, D. A., and John D. Woodbridge, eds. *Hermeneutics, Authority, and Canon*. Grand Rapids: Zondervan, 1986.

Cary, Phillip. *Luther: Gospel, Law, and Reformation.* 24 lectures. Chantey, VA: The Teaching Company, 2004. DVD.
Chappell, Bryan. *Christ-Centered Preaching: Redeeming the Expository Sermon.* 2nd ed. Grand Rapids: Baker Academic, 2005.
Chester, Tim. "Justification, Ecclesiology and the New Perspective." *Them* 30, no. 2 (2005) 5–20.
Chisholm, Hugh. "Supererogation." In *Encyclopedia Britannica.* Cambridge, UK: Cambridge University Press, 1911.
Clark, Gordon Haddon. *God's Hammer.* Unicoi, TN: Trinity Foundation, 1995.
———. *In Defense of Theology.* Fenton, MI: Mott Media, 1984.
———. *Language and Theology.* Unicoi, TN: Trinity Foundation, 1993.
———. *Religion, Reason, and Revelation.* Unicoi, TN: Trinity Foundation, 1995.
———. *Today's Evangelism: Counterfeit or Genuine?* Unicoi, TN: Trinity Foundation, 1990.
Congregation for the Doctrine of the Faith and the Pontifical Council for Promoting Christian Unity. *Response of the Catholic Church to the Joint Declaration of the Catholic Church and the Lutheran World Federation on the Doctrine of Justification.* http://www.christianunity.va/content/unitacristiani/en/dialoghi/sezione-occidentale/luterani/dialogo/documenti-di-dialogo/1999-dichiarazione-congiunta-sulla-dottrina-della-giustificazion/en1.html.
Copi, Irving M. *Introduction to Logic.* 3rd ed. New York: MacMillan, 1968.
Cottret, Bernard. *Calvin: A Biography.* Translated by M. Wallace McDonald. Grand Rapids: Eerdmans, 2000.
Council of Trent. "On Justification." http://www.thecounciloftrent.com/ch6.htm.
Cranfield, C. E. B. *A Critical and Exegetical Commentary on the Epistle to the Romans.* Reprinted with corrections. Vol. 24A of *The International Critical Commentary on the Holy Scriptures of the Old and New Testaments.* Edinburgh: T. & T. Clark, 2004.
Cremer, Hermann. *Paulinische Rechtfertigungslehre im Zusammenhange ihrer geschichtlichen Voraussetzungen.* Reprint, Whitefish, MT: Kessinger, 2010.
Daniels, Richard. *The Christology of John Owen.* Grand Rapids: Reformation Heritage Books, 2004.
Dillenberger, John, ed. *John Calvin: Selections from His Writings.* Oxford: Oxford University Press, 1975.
———. *Martin Luther.* New York: Doubleday, 1961.
Dilthey, Wilhelm. *Leben Schleiermachers.* Vol. 1. Berlin: Georg Reimer, 1870. Logos.
Donaldson, Terence L. *Paul and the Gentiles: Remapping the Apostle's Convictional World.* Minneapolis: Fortress, 1997.
Dooling, D.J. and R. Lachman. "Effects of Comprehension on Retention of Prose." *Journal of Experimental Psychology* 88, no. 2 (1971) 216-22.
Doumergue, Emile. *Calvin and the Reformation: Four Studies.* Reprint, Whitefish, MT: Kessinger, 2008.
Drewery, Benjamin. "Introduction." In *Luther's Works*, edited by Helmut T. Lehman, translated by Philip S. Watson, 33:5–19. Philadelphia: Fortress, 1999.
Dulles, Avery. "Justification in Contemporary Catholic Theology." In *Justification by Faith: Lutherans and Catholics in Dialogue*, edited by H. George Anderson et al., 256-77. Minneapolis: Augsburg, 1985.
———. "Justification: The Joint Declaration." *Josephinum Journal of Theology* 9, no. 1 (Winter/Spring 2002) 108–19. http://www.pcj.edu/journal/essays/dulles9–1.htm.

Dunn, James D.G. *The Epistle to the Galatians*. Peabody, MA: Hendrickson, 1993.
———. *Jesus, Paul and the Law: Studies in Mark and Galatians*. Louisville: Westminster/John Knox, 1999.
———. *The Living Word*. Minneapolis: Fortress, 2009.
———. *The New Perspective on Paul*. Grand Rapids: Eerdmans, 2008.
———. "New Perspective View." In *Justification: Five Views*, edited by James K. Beilby et al. Downers Grove, IL: IVP Academic, 2011. Kindle.
———. "Paul's Theology." In *The Face of New Testament Studies*, edited by Scot McKnight et al., 326–48. Grand Rapids: Baker Academic, 2004.
———. Review of *Justification and Variegated Nomism*. Vol. 1: *The Complexities of Second Temple Judaism*, edited by D. A. Carson et al. *Trinity Journal* 25, no. 1 (2004) 111–13.
———. *Romans 1—8*. Word Biblical Commentary 10. Dallas: Word, 1988.
———. *The Theology of Paul the Apostle*. Grand Rapids: Eerdmans, 2006.
Durant, Will. *The Reformation: The Story of Civilization*. New York: MJF Books, 1993.
Du Toit, Andrie B. "Forensic Metaphors in Romans and Their Soteriological Significance." In *Salvation in the New Testament: Perspectives on Soteriology*, edited by Jan G. van der Watt, 213–46. Supplements to Novum Testamentum 121. Leiden, Neth.: Brill, 2005.
Eberhard, Philippe. *The Middle Voice in Gadamer's Hermeneutics*. Tübingen, Germ.: Mohr Siebeck, 2004.
Eco, Umberto. *Interpretation and Overinterpretation*. Edited by Stefan Collini. Tanner Lectures in Human Values Series. Reprint, New York: Cambridge University Press, 1992.
Edwards, Jonathan. *A Dissertation Concerning the End for Which God Created the World*. Edited by Sereno Dwight. Carlisle, PA: Banner of Truth, 1974.
———. "The Miscellanies." In *The Works of Jonathan Edwards*, edited by Thomas Schafer, 495. New Haven, CT: Yale University Press, 1994.
———. *A Treatise Concerning Religious Affections*. Faithful Classic. N.p.: Prisbrary, 2012. Kindle.
———. *The Works of Jonathan Edwards*. Edited by Edward Hickman. 2 vols. N.p.: B&R Samizdat Express, 2011. Kindle.
Engle, Paul E. and Steve B. Cowan, eds. *Who Runs the Church? Four Views on Church Government*. Grand Rapids: Zondervan, 2004.
"English Bible History: John Calvin." http://www.greatsite.com/timeline-english-bible-history/john-calvin.html.
Erasmus, Desiderius, and Martin Luther. *A Diatribe or Discourse Concerning Free Will*. Edited and translated by Ernst F. Winter. New York: Continuum, 2005.
Erickson, Millard J. *Christian Theology*. Grand Rapids: Baker Academic, 2013.
Evans, Eifion. "John Calvin, Theologian of the Holy Spirit." *Reformation and Revival* 10, no. 4 (Fall 2001) 83–104.
Fackre, Gabriel. "Revelation." In *Karl Barth and Evangelical Theology: Convergences and Divergences*, edited by Sung Wook Chung, 1–25. Grand Rapids: Baker, 2006.
Fagin, Ronald, et al. *Reasoning About Knowledge*. Cambridge, MA: MIT, 2003.
Farnell, F. David. "The New Perspective on Paul: Its Basic Tenets, History, and Presuppositions." *Master's Seminary Journal* 16, no. 2 (Fall 2005) 189–243.
Fee, Gordon D. "The Epistle to the Galatians." 2 MP3 disks. Vancouver: Regent Audio, 1997.

———. *God's Empowering Presence: The Holy Spirit in the Letters of Paul.* Peabody, MA: Hendrickson, 1994.

———. *Listening to the Spirit in the Text.* Grand Rapids: Eerdmans, 2000.

———. *Paul, the Spirit, and the People of God.* Peabody, MA: Hendrickson, 1997.

Fee, Gordon D., and Stuart Douglas. *How to Read the Bible for All It's Worth.* Grand Rapids: Zondervan, 2003.

Ferguson, Sinclair B. *The Holy Spirit.* Downers Grove, IL: InterVarsity, 1996.

Findlay, George G. "The Epistle to the Galatians." In *The Expositor's Bible, Luke to Galatians*, edited by W. Robertson Nicoll, 5:811–925. 6 vols. Hartford, CT: S. S. Scranton, 1903.

Fish, Stanley. *Is There a Text in This Class? The Authority of Interpretive Communities.* Cambridge, MA: Harvard University Press, 1980.

Florovsky, Georges. *Bible, Church, Tradition: An Eastern Orthodox View.* Vol. 1 of *Collected Works of Georges Florovsky.* Belmont, MA: Nordland, 1972.

Forde, Gerhard O. "The Critical Response of German Theological Professors to the Faint Declaration on the Doctrine of Justification." *Dialog* 38, no. 1 (Winter 1999) 71–72.

Forsyth, P. T. *The Cruciality of the Cross.* London: Hodder & Stoughton, 1909.

Freedman, David Noel, ed. *The Anchor Yale Bible Dictionary.* 6 vols. New York: Doubleday, 1992.

Freeman, Curtis. "Toward a *Sensus Fidelium* for an Evangelical Church: Postconservatives and Postliberals on Reading Scripture." In *The Nature of Confession: Evangelicals and Postliberals in Dialogue*, edited by George A. Lindbeck et al., 162–80. Downers Grove, IL: IVP, 1996.

Fretheim, Terence E. "God and Violence in the Old Testament." *Word and World* 24, no. 1 (Winter 2004) 18–28.

———. "Word of God." In *The Anchor Yale Bible Dictionary*, edited by David Noel Freedman, 6:961–8. New York: Doubleday, 1992.

Froude, J. A. *Life and Letters of Erasmus.* London: Longmans, Green & Co., 1900.

Gadamer, Hans-Georg. *Truth and Method.* Translated by Joel Weinsheimer and Donald G. Marshall. New York: Continuum, 1998.

———. *Truth and Method.* Translated by Joel Weinsheimer and Donald G. Marshall. New York: Continuum, 1998. Kindle.

———. *Wahrheit und Methode.* Vol. 1 of *Gesammelte Werke.* Tübingen, Germ.: J.C.B. Mohr Siebeck, 1985–95.

Gaffin, Richard B., Jr. "The Redemptive-Historical View." In *Biblical Hermeneutics: Five Views*, edited by Stanley E. Porter and Beth M. Stovell, Kindle location, 823–1044. Downers Grove, IL: IVP Academic, 2012. Kindle.

Gallant, Tim. "Covenantal Nomism?: A Comparative Review of E. P. Sanders, *Paul and Palestinian Judaism*, and D. A. Carson et al., *Justification and Variegated Nomism*, Vol. 1." http://www.biblicalstudiescenter.org/reviews/nomism.htm.

Ganoczy, Alexandre. "Calvin's Life." In *The Cambridge Companion to John Calvin*, edited by Donald K. McKim, translated by David L. Foxgrover and James Schmitt, 3–24. Cambridge, UK: Cambridge University Press, 2004.

Gathercole, Simon. "What Did Paul Really Mean? 'New Perspective' Scholars Argue That We Need, Well, a New Perspective on Justification By Faith." *Christianity Today* 51, no. 8 (Aug. 2007) 22–28. http://www.christianitytoday.com/ct/2007/august/13.22.html.

Gilbert, Daniel B. "The Pneumatic *Charismata* in the Theology of John Calvin." PhD diss., King's College, University of Aberdeen, 2005.

Gill, Jerry H. *Mediated Transcendence: A Post-Modern Reflection*. Macon, GA: Mercer University, 1989.

Gill, John. *A Collection of Sermons and Tracts*. London: George Keith, 1778.

Godfrey, W. Robert. *John Calvin: Pilgrim and Pastor*. Wheaton, IL: Crossway, 2009.

———. "Law and Gospel." In *The New Dictionary of Theology*, edited by Sinclair B. Ferguson et al., 379. Wheaton, IL: IVP Academic, 1988.

Goldingay, John. *Models for Interpretation of Scripture*. Grand Rapids: Eerdmans, 1995.

González, Justo L. *A History of Christian Thought*. Vol. 3. New York: Abingdon, 2012.

Goodman, Anthony, and Angus MacKay, eds. *The Impact of Humanism on Western Europe During the Renaissance*. Abingdon: Routledge, 1990.

Gräbe, Petrus J. *The Power of God in Paul's Letters*. Wissenschaftliche Untersuchungen zum Neuen Testament 2, no. 123. Tübingen, Germ.: Mohr Siebeck, 2000.

Grace of Calvary Lutheran Church. "Martin Luther." http://www.gocglendora.org/wp-content/uploads/2015/07/Martin-Luther-Quotes.pdf.

Graves, Dan. "Erasmus Loaded the Reformation Cannon." https://www.christianity.com/church/church-history/timeline/1501-1600/erasmus-loaded-the-reformation-cannon-11629916.html.

Gregory of Nazianzus. *Oration 43: Funeral Oration on the Great S. Basil, Bishop of Caesarea in Cappadocia*. Edited by Kevin Knight. http://www.newadvent.org/fathers/310243.htm.

Gregory of Nyssa. *On "Not Three Gods": To Ablabius*. Christian Classics Ethereal Library. http://www.ccel.org/ccel/schaff/npnf205.viii.v.html.

Grenz, Stan. *Revisioning Evangelical Theology: A Fresh Agenda for the Twenty-First Century*. Downers Grove, IL: InterVarsity, 1993.

Grudem, Wayne. *Systematic Theology*. Grand Rapids: Zondervan, 1994.

Gundry, Robert H. "On Oden's 'Answer.'" *Books and Culture* 7, no. 2 (Mar./Apr. 2001) 14-15, 39.

———. "The Nonimputation of Christ's Righteousness." In *Justification: What's at Stake in the Current Debate*, edited by Mark Husbands and Daniel J. Trier, 17–45. Downers Grove, IL: InterVarsity Academic, 2004.

———. "Why I Didn't Endorse 'The Gospel of Jesus Christ: An Evangelical Celebration' . . . Even Though I Wasn't Asked to." *Books and Culture* 7, no. 1 (Jan.–Feb. 2001) 14–15, 39.

Hafemann, Scott. "Paul and His Interpreters." In *Dictionary of Paul and His Letters*, edited by Gerald F. Hawthorne et al., 666–79. IVP Bible Dictionary. Downers Grove, IL: InterVarsity Academic, 1993.

Hansen, G. Walter. *Galatians*. IVP New Testament Commentary 9. Downers Grove, IL: InterVarsity Academic, 1994.

Harris, R. Laird, et al., eds. *The Theological Wordbook of the Old Testament*. Chicago: Moody, 1980.

Harrison, R. K. *Leviticus: An Introduction and Commentary*. Tyndale Old Testament Commentaries. Downers Grove, IL: InterVarsity, 1980.

Hartman, Geoffrey H. *The Fate of Reading and Other Essays*. Chicago: University of Chicago Press, 1975.

Haslam, Peter. *Imputed Righteousness: Or, A Treatise on Justification by Faith*. Edited by Thomas Wood. London: Fisher, and Dixon, 1809. Logos.

Hauerwas, Stanley. *Unleashing the Scripture: Freeing the Bible from Captivity to America.* Nashville: Abingdon, 1993.

Hays, Richard B. *Echoes of Scripture in the Letters of Paul.* New Haven, CT: Yale University Press, 1989.

———. *The Faith of Jesus Christ: The Narrative Substructure of Galatians 3:1-4.* Grand Rapids: Eerdmans, 2002.

The Heidelberg Catechism. In *The Book of Confessions.* Louisville: Westminster John Knox, 1991.

Henry, Carl F. H. *God, Revelation and Authority.* 6 vols. Wheaton, IL: Good News, 1999.

Herford, R. Travers. *Judaism in the New Testament Period.* London: Lindsey, 1928.

Hertz, J. H., ed. *The Pentateuch and Haftorahs: Hebrew Text English Translation and Commentary.* Oxford: Oxford University Press, 1940.

Heyd, David. "Supererogation." In *The Stanford Encyclopedia of Philosophy,* edited by Edward N. Zalta. Stanford, CA: The Metaphysics Research Lab, 2011. http://plato.stanford.edu/archives/win2011/entries/supererogation/.

Hill, David. *Greek Words and Hebrew Meanings.* Cambridge, UK: Cambridge University Press Archive, 1967.

Hirsch, Emanuel. *Die Theologie des Andreas Osiander und ihre geschichtlichen Voraussetzungen.* Göttingen, Germ.: Vandenhoeck & Ruprecht, 1919.

Hodge, A. A. *Commentary on the Westminster Confession.* Escondido, CA: Ephesians Four Group, 1999.

Hodge, Charles. *Systematic Theology.* 3 vols. Oak Harbor, WA: Logos Research Systems, 1997. Logos.

Hoekema, Anthony. *Saved by Grace.* Grand Rapids: Eerdmans, 1994.

Horton, Michael S. *Justification.* 2 vols. Grand Rapids: Zondervan, 2018.

———. *Covenant and Eschatology.* Louisville: Westminster John Knox, 2002.

———. *God of Promise: Introducing Covenant Theology.* Grand Rapids: Baker Academic, 2006.

———. *Lord and Servant.* Louisville: Westminster John Knox, 2005.

———. "Nine Points of Synod: Response to 'The New Perspective on Paul.'" 3 parts. https://www.monergism.com/search?keywords=Michael+Horton%2C+%E2%80%9CNine+Points+of+Synod%3A+Response+to+%E2%80%98The+New+Perspective+on+Paul.%E2%80%99%E2%80%9D&format=All.

———. *People and Place: A Covenant Ecclesiology.* Louisville: Westminster John Knox, 2008.

———. "Traditional Reformed View." In *Justification: Five Views,* edited by James K. Beilby et al. Downers Grove, IL: IVP Academic, 2011. Kindle.

Hoy, David Couzens. *The Critical Circle: Literature and History in Contemporary Hermeneutics.* Berkeley: University of California Press, 1978.

Hunt, Dave and James White. *Debating Calvinism: Five Points, Two Views.* Sisters, OR: Multnomah, 2004. Kindle.

"Integrity." In *Dictionary.* https://www.dictionary.com/browse/integrity?s=t.

Irenaeus. *Against Heresies.* Edited by Kevin Knight. https://www.newadvent.org/fathers/0103438.htm.

Jewett, Robert. "The Law and the Coexistence of Jews and Gentiles in Romans." *Interpretation* 39 (1985) 341-356.

"John Calvin Biography." http://www.notablebiographies.com/Ca-Ch/Calvin-John.html.

"John Calvin: Journalist, Theologian (1509–1564)." http://www.biography.com/people/john-calvin-9235788.

Johnson, Phil. "A Defense of the Old Perspective on Paul: What Did St. Paul *Really* Say?" Jan. 2004. http://www.monergism.com/thethreshold/articles/onsite/new_p.html.

Joint Lutheran-Roman Catholic Study Commission. *Church and Justification*. Geneva: Lutheran World Federation, 1994.

———. "The Gospel and the Church." In *Report of the Joint Lutheran-Roman Catholic Study Commission*, 168–89. New York: Growth in Agreement, 1984.

———. *Justification by Faith*. Geneva: Lutheran World Federation, 1983.

Kalland, Earl S. "399 רָבַד." In *Theological Wordbook of the Old Testament*, edited by R. Laird Harris et al, 178–81. Chicago: Moody, 1999.

Kärkkäinen, Veli-Matti. "Deification View." In *Justification: Five Views*, edited by James K. Beilby et al., loc. 2408–676. Downers Grove, IL: IVP Academic, 2011. Kindle.

———. "The Holy Spirit and Justification: The Ecumenical Significance of Luthers Doctrine of Salvation." *Pneuma: The Journal of the Society for Pentecostal Studies* 24, no. 1 (Jan. 2002) 26–39.

———. "Justification." In *Global Dictionary of Theology*, edited by William A. Dyrness et al., 175–85. Downers Grove, IL: InterVarsity Academic, 2008.

———. "Justification as Forgiveness of Sins and Making Righteous: The Ecumenical Promise of a New Interpretation of Luther." *One in Christ* 37, no. 2 (2002) 32–45.

———. *One with God: Salvation as Deification and Justification*. Collegeville, MN: Liturgical, 2005.

———. "Salvation as Justification and *Theosis*: The Contribution of the New Finnish Luther Interpretation to Our Ecumenical Future." *Dialog* 45, no. 1 (Feb. 2006) 74–82.

Käsemann, Ernst. *Commentary on Romans*. Grand Rapids: Eerdmans, 1980.

———. *New Testament Questions of Today*. Minneapolis: Fortress, 1969.

———. *Das wandernde Gottesvolk*. Göttingen, Germ.: Vandenhoeck & Ruprecht, 1957.

Keller, Timothy. "The Centrality of the Gospel." Jan. 1, 2000. https://redeemercitytocity.com/articles-stories/the-centrality-of-the-gospel.

Kertelge, Karl. "δικαιοσύνη." In *Exegetisches Wörterbuch zum Neuen Testament*, 1:790. Stuttgart, Germ.: Kohlhammer, 1980.

———. *"Rechtfertigung" bei Paulus: Studien zur Struktur und Bedeutungsgehalt des paulinischen Rechtfertigungsbegriffs*. 2nd ed. Neutestamentliche Abhandlungen, n.s., 3. Münster, Germ.: Aschendorff, 1971.

Knight, Henry H., III. *A Future for Truth: Evangelical Theology in a Postmodern World*. Nashville: Abingdon, 1997.

Kramer, Fred. "Martin Chemnitz, 1522–1586." In *Shapers of Religious Traditions in Germany, Switzerland, and Poland, 1560–1600*, edited by Jill Raitt, 46–68. New Haven, CT: Yale University Press, 1981.

Kroll, Paul. "Church History Corner: Vatican II and the Future of Church Unity." *Christian Odyssey* 3, no. 5 (Oct.–Nov. 2007) 18–19.

Kuhn, Helmut. "The Phenomenological Concept of 'Horizon.'" In *Philosophical Essays in Memory of Edmund Husserl*, edited by Martin Farber, 106–23. New York: Greenwood, 1968.

Kuyper, Abraham. *The Work of the Holy Spirit*. Grand Rapids: Eerdmans, 1946.

Lambert, Sylvie and Barbara Moser-Mercer, eds. *Bridging the Gap: Empirical Research in Simultaneous Interpretation*. Klaprozenweg, Neth.: John Benjamins, 1994.

Lane, Anthony N. S. *Justification by Faith in Catholic-Protestant Dialogue: An Evangelical Assessment*. New York: T. & T. Clark, 2002.

Lawson, Steven. "The Biblical Preaching of John Calvin." *Southern Baptist Journal of Theology* 13, no. 4 (Winter 2009) 18–34.

———. "The Preacher of God's Word." In *John Calvin: A Heart for Devotion, Doctrine, and Doxology*, edited by Burk Parsons, 71–82. Sanford, FL: Reformation Trust, 2008.

Lewis, C. S. "Introduction: On the Reading of Old Books." In *On the Incarnation*, by Athanasius. Translated by John Behr. Popular Patristics 44B. Crestwood, NY: St. Vladimir's Seminary Press, 2012.

———. *The Last Battle*. San Francisco: HarperCollins, 2000. First published 1956 by Bodley Head (London).

———. *The Lion, the Witch, and the Wardrobe*. San Francisco: HarperCollins, 2004. First published 1950 by Geoffrey Bles (London).

Loewenich, Walther. *Luther: The Man and His Work*. Translated by Lawrence W. Denef. Minneapolis: Augsburg, 1986.

Longenecker, Bruce W. *The Triumph of Abraham's God: The Transformation of Identity in Galatians*. Edinburgh: T. & T. Clark, 1998.

Longenecker, Richard N. *Galatians*. Vol. 41 of *Word Biblical Commentary*. Dallas: Thomas Nelson, 1990.

Longman, Tremper, III and David E. Garland, eds. *Romans—Galatians*. Rev. ed. Expositors Bible Commentary 11. Grand Rapids: Zondervan, 2008.

Lopes, Augustus Nicodemus and Jose Manoel Da Conceicao. "Calvin, Theologian of the Holy Spirit: The Holy Spirit and the Word of God." *Scottish Bulletin of Evangelical Theology* 15, no. 1 (Spring 1997) 38–49.

Lossky, Vladimir. *In the Image and Likeness of God*. Crestwood, NY: St. Vladimir's Seminary Press, 1985.

———. *The Mystical Theology of the Eastern Church*. Crestwood, NY: St. Vladimir's Seminary Press, 1976.

———. *The Vision of God*. Crestwood, NY: St. Vladimir's Seminary Press, 1973.

Lull, Timothy F., ed. *Martin Luther's Basic Theological Writings*. Philadelphia: Fortress, 2012.

Luther, Martin. *The Bondage of the Will*. Translated by J. I. Packer and O. R. Johnston. Grand Rapids: Baker, 2012.

———. *The Bondage of the Will*. In *Career of the Reformer III*, edited by Helmut T. Lehmann, translated by Philip S. Watson, 3–295. Vol. 33 of *Luther's Works*. Philadelphia: Fortress, 1999.

———. *Church Postil III*. Edited by Christopher Boyd Brown and Benjamin T. G. Mayes, 36–326. Vol. 77 of *Luther's Works*. St. Louis: Concordia, 2014.

———. *D. Martin Luthers Werke, Kritische Gesamtausgabe*. 136 vols. Weimar, Germ.: Böhlau, 1883–2009.

———. "Excerpt on the Mass." In *Martin Luther's Basic Theological Writings*, edited by Timothy Lull. Minneapolis: Fortress, 1989.

———. *The Freedom of a Christian*. In *Career of the Reformer I*, edited by Harold J. Grimm and Helmut T. Lehmann, translated by W.A. Lambert, revised by Harold J. Grimm, 327–78. Vol. 31 of *Luther's Works*. Philadelphia: Fortress, 1999.

―――. *The Large Catechism*. In *The Book of Concord: The Confessions of the Evangelical Lutheran Church*, by Robert Kolb and Timothy J. Wengert, translated by Charles P. Arand, 377–480. Minneapolis: Fortress, 2000.

―――. *Lectures on Galatians, 1519, Chapters 1—6*. In *Lectures on Galatians: 1535, Chapters 5—6; 1519, Chapters 1—6*, edited by Jaroslav Pelikan, 163–410. Vol. 27 of *Luther's Works*. St. Louis: Concordia, 1963.

―――. *Lectures on Galatians, 1535, Chapters 1—4*. Edited by Jaroslav Jan Pelikan et al. Vol 26 of *Luther's Works*. Saint Louis: Concordia, 1999.

―――. *Lectures on Genesis, Chapters 1—5*. Edited by Jaroslav Jan Pelikan. Vol. 1 of *Luther's Works*. Saint Louis: Concordia, 1999.

―――. *Letter to Eobanus Hessus, March 29, 1523*. In *Letters II*, edited by Helmut T. Lehmann, translated by Gerhard A. Krodel, 32–35. Vol. 49 of *Luther's Works*. Philadelphia: Fortress, 1999.

―――. *Letters I*. Edited by Helmut T. Lehmann. Vol. 48 of *Luther's Works*. Philadelphia: Fortress, 1999.

―――. *Luther's Works*. Edited by Jaroslav Pelikan and Helmut T. Lehmann. American ed. 82 vols. (projected). Philadelphia: Fortress, 1955–.

―――. *No. 131: The Duplicity of Desiderius Erasmus—Between November 30 and December 14, 1531*. In *Table Talk*, edited by Helmut T. Lehmann, 19. Vol. 54 of *Luther's Works*. Philadelphia: Fortress, 1999.

―――. *No. 494: How to Preach on the Annunciation of Mary—3/25/1533*. In *Table Talk*, edited by Helmut T. Lehmann, 84. Vol. 54 of *Luther's Works*. Philadelphia: Fortress, 1999.

―――. *Sermon on Two Kinds of Righteousness*. In *Career of the Reformer I*, edited by Jaroslav Pelikan et al., translated by Lowell J. Satre, 293–306. Vol. 31 of *Luther's Works*. Philadelphia: Fortress, 1999.

―――. *Sermons on the Gospel of St. John, Chapters 1—4*. Edited by Jaroslav Jan Pelikan. Vol. 22 of *Luther's Works*. Saint Louis: Concordia, 1999.

―――. *Sermons on the Gospel of St. John, Chapters 6—8*. Edited by Jaroslav Jan Pelikan. Vol. 23 of *Luther's Works*. Philadelphia: Fortress, 1999.

―――. *Sermons on the Gospel of St. John, Chapters 14—16*. Edited by Jaroslav Jan Pelikan. Vol. 24 of *Luther's Works*. Saint Louis: Concordia, 1999.

―――. *St. Paul's Epistle to the Galatians*. Philadelphia: Smith, English & Co., 1860. https://openlibrary.org/works/OL795651W/A_Commentary_on_St._Paul%27s_Epistle_to_the_Galatians.

―――. *What Luther Says: An Anthology*. Edited by Ewald M. Plass. 2 vols. St. Louis: Concordia, 1959.

Lutheran World Federation and the Roman Catholic Church. *Joint Declaration on the Doctrine of Justification*. Grand Rapids: Eerdmans, 2000. https://www.lutheranworld.org/content/resource-joint-declaration-doctrine-justification.

MacArthur, John, Jr, et al. *Rediscovering Expository Preaching: Balancing the Science and Art of Biblical Exposition*. Dallas: Word, 1992.

Macchia, Frank D. "Baptized in the Spirit: Reflections in Response to My Reviewers." *Journal of Pentecostal Theology* 16, no. 2 (Jan. 2008) 14–20.

―――. "Justification through New Creation: The Holy Spirit and the Doctrine by Which the Church Stands or Falls." *Theology Today* 58, no. 2 (July 2001) 202–17.

―――. *Justified in the Spirit: Creation, Redemption, and the Triune God*. Grand Rapids: Eerdmans, 2010.

———. *The Spirit-Baptized Church: A Dogmatic Inquiry*. New York: T&T Clark, 2020.
Machen, J. Gresham. *Christianity and Liberalism*. Grand Rapids: Eerdmans, 1992.
Malloy, Christopher J. *Engrafted into Christ: A Critique of the Joint Declaration*. New York: Lang, 2005.
Manschreck, Clyde L., ed. *Melanchthon on Christian Doctrine: Loci communes (1555)*. New York: Oxford University Press, 1965.
Mantzaridis, Georgios I. *The Deification of Man: St. Gregory Palamas and the Orthodox Tradition*. Crestwood, NY: St. Vladimir's Seminary Press, 1997.
Marmorstein, Arthur. *The Doctrine of Merits in Old Rabbinical Literature*. New York: KTAV, 1968.
Marshall, I. Howard. *Beyond the Bible: Moving from Scripture to Theology*. Grand Rapids: Baker, 2004.
Martin, Douglas. "Krister Stendahl, 86, Ecumenical Bishop, Is Dead." *New York Times*, April 16, 2008. http://www.nytimes.com/2008/04/16/us/16stendahl.html.
"Martin Luther: Founder of Lutheranism." https://www.encyclopedia.com/history/encyclopedias-almanacs-transcripts-and-maps/martin-luther-founder-lutheranism.
Martin, Walter. *Essential Christianity*. Colorado Springs: Gospel Light, 1985.
Matera, Frank. *Romans*. Paideia Commentaries on the New Testament. Grand Rapids: Baker, 2010.
Matheson, Peter. "Humanism and Reform Movements." In *The Impact of Humanism on Western Europe During the Renaissance*, edited by Anthony Goodman and Angus MacKay, 23–42. Abingdon: Routledge, 1990.
Mayhue, Richard L. "Rediscovering Expository Preaching." In *Rediscovering Expository Preaching: Balancing the Science and Art of Biblical Exposition*, by John F. MacArthur, Jr., et al., 3–21. Nashville: Word, 1992.
McCain, Paul T. "A Betrayal of the Gospel: The Joint Declaration on the Doctrine of Justification." *First Things*, Mar. 12, 2010. http://firstthings.com/blogs/evangel/2010/03/a-betrayal-of-the-gospel-the-joint-declaration-on-the-doctrine-of-justification.
McClendon, James W., Jr. *Ethics: Systematic Theology*. 3 vols. Nashville: Abingdon, 1986.
McGoldrick, James Edward. "John Calvin, Practical Theologian: The Reformer's Spirituality." *Outlook* 59, no. 6 (June 2009) 10–15.
McGrath, Alister E. *Evangelicalism and the Future of Christianity*. London: Hodder & Stoughton, 1993.
———. *The Intellectual Origins of the European Reformation*. Grand Rapids: Baker, 1995.
———. *Iustitia Dei: A History of the Christian Doctrine of Justification*. 3rd ed. New York: Cambridge University Press, 1998; Kindle, 2005.
———. *Spirituality in an Age of Change*. Grand Rapids: Zondervan, 1994.
McKim, Donald K, ed. *The Cambridge Companion to John Calvin*. Cambridge, UK: Cambridge University Press, 2004.
Meade, Starr. *Training Hearts, Teaching Minds*. Philipsburg, NJ: Presbyterian & Reformed, 2000.
Meadors, Gary T., et al. *Four Views on Moving Beyond the Bible to Theology*. Counterpoints: Bible and Theology. Grand Rapids: Zondervan, 2009.
Melanchthon, Philip. *Loci Communes, 1543*. Edited by Jacob A. O. Preus. St. Louis: Concordia, 1992.

Mercer, Joe. "The Transitive Property of Congruence." http://ceemrr.com/Geometry1/Transitive/Transitive_print.html.

Meuser, Fred W. *Luther the Preacher*. Minneapolis: Augsburg, 1983.

Montefiore, Claude G. "Jewish Scholarship and Christian Silence." *Hibbert Journal* 1 (1902–1903) 335–46.

———. "On Some Misconceptions of Judaism and Christianity by Each Other." *Jewish Quarterly Review* 8 (1896) 193–216.

———. *Rabbinic Literature and Gospel Teaching*. New York: KTAV, 1970.

Moo, Douglas. *2 Peter, Jude*. Grand Rapids: Zondervan, 1996.

———. *A Commentary on the Epistle to the Romans*. Grand Rapids: Eerdmans, 1996.

———. *Encountering the Book of Romans: A Theological Survey*. Grand Rapids: Baker, 2002.

———. *The Epistle to the Romans*. New International Commentary on the New Testament. Grand Rapids: Eerdmans, 1996.

———. "Israel and the Law in Romans 5–11: Interaction with the New Perspective." In *The Paradoxes of Paul*, edited by D. A. Carson et al, 185–216. Vol. 2 of *Justification and Variegated Nomism*. Grand Rapids: Baker Academic, 2004.

———. "Justification in Galatians." In *Understanding the Times: New Testament Studies in the Twenty-First Century: Essays in Honor of D. A. Carson on the Occasion of His Sixty-Fifth Birthday*, edited by Andreas J. Köstenberger and Robert W. Yabrough, 160–95. Wheaton, IL: Crossway, 2011.

———. *The Letter of James*. Grand Rapids: Eerdmans, 2000.

———. *The Letter to the Romans*. Grand Rapids: Eerdmans, 2008.

———. *The Letters to the Colossians and to Philemon*. Grand Rapids: Eerdmans, 2008.

———. *Romans*. Grand Rapids: Zondervan, 2000.

Moo, Douglas J., and Andrew David Naselli. "The Problem of the New Testament's Use of the Old Testament." In *The Enduring Authority of the Christian Scriptures*, edited by D. A. Carson, loc. 21818–23235. Grand Rapids: Eerdmans, 2016. Kindle.

Moore, George Foot. "Christian Writers on Judaism." *Harvard Theological Review* 14, no. 3 (1921) 197–254.

———. *Judaism in the First Centuries of the Christian Era: The Age of the Tannaim*. 3 vols. Cambridge, MA: Harvard University Press, 1950.

Moore, Rickie D. "Canon and Charisma in the Book of Deuteronomy." *Journal of Pentecostal Theology* 1, no. 1 (Jan. 1992) 75–92.

Moore, Rickie D., and Brian Neil Peterson. *Voice, Word, and Spirit: A Pentecostal Old Testament Survey*. Nashville: Abingdon, 2017.

Moore, Stephen D. *Literary Criticism and the Gospels: The Theoretical Challenge*. New Haven, CT: Yale University Press, 1992.

Morris, Leon. *Apostolic Preaching of the Cross*. Grand Rapids: Eerdmans, 2010.

———. *The Atonement: Its Meaning and Significance*. Downers Grove, IL: IVP Academic, 2012.

———. *The Epistle to the Romans*. Pillar New Testament Commentary. Grand Rapids: Eerdmans, 1988.

Moule, H. C. G. *The Epistle of Paul the Apostle to the Romans*. Cambridge, UK: Cambridge University Press, 1891.

Murray, John. *Redemption: Accomplished and Applied*. Grand Rapids: Eerdmans, 1955.

———. "Systematic Theology." In *The Collected Writings of John Murray*, 2:3–304. Carlisle, PA: Banner of Truth, 1982.

Myers, Jeff and David A. Noebel. *Understanding the Times: A Survey of Competing Worldviews*. Manitou Springs, CO: Summit Ministries, 2015.

Needham, Nick. "Justification in the Early Church Fathers." In *Justification in Perspective: Historical Developments and Contemporary Challenges*, edited by Bruce L. McCormack, 67–127. Grand Rapids: Baker Academic, 2006.

Nestle, Eberhard, et al., eds. *The Greek New Testament*. Stuttgart, Germ.: Deutsche Bibelgesellschaft, 1993.

Nicole, Roger. "B. B. Warfield and the Calvinist Revival." In *Great Leaders of the Christian Church*, edited by John D. Woodbridge, 216–23. Chicago: Moody, 1988.

Niesel, Wilhelm. *The Theology of Calvin*. Translated by Harold Knight. Library of Ecclesiastical History. Cambridge, UK: James Clarke & Co., 1956.

Norris, F. W. "Deification: Consensual and Cogent." *Scottish Journal of Theology* 43, no. 4 (1996) 411–28.

Oden, Thomas C. *The Justification Reader*. Grand Rapids: Eerdmans, 2002.

———. *Systematic Theology*. 3 vols. San Francisco: HarperSanFrancisco, 1992.

"The One Hundred Most Influential Books Ever Written." Wikimedia Foundation. https://en.wikipedia.org/wiki/The_100_Most_Influential_Books_Ever_Written.

Ornstein, Robert E. *Evolution of Consciousness: Of Darwin, Freud, and Cranial Fire: The Origins of the Way We Think*. New York: Simon & Schuster, 1991.

Osborne, Grant R. *The Hermeneutical Spiral: A Comprehensive Introduction to Biblical Interpretation*. Downers Grove, IL: IVP Academic, 2006.

Osiander, Andreas. *Beweisung, daß ich alweg einerlei Lehre von der Gerechtigkeit des Glaubens gehalten und gelehrt habe*. In *Controversia et Confessio Digital*, edited by Irene Dingel. http://www.controversia-et-confessio.de/cc-digital/quellen/modus/ls/10/70/10/ansicht/3850-beweisung-dass-ich-alweg-einerlei-lehre-von-der-gerechtigkeit-des-glaubens-gehalten-und-gelehr.html.

———. *De iustificatione hominis peccatoris coram Deo*. In *Controversia et Confessio Digital*, edited by Irene Dingel. http://www.controversia-et-confessio.de/cc-digital/quellen/modus/ls/10/70/10/ansicht/2803-de-iustificatione-hominis-peccatoris-coram-deo.html.

———. *Disputatio de Iustificatione*. In *Controversia et Confessio Digital*, edited by Irene Dingel. http://www.controversia-et-confessio.de/cc-digital/quellen/modus/ls/10/70/10/ansicht/3318-disputatio-de-iustificatione.html.

———. *Schriften und Briefe 1549 bis August 1551*. Edited by Gerhard Müller und Gottfried Seebass. Gesamtausgabe 9. Gütersloh, Germ.: Gütersloher, 1994.

———. *Von dem einigen Mittler Jhesu Christo und Rechtfertigung des Glauben, lat*. In *Controversia et Confessio Digital*, edited by Irene Dingel. http://www.controversia-et-confessio.de/id/a65f3863-fbba-49ff-bb11-c844c5aa04fb.

———. *Widerlegung der Antwort Melanthonis*. In *Controversia et Confessio Digital*, edited by Irene Dingel. http://www.controversia-et-confessio.de/id/ce7f8e36-a1fb-459c-9f2e-23203f493169.

Packer, J. I. *"Fundamentalism" and the Word of God*. Grand Rapids: Eerdmans, 1958.

———. *God Has Spoken: Revelation and the Bible*. London: Hodder and Stoughton, 1965.

———. "Infallibility and Inerrancy of the Bible." In *The New Dictionary of Theology*, edited by Sinclair B. Ferguson et al., 337–9. Downers Grove, IL: InterVarsity, 1988.

———. *Knowing God*. Downers Grove, IL: IVP, 1993.

———. "Regeneration." In *Evangelical Dictionary of Theology*, edited by Walter Elwell, 1000–1001. 2nd ed. Grand Rapids: Baker, 1984.
———. *Truth and Power: The Place of Scripture in the Christian Life*. Wheaton, IL: Harold Shaw, 1996.
Pae, Sunghyun. *A Study of John Piper's Sermon Preparation: A Model for Pastors Who Emphasize the Supremacy of God in Expository Preaching*. DMin diss., Liberty Baptist Theological Seminary, 2011.
Palmer, Richard E. *Hermeneutics*. Chicago: Northwestern University Press, 1969.
Parker, T. H. L. *John Calvin: A Biography*. Oxford: Lion Hudson, 2006.
———. *Portrait of Calvin*. Minneapolis: Desiring God, 2009. First published 1954 by SMC (London).
Parry, Robin. "Ideological Criticism." In *Dictionary for Theological Interpretation of the Bible*, edited by Kevin J. Vanhoozer et al., 315. Grand Rapids: Baker Academic, 2005.
Peacocke, Arthur. *Theology for a Scientific Age: Being and Becoming—Natural, Divine, and Human*. Minneapolis: Fortress, 1993.
Pederson, Randall. *Unity in Diversity: English Puritans and the Puritan Reformation, 1603–1689*. Series in Church History 68. Leiden, Neth.: Brill, 2014.
"Peter Toon." http://www.theopedia.com/Peter_Toon.
Pelikan, Jaroslav. *The Emergence of the Catholic Tradition (100–600)*. Vol. 1 of *The Christian Tradition: A History of the Development of Doctrine*. Chicago: University of Chicago Press, 1971.
———. *Reformation of Church and Dogma (1300–1700)*. Vol. 4 of *The Christian Tradition: A History of the Development of Doctrine*. Chicago: University of Chicago Press, 1985.
———. *The Riddle of Roman Catholicism*. London: Hodder & Stoughton, 1960.
———. *The Spirit of Eastern Christianity*. Chicago: University of Chicago, 1974.
Perkins, William. *A Commentary on Galatians with Introductory Essays*. Edited by G. T. Sheppard. New York: Pilgrim, 1989.
Pettinger, Tejvan. "Biography of Martin Luther." https://www.biographyonline.net/spiritual/martin-luther.html.
Piepkorn, Arthur Carl. *The Sacred Scripture and the Lutheran Confessions*. Vol. 2 of *The Selected Writings of Arthur Carl Piepkorn*, edited by Philip J. Secker. Mansfield, CT: CEC Press, 2007.
Piper, Bill. *A Good Time and How to Have It*. Greenville, SC: Piper, 1964.
———. *The Greatest Menace to Modern Youth*. Greenville, SC: Piper's Evangelistic, 1980.
———. *Dead Men Made Alive*. Greenville, SC: Piper, 1949.
———. *Stones Out of the Rubbish*. Greenville, SC: Piper, 1947.
———. *The Tyranny of Tolerance*. Greenville, SC: Piper, 1964.
Piper, John. *Brothers, We Are Not Professionals*. Nashville: Broadman Holman, 2002.
———. *Counted Righteous in Christ: Should We Abandon the Imputation of Christ's Righteousness?* Wheaton, IL: Crossway Books, 2002.
———. *Desiring God: Meditations of a Christian Hedonist*. Colorado Springs: Multnomah, 2011.
———. "Evangelist Bill Piper: Fundamentalist Full of Grace and Joy." http://www.desiringgod.org/resource-library/biographies/evangelist-bill-piper-fundamentalist-full-of-grace-and-joy.
———. *Finally Alive*. Wheaton, IL: Christian Focus, 2009.

———. *The Future of Justification: A Response to N. T. Wright*. Wheaton, IL: Crossway, 2007.

———. *God Is the Gospel: Meditations on God's Love as the Gift of Himself*. Wheaton, IL: Crossway, 2005.

———. *God's Passion for His Glory: Living the Vision of Jonathan Edwards*. Wheaton, IL: Crossway, 1998.

———. "Honoring the Biblical Call of Motherhood: A Tribute to Ruth Piper." http://www.desiringgod.org/resource-library/sermons/honoring-the-biblical-call-of-motherhood.

———. "The Inner Essence of Worship." https://www.desiringgod.org/messages/the-inner-essence-of-worship.

———. *John Calvin and His Passion for the Majesty of God*. Wheaton, IL: Crossway Books, 2009.

———. *The Justification of God: An Exegetical and Theological Study of Romans 9:1–23*. Grand Rapids: Baker, 1993.

———. *Let the Nations Be Glad!: The Supremacy of God in Missions*. 3rd ed. Grand Rapids: Baker Academic, 2010. Kindle.

———. *The Pleasures of God: Meditations on God's Delight in Being God*. Sisters, OR: Multnomah, 2000.

———. "Preaching as Expository Exultation for the Glory of God." Originally titled "Why Expositional Preaching is Particularly Glorifying to God." http://www.desiringgod.org/library/sermons/06/042706.html.

———. *Reading the Bible Supernaturally: Seeing and Savoring the Glory of God in Scripture*. Wheaton, IL: Crossway, 2017.

———. *Seeing and Savoring Jesus Christ*. Wheaton, IL: Crossway, 2001.

———. *The Supremacy of God in Preaching*. Grand Rapids: Baker, 2015.

———. "The Supremacy of God in the Life of the Mind." https://www.desiringgod.org/messages/the-supremacy-of-god-in-the-life-of-the-mind.

———. *What Jesus Demands from the World*. Wheaton, IL: Crossway, 2006.

Piper, John, and David Mathis, eds. *With Calvin in the Theater of God: The Glory of Christ in Everyday Life*. Wheaton, IL: Crossway, 2010.

Plantinga, Alvin. *Warrant and Proper Function*. Oxford: Oxford University Press, 1993.

Pohle, Joseph. "Justification." Edited by Kevin Knight. http://www.newadvent.org/cathen/08573a.htm.

Prayson, Daniel. "Works of the Law: Sanders, Dunn and Wright." http://withalliamgod.wordpress.com/2012/11/14/works-of-the-law-sanders-dunn-and-wright/.

Procksch, Otto. "The Word of God in the Old Testament." In *Theological Dictionary of the New Testament*, edited by Gerhard Kittel et al., translated by Geoffrey W. Bromiley, 4:91–100. Grand Rapids: Eerdmans, 1964.

Purdy, Harlyn Graydon. *A Distinct Twenty-First Century Pentecostal Hermeneutic*. Eugene, OR: Wipf and Stock, 2015.

Ramm, Bernard. *Protestant Biblical Interpretation*. Grand Rapids: Baker, 1970.

———. *Rapping About the Spirit*. Waco: Word, 1974.

Ramsay, William M. *Church History One Hundred One*. Louisville: Westminster John Knox Press, 2005.

Rankine, William John Macquorn. "On the General Law of the Transformation of Energy." *Proceedings of the Philosophical Society of Glasgow* 3, no. 5 (1853) 276–80.

Richter, Duncan J. "Ludwig Wittgenstein (1889–1951)." In *Internet Encyclopedia of Philosophy*, edited by James Fieser et al. https://iep.utm.edu/wittgens/.
Ricœur, Paul. *Hermeneutics and the Human Sciences*. Cambridge, UK: Cambridge University Press, 1985.
———. *Interpretation Theory: Discourse and the Surplus of Meaning*. Fort Worth: Texas Christian University Press, 1976.
"The Righteousness of Faith before God." In *The Formula of Concord: Epitome*. https://bookofconcord.org/formula-of-concord-epitome/article-iii/.
Ritschl, Otto. *Dogmengeschichte des Protestantismus*. 4 vols. Göttingen, Germ.: Vandenhoeck & Ruprecht, 1927.
Rupp, Gordon. *The Righteousness of God: Luther Studies*. New York: Hodder & Stoughton, 1968.
Sailhamer, John. *Genesis Unbound: A Provocative New Look at the Creation Account*. Colorado Springs: Dawson Media, 2011. Kindle.
Sanborn, Donald J. "Critical Analysis of the Joint Declaration on the Doctrine of Justification." Edited by Anthony Cekada. http://www.traditionalmass.org/articles/article.php?id=31andcatname=15.
Sanders, E. P. *Paul and Palestinian Judaism*. London: Fortress, 1977.
Sanders, James A. Review of *Holy Scripture: Canon, Authority, Criticism*, by James Barr. *Journal of Biblical Literature* 104, no. 3 (Sept. 1985) 501–2.
Schaff, Philip. *History of the Christian Church*. 8 vols. Grand Rapids: Eerdmans, 1910.
Schechter, Solomon. *Aspects of Rabbinic Theology*. New York: Schocken, 1961.
Schleiermacher, Friedrich. *The Christian Faith*. Edited by H. R. Mackintosh et al. New York: T. & T. Clark, 1999.
Schmid, Hans. *Gerechtigkeit als Weltordnung*. Tübingen, Germ.: Mohr Siebeck, 1958.
Schnelle, Udo. *Apostle Paul: His Life and Theology*. Translated by M. Eugene Boring. Grand Rapids: Baker Academic, 2005.
Searle, John R. *Expression and Meaning*. New York: Cambridge University Press, 1979.
———. *Speech Acts: An Essay in the Philosophy of Language*. Cambridge, UK: Cambridge University Press, 1969.
———. "A Taxonomy of Illocutionary Acts." In *Language, Mind, and Knowledge*, edited by Keith Gunderson, 344–69. Minneapolis: University of Minneapolis Press, 1975.
Seebass, Gottfried. *Bibliographia Osiandrica: Bibliographie der Gedruckten Schriften Andrea Osiander d. A. (1496–1552)*. Nieuwkoop, Neth.: Graaf, 1971.
Seeberg, Reinhold. *Textbook of the History of Doctrines*. 2 vols. Translated by Charles E. Hay. Philadelphia: Lutheran, 1904. Kindle.
Seifrid, Mark A. *Christ, Our Righteousness: Paul's Theology of Justification*. Downers Grove, IL: IVP Academic, 2001.
———. *Justification by Faith: The Origin and Development of a Central Pauline Theme*. Leiden, Neth.: Brill Academic, 1992.
———. Review of *Justified in the Spirit: Creation, Redemption, and the Triune God*, by Frank D. Macchia. *Religious Studies Review* 37, no. 2 (June 2011) 117.
———. "Righteousness Language in the Hebrew Scriptures and Early Judaism." In *The Complexities of Second Temple Judaism*, edited by D.A. Carson et al. Vol. 1 of *Justification and Variegated Nomism*, 39–74. Grand Rapids: Baker, 2001.
Service, Steven R. *Dabar YHWH Gospel Musterion: A Narrative Historical Theology of the Reign of God*. N.p.: Hearts Cry, 2007.
Sheldon, Henry. *History of the Christian Church*. 5 vols. New York: Hendrickson, 1988.

Shepherd, Victor. "Calvin on Justification." http://www.victorshepherd.on.ca/Course/John%20Calvin/the_theology_of_john_calvin39.htm. Site discontinued.

———. "The Theology of John Calvin." http://www.regentaudio.com/RGDL3054S?-category_id=0&search_string=Victor+Shepherd&search_category_id=0. Site discontinued.

Silva, Moisés. "Faith Versus Works of Law in Galatians." In *The Paradoxes of Paul*, edited by D. A. Carson et al., 217–48. Vol. 2 of *Justification and Variegated Nomism*. Grand Rapids: Baker Academic, 2004.

———. "The Law and Christianity: Dunn's New Synthesis." *Westminster Theological Journal* 53, no. 2 (Fall 1991) 339-53.

Sire, James W. *The Universe Next Door*. Downers Grove, IL: IVP Academic, 2004.

Skinner, John. "Righteousness in the OT." In *A Dictionary of the Bible: Pleroma–Zuzim*, edited by James Hastings, 4:272–81. Edinburgh: T. & T. Clark, 1915.

Smith, Huston. "Methodology, Comparisons, and Truth." In *A Magic Still Dwells: Comparative Religion in a Postmodern Age*, edited by Kimberly C. Patton and Benjamin C. Ray. Los Angeles: University of California Press, 2000.

Smith, James E. *The Pentateuch*. Joplin, MO: College Press, 1993.

Smith, Preserved. *Erasmus*. New York: Harpers, 1923.

Snaith, Norman H. *The Distinctive Ideas of the Old Testament*. London: Epworth, 1983.

Soames, Scott. *Philosophy of Language*. Princeton, NJ: Princeton University Press, 2010.

Sproul, R.C. *Faith Alone: The Evangelical Doctrine of Justification*. Grand Rapids: Baker, 1995.

———. *Focus on the Bible: Romans*. Ross-Shire, UK: Christian Focus, 1994.

———. *Knowing Scripture*. Downers Grove, IL: InterVarsity, 1977.

———. "The Reformation Rescued the Gospel." *The Gospel Coalition*, Jan. 23, 2017. https://www.thegospelcoalition.org/article/reformation-rescued-the-gospel/.

Spurgeon, Charles H. *Justification by Faith: Sermon No. 3392*. https://www.blueletterbible.org/Comm/spurgeon_charles/sermons/3392.cfm.

Stanton, Graham N. "Paul's Gospel." In *The Cambridge Companion to St Paul*, edited by James D. G. Dunn, 173–84. Cambridge, UK: Cambridge University Press, 2003.

Stavropoulos, Christoforos. *Partakers of Divine Nature*. Minneapolis: Light and Life, 1976.

———. "Partakers of Divine Nature." In *Eastern Orthodox Theology: A Contemporary Reader*, edited by Daniel B. Clendenin, 183–93. Grand Rapids: Baker, 1995.

Steinmetz, David C. *Reformers in the Wings: From Geiler von Kaysersberg to Theodore Beza*. 2nd ed. New York: Oxford University Press, 2001.

Stendahl, Krister. "The Apostle Paul and the Introspective Conscience of the West." *Harvard Theological Review* 56, no. 3 (July 1963) 199–215.

———. *Final Account: Paul's Letter to the Romans*. Minneapolis: Fortress, 1995.

———. *Paul among the Jews and Gentiles*. Philadelphia: Fortress, 1976.

Stott, John R. W. *The Cross of Christ*. Downers Grove, IL: InterVarsity, 1986.

———. *The Message of Romans: God's Good News for the World; The Bible Speaks Today*. New Testament Commentaries. Downers Grove, IL: InterVarsity Press, 2001.

Stuckenberg, J. H. W. *The History of the Augsburg Confession*. Whitefish, MT: Kessinger, 2009.

Stuhlmacher, Peter. *Revisiting Paul's Doctrine of Justification: A Challenge to the New Perspective*. Downers Grove, IL: IVP, 2001.

Stumme, Wayne C., ed. *The Gospel of Justification in Christ: Where Does the Church Stand Today?* Grand Rapids: Eerdmans, 2006.

Swan, James. "Did Luther Believe Salvation Can Be Lost?" https://beggarsallreformation.blogspot.com/2009/10/did-luther-believe-salvation-can-be.html.

Swanson, James A. *Dictionary of Biblical Languages with Semantic Domains: Hebrew (Old Testament)*. 2nd ed. Oak Harbor, WA: Logos Research Systems, 2001. Logos.

Tamerius, Travis. "An Interview with N. T. Wright." *Reformation and Revival Journal* 11, nos. 1–2 (Winter and Spring 2003) 1037–54.

Tangelder, Johan D. "Calvin and . . . Luther: A Monk and a Minister." *Reformed Perspective* 26, no. 5 (2007): 1, 16–19.

Tavard, George T. *Justification*. New York: Paulist, 1983.

Taylor, Justin. "Gratitude for the New Perspective on Paul but Resistance to Its False Dichotomies." https://www.thegospelcoalition.org/blogs/justin-taylor/gratitude-for-the-new-perspective-on-paul-but-resistance-to-its-false-dichotomies/.

Taylor, Mark C. "Text as Victim." In *Deconstruction and Theology*, edited by Thomas J. J. Altizer, 65. New York: Crossroad, 1982.

Tertullian. *The Two Goats and Christ's Two Natures*. In *Exodus, Leviticus, Numbers, Deuteronomy*, edited by Joseph T. Lienhard. Ancient Christian Commentary on Scripture: Old Testament, 3:185. Downers Grove, IL: InterVarsity, 2001.

Thiselton, Anthony C. "The Supposed Power of Words in the Biblical Writings." *Journal of Theological Studies* 25, no. 2 (Oct. 1974) 283–99.

———. *The Two Horizons: New Testament Hermeneutics and Philosophical Description*. Grand Rapids: Eerdmans, 1980.

Tollington, Janet. "The Ethics of Warfare and the Holy War Tradition in the Book of Judges." In *Ethical and Unethical in the Old Testament: God and Humans in Dialogue*, edited by Katharine Dell, 71–87. New York: Bloomsbury T. & T. Clark, 2010.

Torrance, Thomas F. *The Hermeneutics of John Calvin*. Edinburgh: Scottish Academic Press, 1988.

Vanhoozer, Kevin J. *Biblical Narrative in the Philosophy of Paul Ricoeur: A Study in Hermeneutics and Theology*. New York: Cambridge University Press, 2007.

———. "Discourse on Matter: Hermeneutics and the 'Miracle' of Understanding." In *Hermeneutics at the Crossroads*, edited by Kevin J. Vanhoozer et al., 3–34. Philosophy of Religion. Bloomington, IN: Indiana University Press, 2006.

———. *First Theology: God, Scripture and Hermeneutics*. Downers Grove, IL: InterVarsity Academic, 2002.

———. *Is There a Meaning in This Text? The Bible, the Reader, and the Morality of Literary Knowledge*. Grand Rapids: Zondervan, 2009.

———. "A Person of the Book?: Barth on Biblical Authority and Interpretation." In *Karl Barth and Evangelical Theology: Convergences and Divergences*, 26–59. Edited by Sung Wook Chung. Grand Rapids: Baker Academic, 2006.

Vanhoozer, Kevin J., et al., eds. *Dictionary for Theological Interpretation of the Bible*. Grand Rapids: Baker, 2005.

———. *Hermeneutics at the Crossroads*. Philosophy of Religion. Bloomington, IN: Indiana University Press, 2006.

Vatican II. "Decree on Ecumenism: Unitatis Redintegratio." https://www.vatican.va/archive/hist_councils/ii_vatican_council/documents/vat-ii_decree_19641121_unitatis-redintegratio_en.html.

Vattimo, Gianni. *Beyond Interpretation: The Meaning of Hermeneutics for Philosophy.* Palo Alto, CA: Stanford University Press, 1997.
Vos, Geerhardus. *Biblical Theology.* Grand Rapids: Eerdmans, 1948.
———. *The Pauline Eschatology.* Grand Rapids: Eerdmans, 1952.
———. *Redemptive History and Biblical Interpretation: The Shorter Writings of Geerhardus Vos.* Edited by Richard Gaffin, Jr. Phillipsburg, NJ: P&R, 2001.
Waltke, Bruce K. *A Commentary on Micah.* Grand Rapids: Eerdmans, 2007.
Ware, Kallistos. *The Orthodox Way.* Crestwood, NY: St. Vladimir's Seminary Press, 1995.
Warfield, Benjamin B. *Calvin and Augustine,* edited by Samuel G. Craig. Philadelphia: Presbyterian and Reformed, 1974.
———. *Calvin and Calvinism.* New York: Oxford University Press 1931.
———. "Calvin as a Theologian." Edited by Lance George Marshall. http://www.monergism.com/thethreshold/sdg/warfield/warfield_calvintheologian.html.
———. *Counterfeit Miracles.* Edinburgh: Banner of Truth Trust, 1972.
———. *Faith and Life.* Edinburgh: Banner of Truth Trust, 1974.
———. "Introduction." In *The Work of the Holy Spirit,* by Abraham Kuyper, xxv–xxxix. New York: Funk & Wagnalls, 1900.
———. "John Calvin the Theologian." http://graceonlinelibrary.org/biographies/john-calvin-the-theologian-by-benjamin-b-warfield.
———. *The Works of Benjamin B. Warfield.* 10 vols. Grand Rapids: Baker, 2003.
Warnke, Georgia. *Gadamer's Hermeneutics, Tradition and Reason.* Palo Alto, CA: Stanford University Press, 1987.
Watts, Isaac. *Logic: The Right Use of Reason in the Inquiry after Truth.* Morgan, PA: Soli Deo Gloria, 1998. First published 1724 as *Logick: or, the Right Use of Reason in the Enquiry after Truth.*
Wellman, Sam. *John Calvin: Father of Reformed Theology.* Uhrichsville, OH: Barbour, 2001.
Wells, David F. *No Place for Truth: Or Whatever Happened to Evangelical Theology.* Grand Rapids: Eerdmans, 1993.
Wesley, John. "I Felt My Heart Strangely Warmed." In *Journal of John Wesley.* Christian Classics Ethereal Library. http://www.ccel.org/ccel/wesley/journal.vi.ii.xvi.html.
Westerholm, Stephen, ed. *The Blackwell Companion to Paul.* Chichester, UK: Wiley-Blackwell, 2011.
———. *Israel's Law and the Church's Faith: Paul and His Recent Interpreters.* Grand Rapids: Eerdmans, 1988.
———. *Perspectives Old and New on Paul: The "Lutheran" Paul and His Critics.* Grand Rapids: Eerdmans, 2004.
———. *Understanding Paul: The Early Christian Worldview of the Letter to the Romans.* Grand Rapids: Baker, 2004.
The Westminster Shorter Catechism. http://www.westminsterconfession.org/confessional-standards/the-westminster-shorter-catechism.
Whitaker, Richard. *Whitaker's Revised BDB Hebrew-English Lexicon.* Norfolk, VA: BibleWorks, 1995. Software discontinued.
Wilckens, Ulrich. *Der Brief an die Römer.* Evangelisch-Katholischer Kommentar zum Neuen Testament VI/1. Zürich: Neukirchener, 1978.
Williams, Matt. "What Is 'The New Perspective on Paul'?" *Sundoulos* (Spring 2011). http://www.talbot.edu/sundoulos/spring-2011/lead-article/. Site discontinued.

Wittgenstein, Ludwig. *Philosophical Investigations*. Malden, MA: Blackwell, 1967.
Wriedt, Markus. "Luther's Theology." In *The Cambridge Companion to Luther*, edited by Donald K. McKim, 86–119. New York: Cambridge University Press, 2003.
Wright, N.T. *The Climax of the Covenant: Christ and the Law in Pauline Theology*. Edinburgh: T. & T. Clark, 1991.
———. *Justification: God's Plan and Paul's Vision*. Downers Grove, IL: IVP Academic, 2009.
———. "Käsemann, Ernst." In *The New Dictionary of Theology*, edited by Sinclair B. Ferguson et al., 363–4. Downers Grove, IL: InterVarsity, 2000.
———. "The Letter to the Romans." In *The New Interpreter's Bible*, edited by Leander E. Keck, 10:393–521. New York: Abingdon, 2003.
———. "New Perspectives on Paul." http://ntwrightpage.com/Wright_New_Perspectives.htm.
———. *Paul: In Fresh Perspective*. Minneapolis: Fortress, 1995.
———. "The Paul of History and the Apostle of Faith." *Tyndale Bulletin* 29 (1978) 61–88.
———. "Righteousness." In *The New Dictionary of Theology*, edited by Sinclair B. Ferguson et al., 590–2. Downers Grove, IL: InterVarsity, 2000.
———. *What Saint Paul Really Said: Was Paul of Tarsus the Real Founder of Christianity?* Grand Rapids: Eerdmans, 1997.
Yong, Amos. *Discerning the Spirit(s): A Pentecostal-Charismatic Contribution to Christian Theology of Religions*. Sheffield, UK: Sheffield Academic, 2000.
———. "Primed for the Spirit: Creation, Redemption, and the Missio Spiritus." In *International Review of Mission* 100, no. 2 (Nov. 2011) 355-366.
———. *Spirit-Word-Community: Theological Hermeneutics in Trinitarian Perspective*. Eugene, OR: Wipf & Stock, 2002.
Zetterholm, Magnus. *Approaches to Paul: A Student's Guide to Recent Scholarship*. Philadelphia: Fortress, 2009.
Zizioulas, John D. *Being As Communion: Studies in Personhood and the Church*. Crestwood, NY: St. Vladimir's Seminary, 1985.
———. "Preserving God's Creation: Three Lectures on Theology and Ecology." *King's Theological Review* 12 (1989) 1–5, 41–45; *King's Theological Review* 13 (1990) 1–5.

www.ingramcontent.com/pod-product-compliance
Lightning Source LLC
Chambersburg PA
CBHW070317230426
43663CB00011B/2166